For

Robert Speaight,

with best wishes from

Joanna Richardson

1996

COLETTE

COLETTE
JOANNA RICHARDSON

METHUEN

First published in Great Britain 1983 by
Methuen London Ltd
11 New Fetter Lane, London EC4P 4EE
Copyright © 1983 Joanna Richardson

British Library Cataloguing in Publication data

Richardson, Joanna
 Colette.
  1. Colette – Biography 2. Authors, French –
 20th century – Biography
 I. Title
 843'.912   PQ2605.028Z/
ISBN 0-413-48780-6

Printed in Great Britain by
Butler & Tanner Ltd
Frome and London

For
Janet Vaughan
with love and gratitude

Je voudrais laisser un grand renom parmi les êtres qui, ayant gardé dans leur âme la trace de mon passage, ont pu seulement espérer un instant que je leur appartenais.

Colette

CONTENTS

List of Illustrations	viii
Introduction	ix
Sido's Daughter 1873–93	1
Colette Willy 1893–1906	10
La Vagabonde 1906–12	33
Madame la Baronne de Jouvenel 1912–25	58
The Dark Young Man 1925–35	103
Madame Maurice Goudeket 1935–54	162
Epilogue	231
Notes	241
Select Bibliography	263
Index	271

LIST OF ILLUSTRATIONS

between pages 148 and 149

1. Colette at five
2. Colette as a schoolgirl
3. The earthly paradise
4. Sido and the Captain
5. Colette at eighteen
6. The beginnings of a writer
7. Willy with the 'twins'
8. Colette in her 'squirrel's cage'
9. *Rêve d'Égypte*: Colette and Missy
10. Colette and Missy in the rue Saint-Senoch
11. 'Our Pretty Actresses'
12. 'I have a new heart'
13. Colette at Castel-Novel
14. Colette at Rozven
15. Bertrand de Jouvenel
16. 'The dark young man'
17. 'The human face was always my great landscape'
18. M. and Mme Maurice Goudeket
19. *Dialogue de Bêtes*
20. Colette at work in the rue de Beaujolais
21. Colette, Maurice and Pauline
22. Colette's eightieth birthday
23. Colette with Prince Rainier
24. Colette on the terrace of the Hôtel de Paris, Monte-Carlo

INTRODUCTION

In Saint-Sauveur, in Burgundy, there is a plaque on the house where Colette was born. The street in which it stands is called rue Colette. In Paris there is a place Colette, outside the gardens of the Palais-Royal; and in the Palais-Royal itself, that green-and-white oasis, originally built for Richelieu, we are in the Parisian province which Colette made her own.

The Palais-Royal is now a sad, abandoned, dusty place. It has an atmosphere of melancholy distinction, an air of aristocratic decay. On winter mornings children scamper over the empty pond in the formal gardens, where no fountain plays. On winter nights elderly residents exercise their dogs on the sanded paths. A dog barks, and the bark reverberates round the dim arcades. The visitor walks down the Galerie Beaujolais, past the prestigious restaurant, Le Grand Véfour, which still announces on its windows, in faded letters: 'SHERRY GOBLERS. LEMON SQUASH. ENGLISH SPOKEN.' Inside is a plaque which commemorates Colette's favourite table.

Next door, on the garden side of 9 rue de Beaujolais, is another plaque. It marks the small, first-floor apartment which, even in her lifetime, was part of her legend.

It was from the window here that she used to observe the passers-by ('my bourgeois and provincial side'); it was by this window, under her blue lamp, as bright as moonlight in a theatre, that she wrote *Paris de ma fenêtre*, *Le Fanal bleu* and most of the work of the last sixteen years of her life. It was here, in the Palais-Royal, that her husband was arrested by the Gestapo during the Occupation; it was here that he eventually returned. It was here that Jean Marais came to rehearse *Chéri*, that Anita Loos arrived to discuss *Gigi*, that Cocteau spent long hours in conversation. It was in this courtyard, after her death, that the crowds filed past her catafalque when she was accorded her state funeral.

Colette was among the most original writers in modern French literature. She wrote with difficulty; but her style – which earned the admiration of Proust – is recognised for its classical distinction. She wrote of nature as no-one had done in her native tongue before her. She wrote of certain human relationships with a tact and honesty and wisdom which made her readers feel that only she could appreciate their complexities. Her writing was lyrical, tactile, deeply perceived.

No-one could write like this without a life of intense and diverse experience; and the life of Colette was extraordinary. She was born, obscurely, in Burgundy, two years after the Franco-Prussian War. She died, in Paris, internationally known, eighty-one years later. She had three husbands and a daughter; she had more than one lesbian relationship. She was tempestuous but sane, tough and vulnerable, intensely disliked and profoundly loved. She inspired jealousy, malice, contempt and disgust. She also earned admiration, not only for her charm and for her work, but for her enduring physical courage. The child who was in love with the countryside, the young woman who followed the music-hall troupes, the middle-aged woman who travelled with apparently endless energy, became in time the arthritic cripple who was rarely able to leave her bed. She turned old age and pain and disability to advantage. They gave her a new literary stature. The observer of nature, of human nature, came to build her own philosophy. Faith and hope are not mentioned in her books, but charity abounds there: charity towards the animal which is suffering, towards people who are alone. Colette understood the trial of solitude. No-one could forget the solitude of Chéri.

Like Baudelaire and Proust, Colette looked back to the lost paradise of childhood: a paradise which she unremittingly sought to regain. Yet at the end of her long existence, almost immobile, hard of hearing and with failing sight, she kept her constant, exuberant love of living. She was not concerned about death. 'How could I be concerned,' she asked, 'with anything which is not life?'

INTRODUCTION

This is the first full-scale biography of Colette to be written in English. It is based not only on her published work, and on the mass of secondary sources: letters, memoirs, criticism, biographies and newspaper articles. It is also based on those of her papers which are now available at the Bibliothèque Nationale. It owes much to the practical help of her stepsons. M. Renaud de Jouvenel has answered many queries; he has also sent me notes about his family, copies of articles and of his correspondence with the late Yvonne Mitchell, and with Michèle Sarde. I am above all grateful to M. Bertrand de Jouvenel; he and his literary assistant, Mme Jeannie Malige, gave me generous hospitality, and they bore with all my questions. They showed both patience and understanding, and they have, between them, added a new dimension to this book.

I am glad to thank Miss Kathleen Farrell, for her recollections of Colette; Dr A. M. B. Golding, for his help with medical details; and Mr Graham Greene, for his note on Colette's funeral. I am grateful to Mr Michael Holroyd, who gave me wise advice at critical stages in my research, and to Mr and Mrs James Lees-Milne, who gave me hospitality, lent me letters and shared their vivid recollections. I am indebted to Miss Rosamond Lehmann for describing a visit from Colette, and to Miss Cecily Mackworth (la Marquise de Chabannes) for her illuminating conversation. I am glad to thank Miss Enid McLeod, for her reminiscences of the rue de Beaujolais; M. Claude Pichois, for his practical counsel and for his editions of Colette's correspondence; Dr Alan Raitt, for his expert and constant interest; Mme Claudia Verhesen, for writing to me about Princess Marthe Bibesco; and Dame Veronica Wedgwood, for sending me Bertrand de Jouvenel's tribute to Colette in *Time and Tide*. I am, as usual, indebted to the patient staff at the British Library.

London–Paris   Joanna Richardson
1980–82

SIDO'S DAUGHTER 1873-93

Adèle-Eugénie-Sidonie Landoy – known to posterity as Sido – was born in Paris on 12 August 1835. She was the daughter of Henri-Marie Landoy, a quadroon whom she described as 'the Gorilla', and his wife Adèle-Sophie, *née* Chatenay. Mme Landoy died when Sido, much the youngest of her children, was very small, and Sido was sent to a peasant nurse on a farm at Mézilles, near Saint-Sauveur-en-Puisaye, in Burgundy. When she was eight, she went back to Paris, to live with the Gorilla and her brothers and sister. Her father manufactured chocolate, and she long recalled how the slabs were laid out to dry on the roof every night; next morning they bore imprints like flowers with five hollow petals: the imprints of the paws of marauding cats.[1]

The Gorilla remarried and moved to Lyons. When she was sixteen, Sido went to live with her brothers, who were now established journalists in Brussels. Their friends were artists, poets and musicians, and she grew to love the company of civilised people. At the age of seventy-four she was still to covet that now distant pleasure.[2]

Nothing [wrote Colette] supplanted, in my mother's heart, the beautiful Belgian cities, the warmth of their refined and gentle life, epicurean, and enamoured of the things of the spirit. Certain words from Sido's lips fell on my childish ears, and the sound of them has not faded. At the age of six, when the children in my village were sighing: 'Oh, Paris!', I was hoping 'Brussels,' and I was proud not to say 'Bruqcelles' in the French way.[3]

Whatever her love of Paris and Brussels, Sido returned again and again to visit her old nurse near Saint-Sauveur. It was during one of these visits, in 1854, when she was nineteen, that she met a local landowner, Jules Robineau-Duclos. He was known to the villagers as 'the Savage'.[4]

He lived in a substantial house in the rue de l'Hospice in Saint-Sauveur, alone except for the various maids whom he got with child. His relatives eventually decided that it was time he had a legal heir, and they arranged that he should mary Sido. This he did in 1857.

The marriage was a business transaction which brought her substantial benefits, but she could hardly love her uncouth husband. He was heavily addicted to drink, and one night, in his cups, he assaulted her. Sido was young, but she was not submissive. She threw all the mantelpiece ornaments at him; among them was a candlestick which hurt his face so badly that he never attacked her again.

The two of them grew increasingly lonely. The Savage spent his days away from home; Sido was idle, restless and unhappy in a house where the servants resented her presence. After two years of marriage, she gave birth to a daughter, Juliette; four years later came a son, Achille, whom gossip said was the son of the local tax-collector, Jules-Joseph Colette. On 30 January 1865 the Savage had a stroke and died. Sido wasted no time on regret. On 20 December she married Jules-Joseph at the *mairie* at Saint-Sauveur. The religious ceremony was performed in Belgium in order that her brothers might attend it.

Jules-Joseph Colette had been born at Toulon on 26 September 1829. He had brought a true Provençal panache to his army career. He had trained at Saint-Cyr, and had been commissioned in 1852. He had fought in the Crimean War, been wounded at the battle of the Alma, and, at the age of twenty-six, he had become a captain in the 1st Zouave Infantry. On 9 June 1859, during the Italian campaign, he had lost a leg at Metegnano. 'When the Emperor came to ask after him, he said: "Mother and child are doing well." The child was his left leg, which had just been amputated. He had wrapped it up in a towel.'[5] A fortnight later he was made Chevalier de la Légion-d'honneur.

The loss of his leg meant the end of his promising army career; he could never be content with his sinecure as a provincial inspector of taxes. He was, however, freed from it by his marriage; and he was blissfully happy with his wife. In 1868 she produced a second son, Léopold. On 28 January 1873, after forty-eight hours' labour, she gave birth to her youngest child: another daughter, who was named after herself, Sidonie-Gabrielle. 'With cries of agony,' wrote Colette, 'my mother drove me from her loins. I emerged blue and silent, and no-one thought it worth bothering about me ... I was born half-stifled; I showed a personal determination to live, and indeed to live for a long while.'[6]

Colette was born in Burgundy; she was *méridionale* through her father and she was Parisian through her mother. Through her maternal grandfather she was one-sixteenth negro. 'You know,' she confessed to Francis Jammes, 'my forebears also came from tropical islands, so they came from a distance, like your own, only mine must have been darker ... There, I've a black stain in my blood. Does that disgust you?'[7]

Captain Colette was attached to his children, but he was ruled by his passionate devotion to his wife. Sido abounded with energy and warmth, and with native wisdom. She had a power of love, an originality, an all-absorbing love of nature which made the house at Saint-Sauveur a place of enchantment. The Captain called his daughter Bel-Gazou (a form of *beau gazouillis*, or fine language); even as a child, perhaps, she revelled in words. Her mother called her Minet-chéri. Colette had a childhood that was full of love: a childhood poor in material possessions but astonishingly rich in poetry.

I am leading you religiously to the place where I used to live [she recalled in *Le Voyage égoïste*].
    Come in. I'm going to explain to you. To begin with, you know it's Sunday ... When you wake up, you see, and breathe the warm smell of boiling chocolate, you know that it's Sunday. You know that, at ten o'clock, there are cracked pink cups and flaky flat cakes on the table – here, look, in the dining-room – and you know that you're allowed to go without the big lunch at noon ... Why? I couldn't tell you ... It's a custom of my childhood.
    Don't be alarmed, when you look up at the dark ceiling. Everything protects you here. This old house has so many wonders in it ...[8]

Gently, in recollection, Colette led her visitor to the bedroom she had known as a child; she showed him the cat-door, through which, at dawn, the vagabond cat had ambled in and fallen on the bed, 'cold, white and light as an armful of snow'.[9] Finally she led him into the garden.

I have kept the garden to conquer you. As soon as I open the worn door, as soon as the two shaky steps have moved under our feet, don't you smell the smell of earth, of walnut leaves, chrysanthemums and smoke? You're scenting it like a hunting dog, you're trembling ... The bitter smell of a November garden, the thrilling dominical silence of the woods from which the woodcutter and the cart have gone, the soaking wet path through the forest, where a wave of mist is softly rolling: all that is ours until evening, if you like, since it is Sunday.[10]

The house at Saint-Sauveur was a house of rituals. At Christmas there was always a bunch of winter roses on the table, opening with sudden jerks which surprised the cats and delighted the vigilant child. At Christmas they always ate chestnuts, and revelled in Sido's masterpiece, a white pudding studded with three kinds of raisins.

'It is from Sido,' wrote the critic John Charpentier, years later, 'that Mme Colette gets her spontaneity, her humour, and that instinct or divination which makes her understand both the animal and vegetable worlds.'[11] 'Minet-chéri,' wrote Sido herself, '... you have inherited my tastes, my darling treasure ... I shall die without having my fill of so many splendours ...'[12] From Sido, her mother, Colette learned to study the strange ways of nature. She watched the tortoises go to earth under the cactus stand, to hibernate until the spring. She knew the ponds, blue with shadow in the summer, 'warm here, and icy there from the welling up of a deep source ... They smell of reeds, of musky mud, green flax ...'.[13] She loved the roses, swollen with rain, and cold to the lips; she loved the cool grapes gathered in the dawn, and the last strawberries of October, ripe only on one side. She liked the feel of a frog's cold belly on her hot hands. She developed an imperious and dominant sense of smell: 'a miraculous sense of smell which could invent at will...the aroma of orange-blossom or of bruised bananas, or of the musky melon, over-ripe, which bursts and sheds its sanguine water ...'.[14] She cultivated her sense of taste ('since childhood I have known French wine, and been on intimate terms with it').[15] She developed a sense of touch; she became visually aware. 'O last fire of the year! ... Your wild red peony fills the hearth with a gerbe which perpetually blossoms again ...'[16] She learned, too, the practical ways of country folk. 'Sido made cassis liqueur at home, and, when the berries had yielded all their juice, the residue was thrown into the poultry-yard, all impregnated, still, with alcohol! If you'd only seen the hens! ....'[17]

In time she was sent to the local school. She walked there in the summer term, swinging her long plaits under her big straw hat, and carrying two tame swallows in her pocket. In winter she wore stout wooden clogs, and carried the metal box of live coals and ashes that each child took to school to keep her warm. She never forgot the smell of unwashed country children packed between shut windows and shut doors; she never forgot the black pinafores, the worn, low desks, the stupidity of her classmates. Sometimes she felt frustrated. 'Latin,' she reflected. 'How often I've looked at it "from the outside" with covetous eyes! Far above me ...'[18] She was observant and she was ambitious. Even now, as a child, she hoped that she would be famous.[19] Years later she congratulated Louise Faure-Favier on being the first woman to fly the Channel. 'One must always be first,' she said, 'as one is at school!'[20]

She had heard much from Sido about her family in Brussels; at long last she went to visit them. Her expectations were not disappointed.

At No. 25, rue Botanique there opened to me a house and hearts which Sido had faithfully portrayed. How attractive it was to me, the very architecture of the Belgian house! How I loved its cellar and kitchen, its shining coppers and blue crockery, and the permanent floating aroma of coffee, and the parrot which spoke Spanish almost as well as my aunt ... I loved the salon and its lace curtains closely drawn behind the flower-stands, which were displayed for the admiration of the passers-by. I loved the dining-room wedged between the salon and the conservatory which was facing south, where the birds were singing in their cage, the children were playing, the cat was sleeping under a green plant ... I came from the open country, and from a lovely garden, but there was no rival to the old Belgian conservatory with the constant, sultry temperature kept up by the flaming Belgian coke, and there was no rival to the Belgian gastronomy – which did not feed on illusions![21]

Life at Saint-Sauveur was now less comfortable. Captain Colette had been unlucky with his investments, he had been forced to sell property and to borrow money. Despite their modest way of life, the family were in grave financial trouble. When Colette was twelve, her half-sister, Juliette, married a young doctor. The Captain found himself unable to fulfil the terms of the marriage contract. Dr Rocher and his parents forbade Juliette ever to speak to or to acknowledge her family again. Sido was distraught with misery, Juliette took an overdose of pills, but failed to die. None the less, mother and daughter remained apart. During the next five years financial affairs went from bad to worse. At last, in 1890, when Colette was seventeen, the house in the rue de l'Hospice and all the furniture were sold at auction. For Colette it meant the humiliation of public poverty, the destruction of her childhood paradise.

Her younger brother, Léo, was studying pharmacy in Paris. She and her parents moved to the neighbouring village of Châtillon-sur-Loing, known today as Châtillon-Coligny. They lived in a little house in the rue de l'Égalité with her elder half-brother, Achille. He was now married and a country doctor.

Captain Colette continued to read *La Revue bleue* and *La Revue des Deux Mondes*. Perhaps – for he had literary tastes – he continued to write verse. Certainly he corresponded with Albert Gauthier-Villars, the scientific publisher in Paris. This was the unpredictable chance that shaped his daughter's life. Gauthier-Villars' son came to call at Châtillon-Coligny. He met Colette, and fell in love with her.

Henry Gauthier-Villars – better known as Willy – had been born at Villiers-sur-Orge (Seine-et-Oise) on 10 April 1859. His father, a former pupil of the École Polytechnique,[22] was orthodox and well-to-do. He had sent his son to the Lycée Condorcet and then to the Collège Stanislas. Willy had a versatile mind, and he was given an excellent education; but he was too indolent to fulfil himself. He collaborated at first in various scientific publications; then, suddenly, against his father's wishes, he published a collection of sonnets and a number of literary studies, among them – in 1884 – an essay on Mark Twain.

This was the age of Symbolism, and of the little reviews: the reign of impassioned polemics about literature and art. Critics were idealistic and they were Wagnerian; first and foremost among the polemists was Willy, the intransigent aesthete who signed as Henry Maugis in *La Nouvelle Rive Gauche*. In this review – later called *Lutèce* – he signed alongside Verlaine.

He was increasingly attracted by music criticism and by aesthetics. In October 1889, in *Art et Critique*, he began to publish letters on the Lamoureux concerts, under the flippant pseudonym 'Une Ouvreuse du Cirque d'Été'. He earned a reputation for his casual manner and for his meticulous care in indicating technical errors. His judgments were often based on information which he had accepted from experts: among them Claude Debussy, who maintained that Willy did not know the meaning of a semi-breve. Even now, Willy had his unacknowledged assistants, and he exploited the knowledge of his friends. ('When we recall our past as dupes,' wrote Colette, years later, 'we still refer to our *workroom* days ...')[23] Willy was not only a ruthless entrepreneur. He was already anxious to disguise his personality. He wrote under various pseudonyms; and later, in his novels, he was to record this period of his life, and to conceal the words and deeds of Henry Gauthier-Villars under the old familiar names.

Such was the success of his 'Lettres de l'Ouvreuse' in *Art et Critique* that he continued them in *L'Écho de Paris*. This publication, established in 1884, had an impressive list of contributors, among them the critic Jules Lemaître and the novelist J.-H. Rosny; the literary editors were for a time Catulle Mendès and Marcel Schwob. In the intervals of writing for these periodicals, Willy also acted as music critic for the *Revue Blanche* and the *Revue encyclopédique*. In 1898 he was to join the *Revue internationale de musique*.

This extensive career as a critic naturally brought him enemies. Thanks to his geniality and his apparent frankness, he could still appease enraged musicians and turn rancour into esteem. J.-H. Rosny thought him 'somewhat egotistic and sometimes cruel', but 'always found him pleasant and good company. For the rest, he was complex, subtle, witty, egotistic, and he had incontestable charm.'[24] Rosny was bewildered by the power of Willy's charm ('his ascendancy was extraordinary').[25] The charm was all the more surprising since he was physically repulsive. He was, said Rosny, 'a small man, he was stout at an early age, he had pale blue eyes, and a fat, malicious, cynical face. His voice was rather coarse ...'.[26] Raymond Escholier called him, bluntly, 'one of the most putrid wrecks of the Belle Époque'.[27]

Willy's private life was as unconventional as his career. When he met Colette, he already had an illegitimate son. He was highly-sexed, and patently a man of the world. He was attracted by her youth and innocence. She herself was 'merely surprised that a man who was still young should take such trouble to seem old. He had a filthy pipe, a hat which had gone through a great deal, and a cravat which was beyond all hope ...'.[28] Despite his louche appearance, she was drawn by his sophistication, by the thought of Paris, and by her adolescent longing to discover sexual experience.

Sido did not wholly approve of Henry Gauthier-Villars, and she was reluctant to lose her favourite daughter; but she and her husband were provincial and impoverished. In some ways this decadent *boulevardier* seemed a more distinguished son-in-law than they were entitled to expect.

On 15 May 1893, four months after her twentieth birthday, Gabrielle-Sidonie Colette was married to Henry Gauthier-Villars. The marriage took place quietly at Châtillon-Coligny. Next morning 'a thousand leagues, abysses, discoveries, irremediable metamorphoses' separated her from the previous day.[29] Her life as a woman, she was to write, 'began with this antagonist. A grave encounter for a village girl. Before him – except for the ruin of my parents, and the furniture sold by auction – it was roses all the way. But what should I have done with a life which was nothing but roses?'[30]

Sido was apprehensive. After the wedding, she spent a sleepless night, and, 'when day broke, she was still wearing all her trappings of black faille and jet. Standing in her little kitchen, in front of the stove covered with blue faience tiles, she abandoned her face to an expression of fearful sadness, and pensively made the morning chocolate.'[31]

COLETTE WILLY 1893-1906

Madame Henry Gauthier-Villars looked so young when her husband brought her to Paris that, he maintained, 'I was always afraid that I should be arrested in the street for corruption of a minor.'[1] Colette had not only lost her innocence; she must have known, now, what corruption meant. Willy was experienced, dominating and self-indulgent; his appetites and fantasies both attracted and repelled her.

They settled in the Paris of Toulouse-Lautrec and Zola: a Paris where the Métro had not yet been built, and carriages still outnumbered motor-cars. Maxim's was established this year, and the Eiffel Tower was only four years old. They settled on the Left Bank, which was haunted by Verlaine: in Willy's dark, oppressive bachelor rooms over the Gauthier-Villars' offices. The rooms, at the top of the tall house, were painted bottle-green and brown, and cluttered with erotic German postcards. There was no kitchen and, even if Sido had taught her how to cook, there was nowhere for Colette to exercise her talents. Every morning, at half-past eight, she and Willy would cross the bridge to a modest *crémerie* on the Right Bank and breakfast off croissants, which they dipped into their chocolate.[2] Colette maintained that, apart from these breakfasts, she lived largely on sweets.

From these nightmare rooms, which rattled with every passing omnibus and wagon, she and her husband moved to a third-floor apartment at 28 rue Jacob. It was hardly less disturbing. It never saw the sun; and the previous tenant, who had lived there for half a century, had covered every inch of the walls with multicoloured confetti. He had stuck it on himself, piece by piece. Colette had exchanged her dreams and solitude, her Burgundian countryside, her wild, original family, and the beloved presence of Sido, for this lunatic setting, and for the sinister, prurient company of Willy. 'I remember the lively and ridiculous hope which sustained me,' she was to write in *Mes Apprentissages*. 'This terrible hardship, city life, couldn't last for ever, it would end miraculously with my death and my resurrection, with a conflict which would restore me to my mother's house and garden, and abolish all that marriage had taught me.'[3] Willy took her to the salons which he visited, presented her to friends and acquaintances. But no social life could make amends for domestic misery. She was desperately disillusioned.

Exchanging my state as a village girl for the life which I led from 1894 was enough to drive a child of twenty to despair, if it didn't intoxicate her. Thanks to youth and ignorance, I did indeed begin with intoxication – a guilty intoxication, a terrible and impure adolescent urge. There are many scarcely nubile girls who dream of being the spectacle, the plaything, the libertine masterpiece of an older man. It is an ugly dream, they expiate it when they fulfil it. It is a dream which goes with the neuroses of puberty ...
And so I was punished, harshly, and soon.[4]

Early in her married life Colette decided that her mother must know nothing of her misery. 'I made her the present of a lie: the imitation of happiness. I resisted the terrible longing to go back to her.'[5] She satisfied her own chronic need to see Sido again by writing her a letter every day.

It was, predictably, not enough. She was overcome by depression. She neglected her health and, gradually, she lost the will to live. She was 'swallowed up in day-dreams and in half-light, in hesitation, the habit of keeping silent ...'[6]. At last even Willy grew anxious, and summoned Dr Jullien, the doctor from the Saint-Lazare hospital. Dr Jullien attended her for more than two months. Finally he wrote to Sido that he probably could not save her daughter.

Sido had lost one daughter in marriage, and she did not intend to lose the other. She arrived in Paris, concealed her emotion, slept in the dining-room in the rue Jacob, and looked after Colette with devotion.[7] She did what she alone could do: gave

her back her exuberant love of life. Colette was not to lose it
again.

■━■

One of the earliest visitors to the rue Jacob had been the young
essayist and critic Marcel Schwob. He was a man of wide erudition
and powerful imagination. He also had a flippant, ironic humour
which delighted Colette. She met him in 1893, the year of her
arrival in Paris, and she was fond of him from the first. In the
summer of 1894, from Belle-Isle-en-Mer, where she was convalescing with Willy, paying her first visit to the coast, she wrote to
him repeatedly. She told him about the red-sailed fishing-boats,
the curious fauna of the sea and sand. In September, from
Châtillon-Coligny, she wrote proudly: 'Did I tell you I'd killed a
snake? Perhaps I did, but I am still astonished at my courage.'[8]

One of the friends she mentioned in her letters to Schwob was
Mme Arman de Caillavet. Mme Arman lived in the avenue
Hoche; and, forty years later, Colette still recalled 'the chandeliers
with big crystal drops, the long gallery with its three windows, a
certain low, dark, little room, a refuge for fine old books: a room
which ... received, for several lustrums, the daily visit of Anatole
France. There, in my remarkably tame youth, I used to meet
famous men, whom I can hardly claim to have known, since I
only dared to play the part of a silent figurant at the Sunday
afternoons and the Wednesday dinners.'[9] Anatole France was the
lion of the salon; but Catulle Mendès, Pierre Loüys and Paul Valéry
were also among the guests. So, too, was the young Proust:
charming, troubled, touched by melancholy. Rosny remembered
meeting Colette in the avenue Hoche, 'lit up by her splendid eyes,
which were slightly wild and ready to brave the world'.[10] Fernand
Gregh, the poet and critic, also met her there. 'She was wearing
two pigtails which came down to her waist, and her Burgundian
accent was surprising in a Parisian salon. We had not come to the
end of our surprises with this extraordinary woman, with her
incendiary eyes ... She was going to write French like the greatest
masters. But in those days she was only Willy's wife.'[11]

Mme Arman had come to see her on her sickbed in the rue

Jacob. Not content with her visit, she had sent her a gossipy letter and a brooch in the shape of an insect, with ruby eyes.[12] However, for all her kindness, Mme Arman was not made to be a companion or confidante. It was in 1894 or '95 that Colette met the woman who was to become her closest friend. Marguerite Monceau was two years her senior: she had been born in Paris on 15 September 1871. Her father was Gascon and a teacher of mathematics; her mother was Spanish, and Marguerite had adopted her mother's maiden name, Moreno, when she began her theatrical career. In 1890 she had made her début at the Théâtre-Français. For the next thirteen years she played classical and contemporary parts; and, though she did not stir the general public, she delighted the poets, Mallarmé among them. She became the mistress of Catulle Mendès, the former husband of Judith Gautier. He looked at the same time, it is said, like a lymphatic Christ and like a turbot. He had, however, a real love of poetry; and it was perhaps to him that she owed the art of reciting *Les Fleurs du mal* to perfection.[13]

It was at a *déjeuner* given by Mendès that Colette first met her. 'I had eyes and ears,' she wrote, 'only for the tall, thin young woman ... Everything about her enchanted and humiliated the displaced provincial I still remained. From this first *déjeuner* I admired and loved Marguerite Moreno. What is surprising is that she returned my affection. We were both young enough – we had just come of age – for our friendship to be stamped with the ardour of schoolfriends.'[14]

Colette was now beginning to be familiar to Parisian society. At the 'musical Fridays' of Mme de Saint-Marceaux she met Claude Debussy, Maurice Ravel and César Franck. In Jeanne Muhlfeld's yellow boudoir near the avenue Victor-Hugo – where Lucien Muhlfeld, the novelist, furthered his ambitions – she came to know the new generation of writers: André Gide, Jean Cocteau and François Mauriac. At the Tuesdays of Rachilde, the literary critic, and wife of the founder and editor, Alfred Vallette, she encountered the contributors to the Symbolist *Mercure de France*. On 5 November 1894 Jules Renard, the diarist, recorded her at the experimental Théâtre de l'Œuvre. Renard (one day to write *Poil de Carotte*) had gone to the first night of *Annabella, or 'tis pity she's a whore*. Ford's play had been translated by Maeterlinck, and among the audience was 'Mme Willy, dragging a braid of hair long enough to let a bucket down a well'.[15]

Mme Willy was not the innocent that Renard suggested. She had already begun to write. Willy had decided that his docile young wife might bring some useful money to the household. Willy earned a good deal from his multifarious occupations; he earned 15,000 francs a year from *L'Écho de Paris* alone. But he pretended all his life that he was poor; and his most frequent exclamation was: 'Quick, quick, my dear, there isn't a sou in the house!'[16] Now he told his wife to scribble down recollections of her schooldays. 'Don't be afraid of spicy details, I might do something with it ... Funds are low.'[17] Colette recalled: 'I was getting over a long and serious illness, and I was still mentally and physically lazy. But I found some exercise-books at a stationer's which were like my exercise-books at school, with ruled margins, ... and they gave my fingers back a kind of itch for an imposition.'[18]

Willy dismissed the results of her labours. They were, he said, commercially worthless.

In the summer of 1895 he and Colette spent a holiday at Champagnolle, in the Jura. The standard of comfort was minimal, but at noon the *table-d'hôte* was covered with crayfish, quails, hares and partridge, all of them caught by poachers.[19] Colette took Willy on bicycle rides 'before four o'clock in the morning! It nips you, it's so cold,' she announced to Schwob. 'And there are some very fine colours out of doors at that time of day.'[20] Her husband's comments were not recorded. Her own enthusiasms were not to change.

Schwob himself – now the lover of Marguerite Moreno – was to remain among her dearest friends in the early years of her marriage. In the summer of 1893 he had undergone a serious operation. Since then, his creative energies had been constantly hampered by pain and by physical disability. His life, however, was enriched by the love of Marguerite. In 1900, in London, they were married. She cared for him devotedly until his premature death, five years later.

It was, it seems, in 1899 that Willy took a second look at his wife's account of her schooldays. One glance at her 'imposition', and he understood his error of judgment. In March 1900, signed by Willy, there appeared her impressions of life at a girls' school in the depths of the French provinces.

Claudine à l'école is written by an adult, but it is seen through the eyes of a disabused and cynical adolescent, who feels no affection for anyone, and already understands every movement, every machination, every suggestion in the game of love. Claudine is a virgin, but she already finds the love of men distasteful and the love of women contemptible. She lives in a closed world of schoolgirl infatuations and lesbian relationships; but no-one could deny her shrewdness and her powers of calculation. Nor could they deny her unremitting vivacity. *Claudine à l'école* is written with extraordinary verve. It is wickedly licentious, but, amazingly enough, it never strays into pornography. It is also a *roman à clef*. 'M. Salle, the former principal of the college, figured in the book with his real name. Lerouge was really M. Legouge, inspector of primary schools. And the director Dutertre, who asked such indiscreet questions of the young Claudine, and warmed up so quickly when he stroked her long hair, was none other than the mayor of Saint-Sauveur, Dr M - -, who was to become a Deputy, then under-secretary of State.'[21] The novel created such a scandal that, if Colette's headmistress could be believed, 'Mlle Aimée, the fair-haired assistant teacher, ... missed three marriages with colleagues.'[22]

Claudine à l'école sold 40,000 copies in two months. The little Tanagra silhouette of Claudine became a national figure. 'How she writes, this Claudine!' exclaimed André Beaunier in *Le Journal des Débats*. 'What skill, what wit, what tact! How she contrives to say the most difficult things with a subtle art – subtle and simple, almost classical, if I am not mistaken. Willy can be proud of fostering the first work of this rare and perfect writer.'[23]

Willy was, as usual, ruthless. Confident that he had struck a vein of gold, he locked his wife up for hours at a time in the rue Jacob, to ensure that she continued to write. He also found an original way to advertise the work. He took up a young Algerian actress, Émilie Zouze, known as Polaire; he made her and Colette cut their hair short. He forced them to appear together 'as twin *Claudines à l'école*, the better to illustrate those schoolgirl passions – passions which,' declared Natalie Barney, well versed in these matters, 'neither Colette nor Polaire felt for each other.'[24]

Jacques Gauthier-Villars, Willy's illegitimate son, was seventeen years younger than Colette. He was to leave affectionate reminiscences of the 'illustrious woman of letters, who was my most attractive *stepmother* for some thirteen years'.[25] He had been sent to boarding-school in England. In May 1900, accompanied by a woman friend, Colette went to see him.

My attractive *stepmother* found her stepson changed, more sober in his speech and behaviour. His voice was muffled, and he sprinkled his sometimes hesitant French with anglicisms. This entertained her, as she told Willy in a charming letter: I read it at my father's before it vanished like countless others. In it Colette described her impressions of Mafeking Day in London (19 May 1900), a day of rejoicing to celebrate the relief of this little town in the Transvaal besieged by the Boers and victoriously defended by General Baden-Powell, the creator of the Boy Scout Movement. The tide of rejoicing which unfurled over the British capital was so great that Colette and her friend had a very hard time escaping from the wild assaults of patriots who were mad with joy. Their valiant escort, the Greek consul, had his jacket torn and his top-hat battered in the fray.[26]

Forty-six years later Peter Quennell, the English man of letters, met Colette at a luncheon in Paris. He asked whether she had ever visited England.

Once, she replied. She had spent two or three days at a *château* in the Thames Valley, and she remembered '*une assez aimable petite rivière*' –

here her voice became lightly caressing – that wound its serpentine way across the park. Naturally the house was haunted – she believed that every English *château* had its family ghost; and, while she was staying there, an unfortunate *femme de chambre* ... had encountered the phantom on its nightly rounds and had been discovered next morning, rigid and insensible, just outside the door of the bedroom that she herself was occupying.[27]

At the very end of her life, talking to James Lees-Milne, Colette told another story of her only visit to England. 'She stayed in the country with an Anglo-Indian Colonel Manson who had a dog. To her surprise he always addressed the dog in execrable French. He never spoke to anyone but the dog. The reason was that the only book he had ever read was a French one he had picked up in his club at Quetta when he had nothing better to do ...'.[28] Colette's one visit to England was also recorded by Marcel Boulestin, the future restaurateur, who in 1900 was secretary to Willy.

Boulestin left other comments on Willy and Colette in this year of grace. He soon became a regular guest at their Sunday receptions. Claudine had enriched them; they had moved to the Right Bank. At their new apartment at 93 rue de Courcelles, Boulestin used to see leading musicians, writers, painters, actors and actresses. In the afternoon, when Willy went to his various appointments, Colette and Boulestin used to go out for tea,

sometimes to chic places like the Élysée Palace Hotel or Colombin, sometimes quietly at the British Dairy in the rue Cambon, sometimes at a place which was then frequented by people of doubtful, or hardly doubtful, reputation, the Thé de Ceylan.

We also went to tea parties in studios and private houses (Parisians in those days had tea from five to seven); as long as they were not dull we did not mind if they were a little disreputable.[29]

Jacques Gauthier-Villars recorded his own sharp and somewhat conflicting impressions:

Nearly every afternoon, Willy and Colette went out in the carriage, usually together, on their errands. This carriage was of course horse-drawn, a blue coupé with a bay trotter impeccably driven by Ogier the coachman, with a profile as mediaeval as his name.

I preferred to go out with Colette, since Willy's business calls on publishers or newspaper editors didn't seem madly amusing to me when I was thirteen . . .

However, with Colette there were entertaining expeditions to the big shops, or to sellers of exotic delicacies. Colette had a great fancy for these, and she had no trouble in making me share it . . .

Sometimes Willy asked me to meet him in a fashionable tea-shop. I shared his preference for the English Tea-Rooms . . .

Three or four times a week Willy, the dramatic critic, and Colette, used to go to a theatre or to a soirée . . .

Easter, in the Belle Époque, heralded the spring, to judge by the sudden flowering of straw hats on the heads of passers-by. At the first sign of fine weather, Willy and Colette used to go out riding in the Bois. In the Easter holidays, I joined in these equestrian expeditions which took us from the place Dauphine to Bagatelle and back, by way of the avenue des Acacias. On these riding days, the way of life of the household was changed. At dawn, in other words at about half-past nine, Colette appeared, very elegant in her riding skirt and her felt hat. Willy preferred riding trousers with trouser-straps to boots; he exchanged his legendary topper for a bowler. As for me, I was gaitered like a Canadian trapper.

The faithful Ogier took us in the carriage as far as the entrance to the Bois, where the docile half-breeds of some or other Tattersall were waiting . . .

As we rode our horses in the Bois de Boulogne, Willy and Colette used to meet numerous familiar figures . . .

I remember, too, the insistence of the photographers from the society papers. They took shots of Willy and Colette, very Parisian personalities, the moment that they caught sight of them.[30]

The young Jean Cocteau had a glimpse of them at the fashionable skating-rink, the Palais de Glace des Champs-Élysées:

Round one of the tables sat Willy, Colette and her bulldog. Willy, with his thick moustache and Tartarin imperial, his eyes gleaming under his heavy lids, his fancy cravat, his top hat on its cardboard halo, his bishop's hands folded on the knob of his cane. Beside him, our Colette. Not the solid Colette who offers us succulent salads with raw onions and does her shopping in sandals at Hédiard's . . . No, it was a thin, thin Colette, a kind of little fox in cycling dress, a fox-terrier in skirts.[31]

Bicycles were all the rage, and Willy hired one for *parties de campagne;* he gave Colette a blue one, which he had won in a tombola. It had no mudguards and it had no brakes.³²

■ ▶━━━◀ ■

Claudine was naturally obliged to follow in the footsteps of her creator. In *Claudine à Paris* – which appeared in 1901 – she goes to live in Paris with her father. The book records her longing for her native Montigny (Saint-Sauveur), her illness, her discovery of her aunt, of her homosexual cousin and of his father, Renaud. Renaud, wrote Colette, years later, was 'lighter, emptier and more hollow than the spun-glass balls on Christmas trees'.³³ But Claudine is desperate for love. On her first evening out with him, she asks to be his mistress. Renaud, surprisingly, insists on marriage. In some ways the situation anticipates that of Gigi – the innocent girl who, against all the odds, marries the well-to-do man-about-town. For the first time Colette suggests the power of sexual attraction. But Claudine's love for Renaud is simply physical love; Colette hardly acknowledges the existence of any other kind.

More exercise-books were waiting: two pink, two blue-green, two pale green. (Two of them had lists of household expenses: carriages, cherries at Dijon, paper, stamps and *eau de cologne.*) Willy was impatient. In 1902 Ollendorff duly published *Claudine amoureuse.* Several people, recorded Willy, had read the manuscript, recognised the heroine, and warned her that she would appear in print. Mme Raoul-Duval – known as Georgie – was American by birth, and innocent enough to offer Ollendorff a substantial sum to suppress the book. Ollendorff accepted the money; nearly the whole edition of *Claudine amoureuse* was destroyed. Ollendorff did not, however, warn Mme Raoul-Duval that this blatantly indiscreet novel might be published elsewhere. In fact the Mercure de France accepted the work, and brought it out later in the year, with certain alterations, as *Claudine en ménage.*

It was not surprising that Georgie Raoul-Duval had wanted to suppress the original version. In August 1901 she had been to Bayreuth with Willy and Colette. She had been Willy's mistress. According to him, she had also been that of his wife. In his

Indiscrétions et commentaires sur les 'Claudine', he confessed: 'She was outrageously seductive, this Rézi! A reckless liar. And a traitress, who loved unnecessary danger. She delighted ... in arranging meetings, with Colette and me, in the same room, one after the other, at an hour's interval.'[34] Claudine, it appears, had not been so repelled by lesbianism as she had suggested. Renaud de Jouvenel believes that the thought of her mother making love with the one-legged Captain had affected Colette's own sensibility; very early, he maintains, one can guess her lesbian inclinations.[35]

In *Claudine en ménage*, Colette had given Rézi and her Anglo-Indian husband the name of the English boarding-school which Jacques Gauthier-Villars attended. Perhaps the Anglo-Indian Colonel Lambrook owed something to the Anglo-Indian Colonel Manson, with whom she had stayed on her visit to England.[36] Yet perhaps he looks out at us from a book by Roger Raoul-Duval. *Au Transvaal et dans le Sud-Afrique avec les attachés militaires* was published by Delagrave in 1902; the frontispiece shows the author: a young army officer with a thick moustache, protruding eyes, and a marked resemblance to Lord Randolph Churchill.

Claudine en ménage seems, then, to be largely autobiographical. Married to Renaud, whom she had chosen, Claudine remains unsatisfied. She allows herself to be seduced by the wife of one of Renaud's friends. Renaud, understanding as ever, finds the room where they can make love. Finally, Claudine discovers that he, too, is Rézi's lover. She returns at once to Montigny, to find her roots again, to seek her peace in the Burgundian countryside. Here, within a few days, she asks the forgiven Renaud to join her.

Claudine en ménage is a curious study of corruption, of the various facets of physical attraction. It says all too little about the depths of human relationships. Rachilde was surprisingly enthusiastic. Writing in *Le Mercure de France*, she declared that '*Claudine en ménage* will revolutionise, without revolting, the lovers of naked truths. It is an honest work, and it is written so delectably that it brings tears of joy to the eyes of those who love natural art. These three books, of which *Claudine en ménage* is certainly the most literary and the most audacious, set Willy henceforward in the first rank of French novelists.'[37]

These three novels [wrote Henri Albert, in his pamphlet on Willy], obtained a prodigious success which will count among the most important in modern publishing. *Claudine à Paris* was dramatised, and Willy found a perfect interpreter to incarnate the Parisianised schoolgirl. Mlle Polaire was then only known for her eccentric creations at cafés-concerts, her clothes and her carriage. Willy, despite much resistance, insisted that the part was given to this audacious and inexperienced actress. She rewarded his confidence ... On stage [at the Théâtre des Bouffes-Parisiens], Mlle Polaire did not act, she lived Claudine with a truth, an assurance, a sincerity which was not belied throughout the long run of the play. The double success, both literary and dramatic, popularised the name and the character of Claudine; songs, drawings, fashions propagated the name and likeness of Willy's heroine throughout the world ... Claudine was soon denatured by the public craze. On every side there are now false Claudines à l'École, à Paris, and especially en Ménage.[38]

'The dazzling success of the *Claudines*,' continued another critic, 'exceeded anything one can imagine. It was even confirmed among the *modistes*, the hairdressers and the *pâtissiers* ... The success of a work is rarely explained by its most lasting qualities, form or style. With her over-long eyes and her little schoolgirl's collar, Claudine attracted all her century.'[39]

Early in June 1902 Colette reported to Jeanne Muhlfeld: 'Claudine is about to end a career at the Bouffes which was unhoped-for, if not glorious: 130 performances! But ... none of that is worth the colour of the fifth hour of the morning at Les Monts-Boucons ...'[40]

Les Monts-Boucons was an old Directoire house near Besançon. Since the Claudine books had been a commercial success, Willy had bought the house for Colette (he was later to take it back from her). For three consecutive years she lived there alone from June till November, except for an occasional visit from her husband. Willy enjoyed his freedom in Paris; Colette refreshed herself with country life, and found inspiration for her work. She was there in mid July 1902.

Jeanne Muhlfeld, do you recognise me? I have an apron with pockets, a pink cretonne hood, muddy boots with little studs, no rice-powder, suede gloves to grip the big secateurs, and the heart of a young girl. You can't imagine the pure – and purgative – delight of eating black cherries which the sun has cooked on the tree. It's raining on me, it's shining down on me, I get up at 6 o'clock and go to bed at 9 ... It is my annual orgy of virtue, an almost secret orgy, which brings me down to the moral level of a labourer or a shepherdess.[41]

To Marguerite Moreno she added:

I am very sad to stay here and think that I shall have to go. There is a heavenly smell of mushrooms everywhere. And the ripe apples, whose rather – rather what? – rather baked smell recalls so powerful a memory of last year, and of the others. It is the moment in the year when I amuse myself by thinking about things; I make myself dreadfully sad just for the pleasure of coming round again and seeing that it isn't true.[42]

Jacques-Émile Blanche came of a famous medical family. His grandfather, Dr Blanche, had attended Gérard de Nerval in his periods of insanity; his father had in turn taken charge of the asylum at Passy. Blanche himself was an accomplished artist, a man of letters, and a friend of artists, writers and society figures in England and in France. It was about now that Colette and Willy sat for him for their portrait. The canvas has since disappeared, but the picture remains in the artist's memoirs.

I had Colette, in all her freshness, in my studio. A slight young woman, still almost a girl, with short hair – in advance of the fashion – with her eyes cast down, meditative. She put one of her arms round the neck of a solid fellow with a small fair beard, paunchy, full of zest: the husband of Claudine. Colette and Claudine, Claudine and Colette were the same person, but we did not know it yet.

I was painting the husband's portrait, much more than that of the boarding-school girl in a terracotta dress. Her lord and master dominated her by his lofty height and by his top hat, and he treated her like a child ... Willy, the brilliant journalist, the author of the *Claudine* novels, took good care not to divulge the part that his wife had taken in the creation of these frivolous masterpieces. He trailed her around everywhere, sometimes at the risk of boring the melancholy child. He compelled her to make visits and to dine with dowagers, intellectual or not, in whose company his bourgeois, Parisian snobbery found satisfactions which were incomprehensible to the Burgundian girl. Her eyes were still full of the light of the fields, she was a country girl in love with nature, a dryad fascinated by the pipes of Pan. It was a time of slavery from which the emancipated Vagabond was to emerge, in possession of her great talent as a writer.[43]

It was indeed a time of slavery. Years later, Colette recorded how she had struggled to keep her mother in ignorance of her condition. Sido had once come to Paris in the early days of the marriage, and she had been astonished to find that her daughter did not have a coat in the depths of winter. She had taken Colette to the Grands Magasins du Louvre and had bought her one from her own slender resources.[44] Despite Colette's illness, and despite Willy's evident neglect, she had still found it prudent to keep her counsel. Mother and daughter had continued to pretend that all was well.

I didn't succeed completely in deceiving her [Colette remembered], because she saw through walls. But I did my best to make her believe that I was happy, for thirteen years. My rôle was difficult, especially at the beginning. When I went to see her, at Châtillon-Coligny, ... I felt the much-loved moment approaching when my mother and I would chat alone together ... I was forced to see her sit down in the old armchair beside my bed ...
'Come on, tell me! ...'
She asked questions, watched me with a frightening sagacity. But I was her daughter, and already practised at the game ...[45]

The moment of danger passed. Colette returned to her slavery and to her outwardly dazzling social life. Jacques-Émile Blanche continued:

This singular couple, Colette and Willy, moved in the best and the worst society, but especially in the most elegant, where they propagated musical opinions which were then held to be subversive. The composers they praised were none other than Wagner, Debussy, Chabrier, Frank, d'Indy, Duparc, Gabriel Fauré. No-one knew that Colette was largely responsible for the opinions of l'Ouvreuse. Husband and wife shared the labour of the music critic, obliged to run from one concert to another, from Colonne to the Conservatoire, from the Conservatoire to the Concerts Lamoureux, where there would be simultaneous performances of new music. It was then a question of getting home in time to prepare the Sunday tea. A hundred and one friends climbed the five flights of stairs in a building in the rue de Courcelles to have tea with Colette. The Gauthier-Villars' studio was to be the cradle of the modern arts.[46]

In 1903 there appeared the fourth of the Claudine books, *Claudine s'en va*. The title is misleading, and beyond a doubt it was chosen for commercial reasons. The novel is in fact the journal of Annie, a seemingly colourless young girl whose husband, Alain, leaves for South America. Miserable and apparently helpless, she is taken under the wing of Marthe, her sister-in-law, and swept off to Arriège and Bayreuth. She also becomes acquainted with Claudine and Renaud and with the alcoholic womaniser, Maugis. Maugis was one of Willy's pseudonyms; and Maugis – who had already been a secondary figure in *Claudine à Paris* – is a devastating likeness of the man himself. It was actually inserted in the novel by Willy. 'I think that when he created *the gross Maugis*,' wrote Colette, 'Willy was yielding to one of his megalomanias, his obsession with painting self-portraits, his love of studying himself.'[47] Maugis is affected, malicious and repellent. However, he is also an influential critic, and Marthe elects to become his mistress. She also tells Annie that Alain has long been unfaithful to her. Annie returns to Paris, discovers her husband's love-letters, and leaves him.

Claudine s'en va has none of the brio and style of *Claudine à l'école*. The only characters endowed with a semblance of life are Maugis and of course Claudine, as witty and vivacious as ever. None the less, the book received the plaudits of the press.

What a delightful figure of a woman she really is, this Claudine [wrote the novelist Francis de Miomandre]! With what minute and careful attention she is studied, drawn, examined! Never has *libertine* literature been more serious, never has it been more sincere and purer in its intentions ...

Personally, I have read the *Claudines* with the aesthetic admiration with which I should have studied sketches by Fragonard.[48]

The astonishing vogue of the books continued. So did Willy's fierce publicity.

> Everything in his life, his literary life is [declared a critic] publicity. There is not one of his actions which does not serve as an advertisement ... Willy spends more time on launching a book than he does in writing it ... And Willy writes articles on Mme Willy, and Mme Willy writes articles on Willy, and they both write articles on Mme Polaire, and Mme Polaire writes articles on both of them, or else each of them writes articles on themselves. Publicity, publicity, publicity![49]

Those who read the Claudine books could now buy Claudine lotions, Claudine ice-cream and Claudine perfume; in 1903 they could buy Claudine collars from La Samaritaine. They could buy Claudine hats and Willy rice-powder, even Claudine cigarettes. They could buy picture-postcards of Willy with Claudine wearing button boots and a schoolgirl dress. No doubt they could also buy copies of the photographs taken of the couple by Nadar. It was said that only God, and perhaps Alfred Dreyfus, were as celebrated as Willy. One tradesman in Paris saw beyond the current fashions, and he deserves to be commemorated. A prescient parfumeur, Delettrez, of 15 rue Royale, already offered Le Parfum de Colette.[50]

■ ▸━━◂ ■

From their small fifth-floor apartment in the rue de Courcelles, Willy and Colette moved down the street. At 177, *bis*, rue de Courcelles, they lived, Colette recorded, in half of a private *hôtel*, where their neighbour was Prince Bibesco. [51] One of her visitors here was the poet Lucie Delarue-Mardrus.

> Colette Willy (she pronounced it *Vili*) ... was [recalled Lucie] muscular and slim, and her eyes, which have become still more beautiful with age, already lit up those two little dark blue lamps in the triangle of her face, under the short hair, then unknown, which was her particular distinction.
> We have all learned from *Mes Apprentissages* what her life was at that time. Since I have read the book myself, I have understood better the

attitude that she affected. It was that of a young woman who was constantly giving the hundredth performance of Claudine.[52]

Early in 1904 Colette wrote a novella for her own satisfaction. For the first time she asked to have it published under her own name. Willy refused; he wanted it to be a full-length novel, and he wanted to publish it himself. *Minne* appeared that year as the work of Willy; and Colette was obliged to write a sequel, and to lead Minne astray as he demanded. *Les Égarements de Minne* was published in 1905. Colette was to bring the two works together, under her own name, in 1909, with the title *L'Ingénue libertine*.

Minne – like the early Claudine – is an adolescent whose outward innocence conceals a disturbed and vicious character. The pampered only child of a widowed mother, she dreams of becoming a gangster's moll and the queen of the Paris underworld. Infatuated by a rough young man, whom she chances to pass in the street, she imagines him to be a notorious criminal, and one night she escapes in search of him. She explores Paris in vain and returns home, surprisingly, unscathed. In the second part of the book, she has married her dull but devoted cousin, Antoine. Disillusioned by sexual life, she takes a lover or two, and offers herself, coldbloodedly, to the ubiquitous Maugis, who refuses her. Finally she returns to Antoine; he makes love to her successfully, at last, and Minne is tamed.

L'Ingénue libertine lacks verve; it is plainly written to satsify the commercial appetite for the audacious. It suggests, more clearly than any other book, the degradation of Colette by Willy.

Early in 1904, however, she published her first book under the name of Colette Willy. *Dialogues de Bêtes* established her as an acute, original observer of animal life. 'I didn't know, my dear,' said Willy, 'that I had married the last of the lyric poets!'[53]

Colette was not merely a lover and observer of animals; she understood their characters, almost their speech. She had profound respect for them, she exercised a strange influence over them. At the end of her life she spoke of 'creatures who exchanged a power with me ...'.[54] This power was already recognised by Rachilde. Mme Colette Willy, she wrote in April 1904, 'reveals both an innocent soul and a very curious cerebral complexity. She is a woman of letters in her choice of detail, in the slightly precious novelty of her metaphors, and she is a woman, pure and simple, in her admiration for her animals.'[55] Rachilde – Marguerite Vallette – was generous nowadays to Colette. She was, however, thirteen years her senior, and in time perhaps she came to resent the difference in age, and to resent Colette's distinction. She also came to disapprove of her private life ('I don't know a filthier piece of work'); in laters years she attacked her viciously.[56]

Meanwhile, in 1905, there appeared an enlarged edition of *Dialogues de Bêtes*; it was adorned with a preface by Francis Jammes, known for his writing on nature and rural life. It enjoyed a *succès d'estime*.

Who does not know [asked Henri Albert] that elegant silhouette of an intelligent young woman, who has made herself her husband's collaborator and devoted comrade and has recently published such delightful *Dialogues de Bêtes*? Her image remains inseparable from Willy's. On great days in Paris, at fêtes and first performances, she smiles in the shadow ... of Claudine's father. And, feeling her on his arm, M. Henry Gauthier-Villars seems happier, more benevolent. For, in spite of everything, a great fund of kindness fills Willy's heart.[57]

Willy's public image differed from the private and domestic reality. Colette had soon become aware of his frequent infidelities. As Rosny wrote: 'She knew bitter distress ... And, which I still don't quite understand, she was afraid of her companion ... That Willy could be frightening, I find it very hard to believe. In any case, he dragged her off to meet some rather curious company, and, for years, he reduced her to a kind of slavery.'[58] Willy, who was moved to tears by Wagner's operas, was ruthless in his treatment of his wife.

As Pierre Brisson was to write, she had entered life 'on the arm of an old faun steeped in alcohol, and, in a few years, through him, she had discovered the limits of Parisian depravity.'[59] In this contaminated world – despite her lesbian interlude – she remained a perennial stranger. In mid May 1904, from the rue de Courcelles, she herself confessed to Francis Jammes: 'Everything here is becoming terrible for me, ... and I need to escape so much that the smell of lilies-of-the-valley makes me desperate. Willy is a very good master for a squirrel. The cage is charming and the door is open. He has given me very pretty squirrel's playthings: a trapeze, some parallel bars, rings and ladders ...'[60] It was not enough for him to indulge her taste for gymnastics. In 1905 she observed: 'He makes animals sentimental and women cynical.'[61]

As Sido had surmised, her daughter's marriage was likely from the first to be unhappy. No woman could be happy with Willy. There was, it seems, no question of children. Willy had looked to his young wife for sexual satisfaction and for assistance in his own career. In every way he had exploited her. Now she was all too well instructed in the ways of the world. She had abandoned her poetic childhood and her adolescent dreams of love; she was disillusioned, hurt, and aware that she had missed the pleasures of youth. She had schooled herself to abstain from tears.

Yet Willy had done more than enlighten her curiosity, give her the status of a married woman. He had obliged her, forced her, to write. Had he not done so – as she later told Maurice Goudeket – she would never have written in her life. Never had an author felt less of a vocation. Willy had driven her to her career. He had already given her a sort of associate celebrity; she was beginning to acquire a celebrity of her own. He had done more: he had also introduced her to Paris. She had a world of original and distinguished friends.

Among them was Comte Robert de Montesquiou-Fezensac, the aesthete and man of letters who is said to have been the inspiration of Huysmans' Des Esseintes and of Proust's Charlus. Robert de Montesquiou was a noted homosexual, and he was famous in the literary and fashionable worlds. Colette and Willy publicised his books, and duly welcomed his comments on their own. They delighted in his hospitality. It was at one of his elegant fêtes that Colette encountered the Comtesse de Noailles, whose beauty, poetry and social distinction made her a truly formidable figure.

The first time I saw her [recalled Colette], it was at a fête given by Comte Robert de Montesquiou at the Pavillon des Muses. She had recently married, and she was wearing the dress that you can see in her portrait by Antonio de la Gandara, a very pale dress, the colour of blue silver...

At this time, when her beauty was that of an adolescent, the world was already flocking to her; she accepted homage with the majesty and gravity of a child, and she seemed neither profoundly happy, nor intoxicated, for nothing human cures the melancholy of the elect.[62]

Some people were disconcerted by Anna de Noailles. 'Quite a great lady, but not entirely simple,' wrote Paul Léautaud, the rancorous man of letters. 'Someone asked her what she would like. "To live in a virgin forest!"'[63] Colette refused to be impressed by Mme de Noailles' powers of oratory, and she refused to be overawed by her social status. On their first encounter, Mme de Noailles responded to such stubbornness 'in the decretal form which was her own'.[64] Despite this abrasive introduction, they were to be good friends until the Comtesse died in 1933.

Colette had also come to know a notorious American expatriate: the lesbian Natalie Clifford Barney. Miss Barney was the recipient of Rémy de Gourmont's *Lettres à l'Amazone*; she lived in the rue Jacob, in the house which had once belonged to the actress Adrienne Lecouvreur, and here she presided over a literary salon.

At the beginning of this century [she recalled, years later], when I saw Colette for the first time, she had already ceased to be the slim adolescent with long plaits, lying in a hammock, whom we see in a photograph; she was a young woman, well set on solid legs... She had frank manners, and frank language, but feline silences in her enigmatic triangular face and in her fine bluish-green eyes...

Her favourite companions, a dog and cat - as everybody knows - were no doubt chosen because of their singular resemblance to their mistress. Was her own nature not composed of these two animal natures? She was obedient and devoted to a master, but she was secretly following the instinct of the wild animal which escapes all domination.

She used to exercise her animals in the Bois, wearing button boots for long walks...

I had made the acquaintance of Willy and his wife at the Comtesse Armand de Chabannes', and they asked me to visit them at the rue de Courcelles. What intrigued me most in their apartment was a small gymnasium ... Colette herself worked regularly at the fixed bar, the trapeze, the rings – perhaps with a view to the music-hall to come. But the other workroom, where this schoolgirl, under Willy's guidance, learned to write novels, remained invisible. No doubt it was their bedroom, used for a dual purpose?

Husband and wife did not give themselves the luxury of a private life; they appeared everywhere together.[65]

Miss Barney noticed that, despite his genial manner, or perhaps his false geniality, Willy kept a vigilant eye on the comings and goings of his wife. He was determined not to miss any benefit or pleasure. After Miss Barney moved to Neuilly, she went to ask Colette to a fête. 'Mata-Hari had offered to give another performance of her Javanese dances, but this time entirely naked, and to an audience of women only. Willy was vexed to be excluded, and wanted to give his consent only on scabrous conditions. As we set off, Colette confessed: "I am ashamed that you have had such a close view of my chain." '[66] It was not the only occasion when Colette saw Mata-Hari at Natalie Barney's; she met her there in less exotic mood, armour-plated with whalebone, high-bosomed in a black-and-white check suit. It was an unexpected vignette of the spy who was one day to face the firing-squad.

Another friend of Colette's was a strange and melancholy poet, Pauline Tarn, better known by her pseudonym, Renée Vivien. She had been born in London in 1877 of an English father and an American mother. She and her lover, Natalie Barney, had tried without success to found a colony of women poets at Mytilene in honour of Sappho. In the early 1900s they had settled in Paris. Renée – la Muse aux violettes – drove about in a coupé quilted in mauve satin, her coachman and footmen in violet livery. She also became the lover of Evelina Palmer, an American of pre-Raphaelite appearance. She lived near the Bois de Boulogne, in a ground-floor apartment enhanced by a little Japanese garden. Men were hardly tolerated there. Colette recalled

Renée's long, long body, a body without thickness, slightly stooping. It bore, like a heavy poppy, the head with its golden hair ... Her dresses covered her feet, and she walked, afflicted by a graceful awkwardness, dropping her gloves, her parasol, catching or losing her scarf. People have hardly described – or ill described – her apartment, sombre, sumptuous and changing. Except for a few Buddhas and the old instruments from a music room, all the furniture moved mysteriously at Renée Vivien's. A collection of gold Persian coins was replaced by pieces of jade, by lacquer work, which were soon driven out by glass cases of insects and exotic butterflies. Among these changing wonders, in the darkness of a lodging made sombre by stained glass, curtains, odorous smokes, Renée wandered about, veiled rather than clothed, in black and violet. Three candles wept their brown wax tears in a dining-room on a Chinese table laden with raw fish wound around glass sticks, foie gras, crayfish, sweet and sharp salads, fruit served on jade plates, in hispano-moresque dishes, all washed down by well chosen champagne and cocktails of exceptional stiffness...[67]

Renée herself lived on a piece of fruit, a spoonful of rice and on a glass of champagne, a mouthful of alcohol swallowed when she was fainting from inanition.[68] She died in 1909, at the age of thirty-two.

Colette had already come a long way from Saint-Sauveur. On 17 September 1905 her Burgundian childhood receded even further. Her father died at Châtillon-Coligny. He was in his seventy-fourth year. Captain Colette was buried with his Zouave's tunic draped over his coffin: the wasp-waisted jacket of an officer in the Second Empire. He was given the handsomest of village funerals, and Sido went with him steadily to the graveside: grey-haired, small, and resolute under her widow's veil.[69] A few months later, she was again in mourning. Her elder daughter, Juliette, died at Saint-Sauveur at the age of forty-seven.

By 1905 it was evident that Colette's marriage was over. 'The separation of Colette and Willy seems,' wrote Rosny, 'the most natural thing in the world, and the most necessary.'[70] The twelve-year marriage had been a predictable failure. Colette was now thirty-two, and she had begun to establish her literary renown. She could not yet earn her independent living as a writer.

She was, however, fascinated by the theatre and by the music-hall – which she called the profession of those without professions. Her gymnastics in the rue de Courcelles had kept her supple; she was tempted to seek experience on stage. Willy urged her, warmly, to go on tour.

'It would be an excellent chance to give up this deathly apartment, to make arrangements for a different life – oh, very different ... There's no hurry ...'

There was no mistake [she wrote]. What I had heard was a notice to quit. While I had been dreaming of escape, someone beside me had been dreaming of conveniently showing me the door.[71]

She left the rue de Courcelles. Her husband continued to write to her.

But none of the letters asked me, ever, to retrace the steps which had led me, with my trunk, a few pieces of furniture, the dog and the cat, from the rue de Courcelles to the rue de Villejust. And so, in the little ground-floor apartment, I grew accustomed to thinking that I had reached the place where my whole life must change its flavour, just as the bouquet of the wine changes according to the slope on which the vine is growing.[72]

On 6 February 1906, after various amateur appearances, Colette made her professional début as a mime, and danced at the Théâtre des Mathurins in *Le Désir, l'amour et la chimère*. She took the part of a faun. Years afterwards, Rachilde recalled 'this little faun, a reed flute between its lips, watching a round of nymphs. He was both awkward and mischievous, and yet so pure in his lines, so chaste in his gestures, and so poetic in the rhythm of his slightest movements, that one felt he was flesh and blood in this cheap cardboard setting. One believed in him, despite the electric moonbeam. He was no longer dancing. He was living his dream.'[73] Colette continued her career at the Théâtre-Royal and the Olympia. Now that she had separated from Willy, she also became the mistress of the Marquise de Belboeuf.

LA VAGABONDE 1906-12

Sophie-Mathilde-Adèle-Denise, the fourth and youngest child of the Duc de Morny, had been born on 26 May 1863.[1] Through her father she was the great-granddaughter of the Empress Josephine – and the niece of Napoleon III. Through her mother, the former Princess Sophie Troubetzkoi, she was descended from Louis XV.

Her father had died when she was only two. Her mother had thought the child's nose was too long, and she had dismissed her as 'the tapir'. She had spoilt her less than her brothers and sister; indeed it was said that she found her so unattractive that she had left her upbringing to the servants. Louise Weiss, the journalist, in her memoirs, records: 'La Troubetzkoi seems to have been tyrannical and crazy. She made her children and all her household eat oysters for breakfast. They gave Mathilde a serious attack of typhoid and a horror of her mother which lasted until her death.'[2] Her mother married again, this time a Spaniard, the Duc de Sesto. He was very fond of Mathilde, and she was grateful for his affection, but her mother's cruelty had destroyed her.[3]

Missy, as Paris called her, now, had been unlikely, from the first, to make a satisfactory marriage. Years later, staying with Liane de Pougy, then married to the Roumanian Prince Georges Ghika, she caused 'a great sensation'. 'Children,' she announced, 'I have a confession to make ... Well, listen: twice in my life I have slept with men ... One of them was my cousin Alexis Orloff. He said he would kill himself if I resisted, so – well, I didn't resist, but I refused any repetition. The second and last was Lord Yume [sic]. He was a very good-looking boy and he adored me, he wanted to marry me. He wore me down, so at last I said "Let's try," and I was his mistress for ten days. Then I'd had enough so I refused his proposal.'[4] Eventually, in 1903, at the age of forty, Missy married the Marquis de Belboeuf. He was immensely rich and he had estates in Normandy. Legend says that after one night with her husband, she avoided men, and loved only women.

She was 'dark-haired, and not bad-looking, with dark, incandescent eyes',[5] but she was strangely masculine in appearance. She dressed in a dinner-jacket when she was entertaining (almost exclusively women), or in mechanics' overalls during the day. It is said that, as her ankles were slim, she wore three or four pairs of woollen socks to give herself a more manly appearance.[6]

Missy de Belboeuf threw to the winds all that her birth and upbringing should have led her to respect. She created herself a character in a world which was of her choosing. I won't go so far as to say that Missy was a *monster* [wrote the socialite André de Fouquières]. She was in fact inspired by her anxiety to *épater le bourgeois*, and vice, with her, was contrived rather than natural...

One evening, I was invited to dinner with her. I was the only man among several female couples, and I was seated on the right of the mistress of the house. At the very beginning of the meal, my neighbour pulled her skirt right up, without the least embarrassment, and, holding it up in this position, she continued the conversation and gave herself several injections of morphine. She smoked enormous cigars incessantly. She sacrificed to her gods in company with a big and handsome blonde, Princess Poniatowska.[7]

Catherine Poniatowska was one of the notorious lesbians of the age.

Liane de Pougy was intensely lesbian; yet even she observed Missy with bewilderment. Missy, she said, used to flatten her breasts under a wide rubber band. 'She would have let her moustache grow if she'd had one! She exchanged the name Mathilde for the debonair "Uncle Max". At bottom she was a charming, childlike creature, a bit simple, well brought-up but an exhibitionist and a worry to her family... Max-Mathilde loved dressing up and giving fancy-dress dances; her whole life was a masquerade.' She was finally to be ruined by it.[8]

And yet, despite the masquerade, her natural aristocracy remained. 'She formed a school,' wrote Louise Weiss. 'It was she who sent mounds of Parma violets to Renée Vivien's apartments:

the violets which later became the symbol of *ces dames* ... Mathilde de Morny had been a sort of pioneer, whose manners these ladies later imitated although they did not succeed in matching her distinction, her class, her correctness of bearing and language ... She was a great lady, and she brooked no breach of protocol ... She entertained surrounded by her Napoleonic mementoes ... In spite of the freedom of thought and the free behaviour of *ces dames*, there were castes at Lesbos.'[9]

Despite her masculine appearance, Mathilde de Belboeuf appears to have had a strong maternal instinct. She was ten years older than Colette, and she protected her. She was also her lover. In *Les Vrilles de la vigne* – in 1908 – Colette explicitly describes their relationship. In 'Chanson de la danseuse', the sex of the lover is not specified, but the internal evidence makes it plain.[10] In 'Nuit blanche', Colette recalls herself in bed with the woman she loves. When she is tense, and cannot sleep,

... I know quite well that you will hold me closer still, and that, if the cradling of your arms is not enough to soothe me, your kiss will become more tenacious, your hands more amorous, and you will grant me sensual pleasure as relief, as the sovereign exorcism which drives from me the demons of fever, anger and anxiety ... You will give me sensual pleasure, bending over me, your eyes full of maternal anxiety: you who seek, in your passionate friend, for the child you have not known...[11]

Missy had 'enchanter's hands' and, wrote Colette, 'an overwhelming gaze'.[12]

Willy had encouraged Colette to write about lesbianism, he had encouraged her to mix in homosexual society. Lesbian relationships were actually in fashion. In the early 1900s lesbians became increasingly uninhibited, in private and in public. Even courtesans like Liane de Pougy and Émilienne d'Alençon consoled themselves with women for the company of men. Colette had not forgotten her affair with Georgie. It is said that in time she was drawn to Musidora, a dancer at the Folies-Bergère, to the actress Thérèse Robert and to her own secretary, Claude Chauvière.[13] However true these statements are, Colette was physically drawn to Missy. But, with Colette, as Pierre Brisson has acutely observed, it was never a question of sexuality, but of sensuality.[14] She felt an urgent need for sensual comfort. And, above all, she remained Sido's daughter. No doubt, above all, she needed a maternal figure. She was 'a nervous child who is returning invincibly, innocently, to feminine warmth, a child who wishes only for the loving shelter and the motionless caress of two enclosing arms'.[15]

Colette was clearly bisexual, at least in her early years; yet even this statement does not wholly explain her character. She herself gave the most illuminating explanation of her nature in a letter to Robert de Montesquiou. The breakdown of her marriage, and her liaison with Missy, had not affected her lively friendship with him. She eagerly accepted his invitation to the Pavillon des Muses, she asked him to *déjeuner* in her apartment. Montesquiou's study of the complex and disturbing art of Aubrey Beardsley assured her that he would understand her own outrageous and frustrating life. Willy had corrupted her, but even the Marquise did not satisfy her secret desires. Colette was drawn by the thought of concealed or indeterminate sex. She felt herself a passionate hermaphrodite. She was excited by the abnormal, by the *voyeur*.

At least three times [she wrote to Montesquiou] I have read your study of Beardsley, for whom I have an almost guilty passion, the drawings of this very young and rather mad young man correspond so closely to what is hidden in me. I have so longed to live, if only for an hour, in front of that garlanded dressing-table, whose mirror would reflect, behind my shoulder, the black velvet mask of the creature in disguise: the creature who has such pointed fingers.

I should very much like to know the name of the Lady who liked the faun. I have so few friends, Monsieur. This is not a complaint, it's certainly not! But I live, I'm told, in an unusual way, and I know that I am very much blamed for it. I am very much blamed especially because I don't give sufficient explanation of my reasons for breaking with nearly everything that is sensible or that is said to be so. But I assure you that I am not wicked, and that there is not a single ulterior motive for my behaviour! That doesn't matter to you, but I don't like to be misunderstood by a certain quality of people ...

Believe, dear Monsieur, in the real sympathy of

COLETTE WILLY.[16]

Georges Wague had made his theatrical début in 1898 with Christiane Mendelys, who became his wife. He had revived the art of mime at the turn of the century. Early in 1906 he had given Colette her first lessons in mime, and later that year a drama by the Belgian poet Charles van Lerberghe was performed at the Théâtre de l'Œuvre. Wague took the title-part in *Pan*, and Colette Willy, almost naked, appeared as Paniska among the bacchantes and the satyrs. The performance did not only establish her in the theatre; it helped to cement a close friendship with Wague, which was to last for the rest of her life.

In 1906 another intimate friend made his appearance. Léon Hamel was fifteen years older than Colette. He was a well-to-do and widely-travelled dilettante. His wisdom and integrity made him a natural confidant, and until his death in 1917 Colette confided in him without reserve. No-one, except Marguerite Moreno, was to be more informed about the vicissitudes of her private life.

A few authors' quarrels with her husband, and her liaison with Missy, had made Colette a favourite subject for the gossip-writers. Willy did not fail to get publicity from his wife's career. He used, it is said, to travel in 'Ladies Only' compartments in trains. When someone pointed his error out, he answered: 'I am the Marquise de Belboeuf.'

He exploited the situation in a more practical way. Colette and Missy belonged to a lesbian club in the avenue Victor-Hugo; from time to time the members performed pantomimes for one another. Willy visited the club out of curiosity. He persuaded Missy to make a public appearance.

He had taken Georges Wague into his confidence; and Vuillermoz, who took part in the rehearsals as a pianist ... Missy agreed to present *Rêve d'Égypte*, a pantomime which she signed with her anagram, Yssim. The project interested Mayrargue, then director of the Moulin-Rouge. Foreseeing the publicity which he would get out of it, he suggested to Mme la Marquise that she introduced the Yssim pantomime into a revue which had already had some 60 performances ... Colette Willy was to figure as a mummy ...

The subject evoked the customs of ancient Egypt. An elderly scholar – this was the Marquise – inspired by the love of learning, saw her sculptures and statuettes move like *tableaux vivants*. Then Colette came out of her sarcophagus and charmed the good man with her songs and dances ...[17]

Marcel Boulestin recalled that

days before the performance there was not a seat to be had at any price. The first-night audience was composed of several elements besides the professional first-nighters, and those who had only come out of curiosity; members of the Bonapartist party, who were shocked and angry at the idea of the Marquise's exhibition; members of the *demi-monde* and ladies from Maxim's who had suddenly been seized with a fit of moral indignation; and Society people, or rather their servants whom they had sent in their stead. All had come with the intention of making a row, and armed with oranges, apples, and various vegetables.

I suppose it is true to say that there had never been such a scandal in a Paris theatre.[18]

The moment that the curtain went up, on 3 January 1907, the overheated audience grew explosive. The Marquise, in her blue velvet suit, was greeted with ribald comments from every side. The ribaldry increased when Colette emerged from her sarcophagus. She was swaddled in bandelets which fell of their own accord, to reveal her blue Egyptian dress. The climax was the moment when the Egyptologist gave the resurrected mummy a prolonged and passionate kiss. At this, a hail of orange-peel, cigarettes, match-boxes and vegetables rained upon the stage.[19] Liane de Pougy, the courtesan, and Suzanne Derval, the actress and *demi-mondaine*, withdrew into the shadows of their box.[20] Willy, who was in a stage-box, had to be rushed to safety by the police. Boulestin met 'a few English acquaintances, Cosmo Gordon Lennox and Harry Melvill, so excited that they both talked at the same time; and Gerald Kelly, so thrilled that he said he was coming to the second performance. But there was no second performance, at least with the Marquise.'[21]

Next day M. Lépine, the Prefect of Police, summoned the administrator of the Société du Moulin-Rouge. He informed him that the performance of *Rêve d'Égypte* was banned by prefectural decree. He also threatened that he would have his establishment closed if the announcement remained on the poster. That evening Mme Yssim was replaced by Georges Wague.

On 9 January, at the offices of *Le Mercure de France*, Paul Léautaud saw Colette Willy. She was now highly scandalous 'because of her exhibitions at the Moulin-Rouge'.[22] She was talking to the editor about a final *Claudine* which she was going to publish under her own name.

La Retraite sentimentale made its appearance later in the year. It bore a note to the reader: 'For reasons which have nothing to do with literature, I have ceased to collaborate with Willy.'

The novel was published as the work of Colette Willy. It is set in Annie's country house at Casamène, clearly recognisable as Les Monts-Boucons. Claudine has come to stay with Annie. As the two women grow intimate, Annie reveals her past. The break-up of her marriage has turned the naive young wife into a promiscuous woman; and, when Claudine's stepson comes to stay, Annie makes physical advances to him. Marcel is homosexual, the episode is disastrous, and Annie leaves Les Monts-Boucons, to search abroad, again, for the love which constantly eludes her. Renaud has been gravely ill in a sanatorium in Switzerland. He returns to Switzerland, a dying man of fifty. He dies, and Claudine lives on, alone, deep in the countryside, aware at last of the nature of love.

The author of *La Retraite sentimentale* was now immersed in her second career. In 1907 Georges Wague began rehearsals of his new mime, *La Chair*, for the Apollo. The plot would raise a disbelieving smile from the modern spectator; but it was not then considered ludicrous. A man was deceived by his wife and prepared to kill her in his fury. He knelt before her, vanquished, because – unbelievably – he saw her naked for the first time. She taunted him with her beauty and refused to yield to him. In despair, he killed himself. Wague played the husband and Christine Kerf the lover. Colette played Yulka, the triumphant mistress. *La Chair*, with music by Albert Chantrier, was first performed in Paris on 31 October 1907. It was warmly received and 'taken off, still warm, to Nice, and revived in Paris in April 1908. In Nice, at the Palais du Soleil, the surroundings helped, and Colette showed herself neither more or less modest.'[23]

For several years Colette, Christine Kerf and Wague found themselves on tour. They played *La Chair* not only in Paris and Nice, but in Monte-Carlo, Bordeaux, Rouen, Marseilles, Lyons and Brussels. They also performed it in Grenoble, Geneva and Le Havre. *La Chair* reached more than 250 performances.

It was at the Casino de Lyon that the young Maurice Chevalier found himself advertised on the same poster as Colette Willy. He thought her highly desirable, but did not dare to declare himself.

I became her friend – many years later [so he recalled]. She had become the great Colette. I finally confessed to her that once, in Lyons, my feelings for her had become very disturbing.

'You really mean that, my dear Maurice? ... Oh, how ridiculous! You should have told me. What a pity, I'm a fat old woman now ... It's too late. There you are, it's too late!!!' ...

I am [continued Chevalier] very proud of the friendship and the interest that she did not cease to show me in the later part of our lives ...

I shall content myself with having found her very desirable in her youth and very admirable in later life.[24]

Meanwhile, in her early years, Colette did not restrict herself to mime. She acted in her own short play, *En Camarades*; she performed at the Théâtre des Arts and at the Comédie-Royale. She went on tour in the provinces with *Claudine à Paris*, a three-act play by Willy and Lugné-Poë. But she was, above all, drawn by the music-hall and by the café-concert. In these pre-war years, the caf-con' was flourishing. In Paris, the Gaîété-Rochechouart, the Cigale and the Scala were considered fairly respectable. The most widely popular café-concerts were Ba-ta-clan, the Casino Montparnasse, the Eldorado and the Casino Saint-Martin. They attracted a local public who could be obstreperous and demanding. At Ba-ta-clan,

Colette revived *Aux Bat' d'aff*, a mimodrama which she had created at the Gaiété-Rochechouart.

The years 1906-11 were, for her, the music-hall years. In Paris, and on tour, she continued to live with Mathilde de Belboeuf. Some said that she wore a bracelet engraved with the words: 'I belong to Missy.' Maurice Martin du Gard, who called on her in Brittany, was greeted by 'a gentleman of a certain age, paunchy, with white trousers, a black alpaca jacket; a slight stubble of grey hair, a lorgnette... This gentleman was the Marquise.'[25] Boulestin recalled Missy, dressed in masculine attire, drinking green chartreuse and being addressed by waiters as 'monsieur'. One Christmas Eve he was invited to the *réveillon*, or midnight supper, at Missy's apartment. It was, he remembered, 'just a quiet, greedy supper with pounds of beautiful truffles quite plain, cooked under the ashes, of which Colette and myself ate an enormous amount.'[26] As for Missy, wrote Colette, 'she lives above this world and feeds on the smoke of havanas.'[27] Liane de Pougy echoed the comment. Missy's cigars gave her a headache; and, in years to come, when Missy arrived 'in her beautiful red car with her chauffeur and her maid', she also proved an impossible guest. 'I can't eat eggs, or fish, or peas, or beans, or tomatoes, or veal, or pork ...'[28]

While she was living with Missy, and immersed in her music-hall career, Colette continued to write books which brought her increasing recognition. In 1908 she published *Les Vrilles de la vigne*: a collection of autobiographical essays and stories. She had written them in her dressing-room at the Théâtre-Marigny during the intervals of *Pan*. In 1909 came *L'Ingénue libertine*. She sent a copy to Marguerite Moreno, now living with Jean Daragon, her second husband, in Buenos Aires. 'What talent you have, my dear Colette!' answered Marguerite. '... Write on, write on for ever for the pleasure of those who love to read, and especially for mine ... If you have a moment, write and tell me if you are working on something and if you are *content*.'[29]

Colette was no doubt content to be separated from Willy. Even now, she was learning more of his gross and selfish behaviour.

'Unknown to me, he sold *all* the Claudines to the publishers for almost nothing,' she told Léon Hamel early in 1909. 'And these books which (morally) almost entirely belonged to me are lost for ever to him and to me ... Just think that, after 3 years of separation, I still very often hear of betrayals that I hadn't known ...'[30]

At her new apartment at 25 rue Saint-Senoch, she continued to work at the novel which she had been writing on tour: *La Vagabonde*, her account of her music-hall years. In May 1910 – long before she had finished the book – the serial version began to appear in *La Vie Parisienne*. At Le Crotoy, on the coast near Le Touquet, where she spent part of the summer with Missy, she continued, desperately, to write it. On 28 July she told the critic André Rouveyre: 'I must – I mean *must* finish my novel in ten or twelve days! ... Missy is well, thank God, and she quietly suffers the sudden changes of wind and rain – and mine.'[31]

The relationship continued; yet *La Vagabonde* contained an observation which may reflect something of its author's mood. 'What use explaining to him?' asked the heroine. 'For him [her admirer], two women in an embrace will always be a licentious group, and not the melancholy, touching picture of two weaknesses, taking refuge perhaps in each other's arms to sleep there, weep there, to escape man who is often bad, and to enjoy, more than any pleasure, the bitter happiness of feeling themselves akin, and insignificant, and forgotten ...'[32]

On 21 June, at last, she obtained her divorce from Willy. Later in the year, Jacques Gauthier-Villars returned from Spain to do his military service. Willy told him 'that his relations with Colette were no longer strained, ... they were broken. "A pity," I said, impassive but very sorry. "Yes, a pity," was Willy's comment, "for her and for me." '[33]

· ——— ·

As for Colette, her private life had now become decidedly complex. She was still living with Missy, but she was encouraging Polaire's former lover, Auguste Hériot. Polaire, in her memoirs, was to write so bitterly of Hériot that one wonders if he had deserted her for Colette. 'Four years of hell!' declared Polaire.

'And yet he represented everything that can contribute to a woman's happiness. However, he showed a possessiveness which clashed with my independent nature. He used to talk of nothing except marriage.'[34] It is strange that, if her life with him had been so infernal, Polaire had borne with him for four years. It is also strange that an actress of passing notoriety should have rejected such a brilliant match. However, their liaison was now over; and this vastly wealthy young man, whose family owned a department store in Paris, was ardently in love with Colette.

Sylvain Bonmariage, in his scandalous *Willy, Colette et moi*, recorded that

young H—— was the son of Chauchard's partner at the Grands Magasins du Louvre. He was some thirty years old, and, with his wit, his perfect education, the lissom, masculine elegance of a cavalry officer, and the millions which backed the overwhelming power of his physical charm, he was one of the most attractive people in Paris. His misfortune was to abuse strong drink, and at times to lose his self-control.

He was immature, capricious, changing in friendship, absolute in love. An orphan, and a bachelor, he lived in an imposing *hôtel*, the one in which the Legation of the Argentine Republic was to be installed two years later.

There was a Louis XV salon there, signed Ries[e]ner, on the walls of which were displayed two Gobelins tapestries, taken from Fragonard cartoons. These were sold for 1,500,000 (gold) francs to Mr Pierpont Morgan. In this salon - his mother's - just as it was, H—— had an American bar installed, and he had engaged the best barman in Paris, Francis, in his service ...[35]

Robert Chassériau told Bonmariage that 'H——'s introduction to Colette was a sort of revelation for him. He abandoned all his friends, all his fantasies, prepared to devote all his powers and his fortune to the enterprise of loving her, of making himself beloved by her and assuring her happiness. He adored her faithfully for at least two years. Was he happy? He avoided every question, stubbornly, and in ferocious silence.'[36]

Late in 1910 Colette took a brief holiday in Naples with Hériot.[37] 'My young companion sends you his greetings,' she announced to Hamel on 19 November. 'He is a nice boy when he's alone with me. He'll never be happy, because he's built on a foundation of sadness.'[38]

Late in 1910 *La Vagabonde* was published in book form. It is a rich and delicate impression of a music-hall existence: the crude, endearing comradeship, the poverty, the squalor of provincial lodgings and provincial theatres, the coarseness of the audience, the loneliness, the bitterness and indignity. It is also a panorama of the changing landscapes through which the actors move, presented with vibrant sensibility. It is written from the heart, because it is written from experience and, at times, with lyrical power. Cocteau later noted, with a certain dramatic licence, that Colette's celebrity had been born 'in the humble corridors of the music-halls: slowly and obscurely, as on the straw of a manger'.[39]

One astonished reader of *La Vagabonde* recognised himself in the book. 'She talked about me,' wrote Maurice Chevalier, 'and she had distorted me not a little in one of her characters whom she called Cavaillon.'[40]

Colette, it has been said, cannot imagine a happy relationship; she analyses failure, and she speaks of what she knows. Yet the unfulfilled love-affair between Renée Néré and Maxime Dufferein-Chautel (based, it is said, on Auguste Hériot) lacks the poignant authenticity which will mark Léa's relationship with Chéri. Renée is, at first, annoyed by her persistent admirer; then she is bored by him. Yet she does not simply dismiss him. She allows him to continue his visits, she accepts his flowers, she flirts with him, and she falls in love with him as soon as he makes a physical advance. It is hard to believe in her vexation, her boredom, or her love. She seems to delude both herself and the reader. Yet, from her letters to Max, certain patent truths still emerge. She is terrified of growing old, and of the temptations that this would bring him; she has been so hurt by marriage, by the infidelity of the husband whom she continues to love, that she has no heart for a second alliance. She longs for physical passion and for companionship, but she cannot bear the thought of a master. She must see her life through her own eyes, keep her dignity and freedom. *La Vaga-*

bonde expresses all that is incomprehensible, all that is irremediable, in love.

La Vagabonde, said Rémy de Gourmont, confirmed the originality of Colette. 'It is not perhaps a work of art, it is a treatise of feminine psychology. It is woman laid bare with her eternal way of wanting what she does not want, of no longer wanting what she is offered and what she desires, of tearing herself away from life through her pride in living.'[41]

La Vagabonde – like the book submitted by Guillaume Apollinaire – was an unsuccessful candidate for the Prix Goncourt. But whatever her fortunes might be at the Académie-Goncourt, Colette was now discussed in a more august, more awesome setting. On 5 January 1911 certain members of the Académie-Française were talking about the election of women.

'Have you read *La Vagabonde* by the author of the *Claudines*?'
'No.'
'Then read it. Perhaps you would vote for Claudine.'
'You're joking.'
'Not at all. I'm not joking. And look at Mme Curie. She's going to open the door to many ambitions and countless fantasies. There's no doubt Mme Curie will be elected...'[42]

On 2 December 1910, with boundless energy, Colette had embarked upon a third career. She had begun to write regularly for a leading Paris newspaper. Her name was thought too notorious for a family paper like *Le Matin*, and at first she signed with an enigmatic mask. On 27 February 1911, next to the mask, was written: 'C'est moi, Colette Willy.' Her chronicles appeared under the title 'Contes des Mille et un matins'.

That month she found herself installed at the Majestic Palace Hotel in Nice, with the faithful Auguste Hériot; there they were joined by another admirer, Lily de Rême (who was to be the model for the giddy, limited, vulgar May in *L'Entrave*).

The little de R ... came to join us two days ago [Colette reported to Hamel on 14 February], and our trio would interest you. These two children in love with me are remarkable – for the very fact that they love me ... But I'm not very happy about young H. Dear Hamel, how I've wanted to talk to you about it! And who can I talk to frankly, if not you? The die is cast, you're the one I'll ask for secrecy and advice, because the love-affair seems to me to be serious, especially for him, I am not emotionally in danger. I must talk to you ...[43]

In the meanwhile she enjoyed the devotion of Hériot and of Lily de Rême, and indulged in a verbal flirtation with the popular novelist Claude Farrère. 'Dear Claude Farrère [this on 22 February], I shan't be able to come and see you ... I'm going to Brittany to meet Missy and then I'm going to Tunis. If you were to come to Tunis ...'[44]

She went to Tunis with Lily de Rême. On 21 March she reported their arrival, 'exhausted and content'.[45] They were not to be content for long. Ten days later, from Rozven, near Saint-Malo, she told Hamel 'how impossible Lily was in Tunis, in Marseilles and everywhere. It's terrible! When I think that she has suggested that we go to India together! I'd rather burst.'[46]

The life of the vagabond continued. On 25 June, from Geneva, she told André Rouveyre that she was performing there until 1 July, and that she might go on to perform in Lausanne and Interlaken and Lucerne.[47]

Within the next month the era of Missy – and Hériot – was over.

■━━■

Bertrand Henry Léon Robert de Jouvenel des Ursins descended from Limousin barons.[48] The name Jouvenel des Ursins had entered history at the end of the Hundred Years' War, in the third generation of Henry's known forebears. His earliest ancestor on record was Pierre Jouvenel, a prosperous draper in Troyes towards the end of the fourteenth century. Pierre provided his son, Jean Jouvenel, with an education in law and a drapery trade in Paris. Jean rose to prominence in the reign of Charles V, and became king's advocate in the *parlement* of Paris, president of the *parlement* of Toulouse, and first president of the *parlement* of Poitiers. The best-known of his many children was his namesake Jean, who fought under the banner of Joan of Arc and lived to become Archbishop of Rheims and Peer of France. It was he who spelt his name Juvénal, and added 'des Ursins' to it, to signify his descent from the Orsinis, but his claim has always been contested.

After the death of Jean Juvénal des Ursins, the family name reverted to the form Jouvenel. In the reign of François I, the family was converted to Protestantism. It lost favour with the Court and took refuge in the south of France. The Jouvenels who survived the Wars of Religion sank to the condition of the peasantry.

In the nineteenth century, Léon de Jouvenel des Ursins restored his family to prominence.[49] He married a relation of the politician Casimir-Perier. Then, in 1844, a Corrézien by birth and a Corrézien at heart, he bought the *château* of Castel-Novel, near Varetz. He was to live there for nearly half a century. In 1848, when the monarchy collapsed, he ran as a royalist candidate for the Constituent Assembly. He was defeated and rallied to the Republic. Under the Second Empire he was elected Deputy for the department of Corrèze. In 1876 he withdrew from politics and retired to Castel-Novel.

Léon's son, Raoul, married a daughter of the progressive Deputy De Janzé, and became the Prefect of Côtes-du-Nord: one of the youngest and most lavish Prefects of the Second Empire. Like his father, he wanted to see the House of Orleans restored after the fall of Napoleon III. As France settled down under the Republic, he, too, withdrew from public life and returned to his native Corrèze. There, in the town of Brive-la-Gaillarde, on 2 April 1876, his son Henry was born. A second son, Robert, followed five years later.

Léon died in 1886. That year the Comte de Paris, Orleanist Pretender to the throne, was banished from France, and Raoul wanted to follow with his family into exile. His wife demurred; and Raoul vented his bitterness and his frustration on her. She pleaded for a divorce; he refused. She deserted him – but he refused a divorce to the last.

Henry de Jouvenel spent his childhood at Castel-Novel. When he was seventeen, his father took him to Paris, settled with him in the rue du Faubourg Saint-Honoré, and sent him to the Collège

Stanislas, to prepare for his *baccalauréat*. In the autumn of 1895 he entered the École Normale Supérieure. A few months later, he was conscripted for military service; in 1899 he left the army as a corporal and began to make his career.

He was romantically handsome; he was elegant, charming and highly intelligent, and he already had a gift for making himself loved. He soon conquered Paris, fought duels where necessary, and associated with other young beginners in politics. He became the secretary-general of the Democratic Conferences Committee. His speeches at the Cercle républicain impressed Alfred Boas, a wealthy Jewish industrialist, who was also an influential Radical and Freemason. Boas secured him an appointment as cabinet secretary to the Minister of Justice, Valle, in the Radical government which was formed by Combes in June 1902. Jouvenel – still only twenty-seven – then applied for a post on *Le Matin*. The owner of the newspaper, Maurice Bunau-Varilla, hired him at what was said to be an astronomical salary. He became one of the two alternating editors-in-chief – they worked for a fortnight at a time – with Stéphane Lauzanne. He was to turn *Le Matin*, which was still in its early days, into a newspaper with a big circulation.

In 1902 he also married Claire Boas, his patron's daughter. They spent the first year of their marriage living with his father; then they took a house of their own. But they had little in common, and there was much on which they disagreed. In 1903 she bore him a son, Bertrand; soon afterwards, the marriage foundered, and in 1906 they were divorced.

Claire Boas de Jouvenel never remarried; instead, with the help of the politician Philippe Berthelot, she rose to 'the head of the zealous battalion of Quai d'Orsay ladies', as 'a sort of diplomatic and republican squad leader'.[50] She was undoubtedly influential. In the spring of 1916, recorded Édouard Beneš, 'Milan Štefánik had introduced me to the salon of Mme de Jouvenel, where I met some political celebrities: M. Philippe Berthelot, the deputies Picard, Lémery, Louis Martin, Paul-Boncour, M. Kammerer, journalists, ministers plenipotentiary, military men ...'[51] In 1917, as the Austro-Hungarian Empire was secretly offering to surrender in return for a guarantee of its integrity, Claire Boas de Jouvenel brought together the Czech Beneš, the Slovak Štefánik and the two

Quai d'Orsay specialists in Slavic affairs, Ernest Denis and Louis Léger; and the four of them improvised a joint Czech and Slovak state. 'She received the most important people in the Government; she was convinced,' wrote one of the Jouvenels, 'that she had brought Czechoslovakia into the world. Her apartment in Paris was an unbelievable bazaar, and God knows how she managed to buy herself a Rolls. One suspects that she lived on various subsidies, and especially on secret funds from the Ministry of Foreign Affairs. She was certainly exasperating because she meddled with everything, always wanted to play an important part, to cut a figure.'[52] She was maddening, but she deserved consideration. After the war, she founded La Bienvenue Française, an organisation for the reception of foreign visitors to France; she launched La Journée Pasteur, to raise money for scientific laboratories, and she created exchange scholarships and welfare funds by the dozen. Berthelot's retirement somewhat limited her access to ministries in Paris and to chanceries abroad; she used her remaining influence unsparingly to urge war against Hitler.

Henry de Jouvenel's first direct relations with French politics lasted less than four years. They were confined to the Ministry of Justice until January 1905, when Combes lost the confidence of the Chamber of Deputies. Jouvenel then became chief secretary to the Radical-Socialist Dubief, Minister of Commerce in the Rouvier administration. When this government fell, in turn, he broke off his formal political activity. Journalism was more satisfying. His first expenses as chief secretary had been defrayed by his earnings as editor. By 1907 he was said to run *Le Matin*.

He divided his time between Paris, where he edited his paper, and Corrèze, which he always regarded as his home. He sought out the company of the well-read in preference to that of the well-born. He led an intensely social life, spent money like a prince, and his successes with women earned him a lasting reputation.

Physically [wrote one of the family], he was quite a tall man, with a tendency to stoutness; he had a proud glance, an aquiline nose, of which there are many in central and south-western France since the Arabs passed that way. He had a generous mouth and proud moustaches which he was to shorten later. He had undeniable presence; he had what people called a dashing air. He had a 'tone of voice' (the expression is his own) ... which had a great effect on women and on senators. He used it. A tyrannical father and friend, he was irascible, suddenly stung into terrifying rages. Deep down, he was sensitive, indeed a weak man who hid his weakness under a crusty manner ...

He was a real spendthrift, he led a life which was nearly always magnificent. He has been compared to a Florentine nobleman of the Renaissance. In my opinion he was also, perhaps above all, a Rastignac.[53]

Small wonder that Henry de Jouvenel soon became a lion of the Parisian *gens de lettres*. Women used to call him 'the Tiger'. Among them was Mme Pillet-Will, Comtesse de Comminges. She was 'perhaps an unstable, excessive character, but very cultivated', and beautiful, and she was herself known as 'the Panther'.[54] She presented him with a second son, Renaud, in 1907.

■———·■

My mother, Isabelle de Comminges, was born [wrote Renaud] at the Château de Saint-Marcet (Ariège), at the foot of the Abbey of Saint Bertrand de Comminges, one of the most beautiful in France, looking over a very fine Pyrenean landscape. Her father, a dashing officer with splendid moustaches, ... had married a Polish woman, Princess Lubomirski, I don't know where he had found her and she must have been bored, so far from her marshes, since the family came from the neighbourhood of Pinsk. It was probably the only break in a tradition of all-French marriages, for the Comminges were allied to a number of the best aristocratic families in France.

The Comminges belong, in fact, to one of the most ancient families, earlier than the hereditary kings, and, for my mother, the Bourbons were usurpers ...

Grandfather Comminges was not rich, he married his daughter to Comte Pillet-Will, a wealthy Parisian banker, by whom she had three children whom I have never even seen. 'He was a madman,' she wrote to me, and she felt contempt for him because this Comte or his father had bought his title. One day, this Pillet-Will shot my mother's dog dead with a revolver: he was afraid of the Great Dane. The Comtesse looked at him with disdain, insulted him, had her trunks packed, and left at once.

She must have had a proud appearance when she rode on horseback in the Bois de Boulogne, in her riding-habit, with her bronze eyes and

her hair which verged on red . . .
    She was very fond of animals, had dobermans and even a black panther. As for me, my first playmate, in a garden in Passy, was a young puma. She never remarried.
    I don't know how she met my father, but . . . I have a feeling that this love was a sort of confrontation, a sort of duel in which my father did not get the upper hand. The Comtesse certainly loved him, but in her own way, condescendingly. 'You don't sit a horse well,' she used to tell him. 'You should buy a buggy.' Many years later, she asked me: 'Does your father still eat mutton with his fingers?' And my father asked me: 'How is your mother?' as if he still felt the effects of her claws.
    One day, it seems, Jouvenel left the Panther . . . for Colette.[55]

Sidi – as she called him – was three years younger than Colette. No doubt his irregular past was part of his attraction; but she could hardly have failed to be attracted by this prestigious man.
    Renaud de Jouvenel later reflected, with bewilderment, on his father's relationship with her.

At the time they fell in love, she must have looked very like the nymph stretched out on a velvet couch, the photograph which was reproduced on a postcard inscribed: *Our Pretty Actresses: Mme Colette of the Olympia*, and subtitled *I am entirely yours*.
    As for my father – whom she called Pasha or Sidi or both – he belonged to a quite different race. An aristocrat who was somewhat infatuated by nobility, and a radical-socialist of the old school – sincerely democratic – he hardly swerved, to my knowledge, from his haughtiness, or from his bourgeois prejudices, because one can be both a bourgeois and an aristocrat . . . He had a lofty idea of his duties as a statesman, as an ambassador for his country in his own life as well as in an embassy, in the Senate, or elsewhere . . . He was of such a different order [from Colette] that I cannot make out what pleased him, contemporary aesthetics apart, in this literary débutante . . . Perhaps he had repressed plebeian instincts, as my mother, a countess, used to tell him to his face, and perhaps he was eager to show them – in a spirit of compensation – after his affair with the woman who was called the Panther . . . She was always ready to throw her genealogy at you, and she did not forget that the Comminges had come three centuries before the Jouvenels . . .[56]

It was astonishing that Jouvenel should have been in love with Colette. Yet so it was; and Renaud was to keep letters from Colette to his father, which he steadfastly refused to publish. They proved, he said, a love which bordered on humility.[57]

'Dear Rouveyre,' wrote Colette on 22 July 1911, '... I'm spending a few days in Paris. Events are rather disturbing at the moment.'[58]

Events were indeed disturbing. On 30 June Jouvenel had fought a duel with a representative of *Le Journal*; it was alleged that the paper had insulted *Le Matin*.[59] Next day, with his arm in a sling, he had appeared in Lausanne, where Colette was performing, to say that he could not and would not live without her. At the same time, so Colette reported to Léon Hamel,[60] Hériot had wanted to join her in Switzerland, and she had been obliged to stop him with frantic, lying and contradictory telegrams. Jouvenel, she said, returned to Paris, and he confessed to the Panther that he loved another woman. The Panther declared that she would kill her. Colette claimed that she boldly went to see her and told her that she was the woman in question. Mme de Comminges – she continued – pleaded with her to leave Jouvenel. Two days later she became aggressive again and told Jouvenel that she would knife Colette. It made a dramatic narrative; but, as Renaud observed,

> Colette could allow herself to be so carried away by her lyricism that she forgot the reality of things. I cannot possibly imagine Colette visiting the Comtesse-Panthère, and, still less, the Comtesse falling on her knees before her. She, who was coldness itself, and cold even in her anger! ... This very problematical visit would absolutely contradict the interview which I organized, long afterwards, between the two women at the Hôtel Claridge.[61]

However – so Colette maintained – Jouvenel instructed a friend, Charles Sauerwein, to drive her to Rozven, and the three of them arrived to find Missy, not surprisingly, icy and disgusted. The two men returned to Paris, and another friend was left to mount guard. Missy departed for Honfleur. Three days later, Jouvenel summoned Colette to Paris, and Sauerwein drove back to fetch her, while Mme de Comminges – she said – was prowling round in search of her with a revolver. Colette maintained that she was forced to live in semi-imprisonment in Paris, guarded by Jouvenel and by the Sûreté.

Whatever the facts of the case, this period was suddenly ended by a providential and unforeseen event. Auguste Hériot sought consolation from Mme de Comminges. They embarked on a yacht, the *Esmerald*, for a cruise of at least six weeks.

The situation was as complex as any in a novel, for Missy – so Colette maintained – was devoted to Hériot, she had prepared a room for him at Rozven, and she had intended to impose him almost conjugally on her.[62] It is a remarkable statement. If it is true, it can only mean that Missy wanted to be rid of her, or that she was purely maternal, and wanted Colette to make 'a good match'.[63] Perhaps she was maternal about Colette and paternal about Hériot. Liane de Pougy, who had recently married Georges Ghika, recorded in her *cahiers bleus*: 'It was Missy's way to call nice-looking boys her "sons". So when I became the wife of her "son" she called me "daughter" and signed herself "your father-in-law." '[64]

Whatever Missy's feelings, her eager championship of Hériot would have been enough in itself to end Colette's relationship with him. Jouvenel, however, showed his own determination by having his house fitted up for his new mistress. Missy bought a villa three kilometres from Rozven: an action which looked like an epilogue. Jouvenel, exultant, drove Colette to Castel-Novel.[65]

For the de-classed woman who performed in music-halls, it seemed a romance out of fiction. Yet it was real enough. Years later, she still remembered that evening in the summer of 1911,

a Limousin summer compared with which July in Provence is all freshness and dew, at nightfall, the black towers against the pale sky, the ground floor with candles and paraffin lamps, some very well-polished silver, an imposing valet in a whitish dress-coat, the big rose-trees not pruned – it was all obscure, crumbling, enchanting. In the Lions' room, where I left the doors and windows open at night in the hope of a breeze, the bats were flitting to and fro between the pillars of the four-poster bed. I was – for more than one reason – dazzled.[66]

Back in Paris, she wrote to Hamel: 'I have a new heart.'[67]

She was physically very much in love with Jouvenel, and she chose to proclaim the fact to all the world. 'Who tells you that I am neglecting physical culture [this to Christiane Mendelys, on 29 August]? I have a new method, that's all. The Sidi method. Excellent. No public lessons. Private lessons – extremely private ...'[68]

By October she and Sidi were living at 57 rue Cortambert, an old wooden Swiss châlet in the fashionable district of Passy. It was from here, apparently, that Sidi sent an invitation to Sido. 'Your invitation,' came the answer, 'is so gracious that for many reasons I've decided to accept it. Among these reasons there is one which I never resist: the sight of my daughter's dear face, and the sound of her voice. And then I want to meet you, and to judge as far as I can why she has been so eager to kick over the traces for you.'[69]

On 3 December, at the Gaiété-Rochechouart, Georges Wague presented a mimodrama by himself and J.-M. Allène, with music by Albert Chantrier. Colette played the title-rôle in *L'Oiseau de nuit*, that of 'a young beggar-girl, pitiful and seductive, woman and demon'.[70] In April 1912, more disturbing than ever, she appeared in the mime *La Chatte amoureuse*, at the music-hall in the boulevard Voltaire. Dressed as a cat, in black fleshings, she displayed a 'divinely provocative' silhouette.[71]

Her tempestuous love-affair continued, though even she was uncertain how it would end. On 1 August Sidi left for a week of aviation at Brive; he put her in charge of certain interior decoration in the house, as if she were going to end her days there. She herself dared not think that the relationship would be permanent; but on 17 August, when Sidi had returned, she confessed to Hamel: 'I'm letting myself enjoy an ephemeral animal happiness which damn well has its value. You know yourself how precious it is, after days and weeks of disaster: the *presence* of the necessary person.'[72]

It was one of the rare moments in her life when Colette was not dreaming of Saint-Sauveur, or of Sido – now an ailing old woman at Châtillon. Indeed on 26 August she told Wague, with a certain asperity: 'I'm leaving for Châtillon, where my blessed mother is insufferable, not that she is more seriously ill, but she is having an attack of "I must see my daughter." Sidi is granting me three days – maximum.'[73] She left for Châtillon next day, for a visit of forty-eight hours. On 29 August, just before she returned to Paris, she told Christiane Mendelys: 'Mother isn't marvellous, but she can still survive, which is all one asks of her.'[74]

Sido could not survive much longer. She was suffering from cancer. Larnac, in his book on Colette, said that her death had long been expected.[75] On 25 September she died. 'Dear Hamel,' wrote Colette, '... I am not going to the funeral. I am telling hardly anyone about it, and I'm not wearing any outward mourning. At the moment it is fairly all right. But I am tormented by the stupid thought that I shan't be able to write to mother any more as I so often did ...'[76] She had written to her two or three times a week.

'If she had really loved Sido,' Renaud de Jouvenel has written, 'my father would not have prevented her from going to her funeral. Perhaps ... she only began to be interested in Sido later in the day, and it is an exploitable subject in the literary sense ...'[77] It is easy to accuse Colette of lack of feeling; but in fact she could not bear to acknowledge the fact of Sido's death. Writing to Léopold Marchand, the dramatist, when his mother died, she confessed: 'When it was a question of my mother, I had less courage than you, because I only wanted to know her when she was alive.'[78]

Sido was to remain to her marvellously alive. Thirty years after Sido's death, Colette was to write of 'my mother, the mother I never loved enough, or well enough.'[79] In 1945, in *Belles Saisons*, she still dreamed of 'a small woman, plump and vivacious, bearing on her woollen dress the smell of the wood fire, the chrysanthemum border ...'[80] She was always waiting, as she had waited in her childhood, for Sido. She still recognised that Sido was 'the most important person in all my life.'[81] No husband, lover or child was ever to inspire her with the same profound, complete devotion. Sido remained her comfort, her inspiration and her strength.

■ ▬ ■

In the autumn of 1912 Sidi tried to comfort her by taking her back to Castel-Novel, where his family looked after her. The days of uncertainty were over. He had now, it seems, decided to marry her. On 14 October, from the *château* in Corrèze, she reported to her usual correspondent: 'Dear Hamel, ... Everyone is charming to me. My mother-in-law, as Sidi calls her, is youth and gaiety itself.'[82]

Passionate, amusing, and fiercely unorthodox, Mamita had much in common with Colette; but she is perhaps best recorded by Renaud.

At the summit of the family pyramid as I knew it [so he writes], there is the Dowager Baronne, my paternal grandmother, called Mamita.

When I saw her, I mean saw her, she was already old. She suffered from emphysema and rheumatism and walked with the aid of sticks, but she was merry and amusing. She smoked cigars, drank big glasses of brandy, and said: 'They refuse me everything,' she was confessed at home by the famous Abbé Mugnier, who absolved her on principle, that Abbé Mugnier who converted Huysmans and whom I called *Riquet à la houppe* because of the little white toupet on his head. This abbé was a remarkable man, a friend of Bergson, of Princess Bibesco, of many other celebrities, including the Duchesse d'Uzès and the little Duchesse de Castries ...

When she was still young, Mamita had had an affair with M. Chevandier de Valdrôme, by whom she had a daughter, Edith, who died young, probably of tuberculosis, perhaps of leukaemia, I don't know. However it was, she brought her back to the family *château* and, thanks to a photograph, one can see on the *château* terrace: Mamita, the cuckolded grandfather, Edith and my father, who seems to have taken the thing very well.[83]

Raoul de Jouvenel had now died; but, on this visit to the *château*, Colette met all the rest of the family.

There's Robert, there's the young sister who is an enormous, gentle child and contrives to look like Sidi in a striking way. There is the sweet and classic English governess, who gets up at night – I am hardly exaggerating – to bring me aspirins. And finally there is a bright and burning sun which warms my wretched cold, and Castel-Novel is worthy of the countryside around it. All the same, this way of life, this 'resting in the country', would overtax people who were well in training, if one didn't go to bed early. At 8 o'clock in the morning, everyone is bustling about, Sidi is on the farm, his mother playing tennis, I am wherever you choose to imagine me. The day before yesterday there was an excursion to Curemonte, the *château* which Robert has bought (it needs a hundred thousand francs on repairs before there is any thought of furniture) ...[84]

From her *château* life she returned – no doubt for financial reasons – to her music-hall career. She was earning a good living. Later that month she went to Geneva, where *L'Oiseau de nuit* was presented at the Apollo. After this, she abandoned the music-hall.

Since she had first performed in *La Chair*, five years had passed. Her success had been prolonged. She had owed it to her half-nakedness, to the crude charm of her gestures, the authority of her inviting eyes. She knew that this success and its causes would not last for life.[85] There was another, more imperative reason why she left the stage. By November she was pregnant.

'There are,' wrote Renaud, 'two versions of the reasons for this marriage: those of M. de Cizancourt and my sister. According to the former, Jouvenel said: "I am the only man in Paris capable of marrying that woman." According to my sister, her mother had been pregnant; but it is not the custom in our family to marry all the women we get pregnant. Where should we be?'[86]

Whatever the reason, Colette and Sidi were married on 19 December.

MADAME LA BARONNE DE JOUVENEL 1912-25

I

Two days after Christmas the new Baronne de Jouvenel confessed to Christiane Mendelys that she was unmistakably getting fatter. Since their marriage, she and Sidi had been celebrating constantly, and going from lunch to dinner and from dinner to supper. No doubt their child would prove to be the most ignoble rake.[1]

Sidi had no fortune, and he depended on his salary from *Le Matin*. He was overworked, and Colette was now uncomfortably pregnant. Late in January they left for the South of France, but they were not to have a belated honeymoon. On the eve of their departure, Colette announced to Wague that she hoped to work at her novel.[2]

L'Entrave was the sequel to *La Vagabonde*; at times she wondered which would end first: her novel or her pregnancy. It was the novel which was set aside. On 3 July 1913, at the age of forty, Colette gave birth to her only child: her daughter Colette de Jouvenel, known – as she herself had been known – as Bel-Gazou. A few days later she told Rouveyre that the little girl was beautiful, and she herself was recovering rapidly.[3]

Once her convalescence was over, Colette returned to her social duties as Sidi's wife. The President of the Republic paid an official visit to Corrèze, and she was obliged to entertain him. She and Sidi had lunch with him and his wife at Brive, Mme Poincaré was charming and wanted a Siamese cat, and she herself gave a dinner for eighty-seven people.⁴ Such illustrious activities did not keep Colette from her novel. On 16 September she announced to Hamel that she had finished *L'Entrave*, and that she was exultant with relief.⁵

The year 1913 saw the publication of *L'Envers du Music-Hall*. This collection of thumbnail sketches and vignettes of backstage life, these miniature conversations, are full of affectionate nostalgia. Even now, Colette looks back, regretfully, at her music-hall days. She suggests the camaraderie which was born of the theatre and of its exacting communal life. Constantly travelling, rarely resting, ill-paid, often underfed, living in squalid hotels and working in down-at-heel theatres, the music-hall artists had been drawn close to one another by the very harshness of their existence. Sometimes their private lives remained mysterious, sometimes they proved to be tragic; they themselves kept their reticence and their immodesty, their personal secrets and their fraternal confidences. The Claudine books had been devised to satisfy Willy and to make money; *La Vagabonde* and *L'Envers du Music-Hall* hardly seem to be the work of the same author.

The year also saw the publication of *L'Entrave*. 'A dog which has been tied up for a long time doesn't frisk about if one takes it off the lead,' wrote Colette. 'It still moves in a regular way, instinctively calculating the length of an illusory impediment.'⁶ This impediment, *L'Entrave*, explained the title of the novel. *L'Entrave* is the trammel of a woman's love, the emotional impediment which turns the vagabond into a faithful mistress.

Renée Néré, the heroine of *La Vagabonde*, is staying in Nice; and there, by chance, she sees her abandoned lover, with his wife and child. Maxime has found consolation for her departure; she herself is now thirty-six, she has no lover and she is incurably restless. Yet in the past year she has come to wish that her days of wandering were over. She seeks 'the illusion not of arriving, but of returning'.⁷ With her, in Nice, is her young friend May (based, it is said, on Lily de Rême) with her lover Jean. Jean is drawn to Renée. When she leaves for Switzerland, he follows her; on their return to Paris, she goes to live with him, and she comes to understand 'the wonder of the *presence*, the inexplicable security of all the senses'.[8] Colette had used much the same words of Sidi. Louise Weiss insists, in her memoirs, that Sidi had been the hero of *La Vagabonde*;[9] but the novel had been published before Colette had met him. It is much more probable that Sidi inspired the lyrical love which is so evident in the sequel. When Jean leaves Renée, his absence proves that her vagabondage is truly over. She waits for him, prepared to accept him on the terms he chooses. He thinks that she wants nothing but physical love; she lets him think that this is all that she wants to give or to receive. In fact she belongs to him entirely. He will now be the vagabond; she herself is trammelled for ever.

Colette herself was later to pass a harsh and clear-eyed judgment on the heroes of her early novels.

Not a jotting, not a notebook, not the slightest scribble to guide me. Where, then, did they come from, my heroes without footprints? The first hero of all, that Renaud whom Claudine married, was inconsistency itself. This mature seducer sprang from the imagination of a young woman who was still enough of a young girl to believe in mature seducers. I had no sooner created him than I took a dislike to him, and, the moment he laid himself open to attack, I killed him. His death gave me the impression of ending a sort of literary puberty ...

But the Maxime of *La Vagabonde*, the Jean of *L'Entrave* were hardly the better for it. Neither of them goes beyond the level of a virile dummy.[10]

Renaud de Jouvenel was to pass an even sterner verdict. 'In some of her works, ... man is presented much more stupid, irresponsible and incomprehensive than he can be. She is so inward-looking that she does not see him. I don't imagine her having [physical] pleasure, and perhaps she always missed a possible love, which was made impossible by her monstrous egotism.'[11]

In 1914 Colette was not only writing books and contributing to *Le Matin*. She also embarked on her career as a lecturer.

Lecturer [repeated Claude Chauvière, sometimes her secretary]? Lecturer? The word is inaccurate. Colette does not give lectures. She gives her audience a dazzling conversation.

She tries to learn her text by heart, and she rehearses it, she writes it

out in large letters on loose pages so that she can follow it, on the
platform, without glasses ...
But the moment she is settled behind the carafe and the glass of
water, she muddles up the pages and notes ... She abandons the
subject, and trusts to inspiration... In fact she begins to chat, and the
charm works. It is the charm of intimacy.[12]

Colette might be charming, but she was not always qualified to
lecture. On 7 February, at the Théâtre Fémina, she introduced a
performance of *L'École des Femmes*. She was not drawn to Molière,
indeed she knew hardly anything about him. 'Damn Molière!' she
wrote to Marguerite soon afterwards. 'Damn Molière! That's all I
want to say to you to-day. I have a horror of talking about things
that I don't know ... At the end I yielded to a fit of sincerity, and
dared to admit that I could live without Molière ... Well, that's
over!'[13]

In April 1914 she and Sidi escaped to Rozven, to the house which
Missy had given her, on the wild coast between Cancale and
Saint-Malo. There were still improvements to be made, and the
builders and decorators were at work. She and Sidi were forced to
sleep in a barn, and her feet were pricked by upholsterer's tacks
and covered in polish from the parquet floors.[14]
That spring they escaped again, this time to Castel-Novel.

No postcard [writes Renaud de Jouvenel] could convey the charm of
this little *château* ... When I was young, it seemed to me to belong to
the world of *Le Grand Meaulnes* by Alain Fournier ... None of my
friends has been able to forget it.
It stands on a hill, a little Mont Saint-Michel on land, surrounded by
a very beautiful wood, very thickly planted, very dense, with a little
romantic lake; and, to get to it, you go up a shady road, pass under a
vault of shadow, before you find yourself in front of it. Built of local
stone, pink or very pale green, it is a hybrid. The big tower on the left
is built flush with the rock, and, originally, there must only have been a
small part of a building. Later on, in the eighteenth century, they
added the right-hand part and the return wing. The façade was eaten
up by wistaria and the back wall was almost entirely covered by
centennial ivy, which gave it a romantic appearance and, for a child,
the appearance of a haunted castle. Inside it was sombre, indeed severe.

The walls of the big dining-room were covered with a fabric which imitated Cordoba leather and was scattered with *fleur de lys* in bad nineteenth-century taste. It was so cold in the big drawing-room that we used to take refuge in my father's library, where a big log fire was burning. No electricity, no running water. Every night everyone equipped themselves with a paraffin lamp (which cast shadows on the high walls) and they washed themselves in basins or zinc tubs. The water was brought up in big barrels on ox-carts from the farm. On the second floor, on the right, Colette had an enormous bedroom hung with *toile de Jouy* with a pink pattern on a white ground, with two windows and a view over the tree-tops and the surrounding country ... To the left of her room was the huge attic full of odd things, of toys, enormous trunks which had belonged to my grandfather and my great-grandfather, an ideal place for children's fantasies. That is the setting for the story by Colette which describes our hunt for ghosts; it was a great horn-owl which was striding up and down the attic ...[15]

On 4 August 1914 England and France declared war on Germany. Bel-Gazou was to stay for much of the war at Castel-Novel, in the charge of Miss Draper, known to the family as Nursie-dear. A classic English nurse, Miss Draper earned the devotion of Bel-Gazou and brought her up with firmness and affection. Colette recorded that Nursie-dear remained at Castel-Novel throughout the war. 'This harsh, cross-grained, grumbling foreigner, hard on others and on herself, exiled herself voluntarily into the country alone with a small child, defended what I possessed, turned gardener, doctor, cook – and refused her wages.'[16] Here, once again, so Renaud writes, Colette embroidered on the truth. 'During the War, Nursie-dear didn't have so much to do ... Castel-Novel was not only a *château*, but a big estate (at least 150 hectares), with cows, calves, pigs, poultry, land which was rich in various crops and vines, all of it very well farmed by an excellent manager.'[17]

Colette made another, more notable error. Nursie-dear was not alone at Castel-Novel. A thirteen-year-old local girl stayed there as maid to the nurse and the baby. Pauline Verine was to be Colette's devoted friend, servant and companion for forty years.

The Jouvenels' life was immediately transformed by the declaration of war. On 30 August Colette reported that Sidi was at Verdun. He was a second-lieutenant in the 44th regiment. Their means of existence were now much reduced.[18] She herself remained in Paris, writing dramatic criticism for one paper and a weekly 'Journal de Colette' for another. She also became a night-nurse at the Lycée Janson-de-Sailly, which had been converted into a hospital. She worked for thirteen hours at a stretch, and she was much relieved when male nurses took over the night shifts.[19]

Her writing and her nursing did not keep her thoughts from Sidi. That winter, almost unbelievably, she managed to join him at Verdun. She went as a nurse, but – so she said – under a false name and with borrowed papers. 'The least troubled hours were those of the "black train", which crawled along, all its lights extinguished, between Châlons and Verdun, slowly, slowly, as if it were groping, restraining its wheezing and its whistle. Long hours, perhaps, because I was impatient to arrive, but crowded, anxious hours, illuminated by the northern light of an endless cannonade...'[20]

Her presence at Verdun had of course to remain officially secret, and she spent many days indoors, in hiding. Through the slats of her shutters, she saw the German prisoners-of-war passing in shabby procession through the town. She became accustomed to the air-raids, morning and afternoon. In the evening Sidi returned to his 'harem', and sometimes at night she ventured out of doors. On 20 December she reported to Hamel that the order for a general offensive was a delight to her heart and her ears. That morning the cannonade had begun, an uninterrupted rain of shells which shook the doors and windows.[21]

She spent several weeks with Sidi at Verdun; she was still there, in hiding, in February 1915.[22]

Her days of nursing were now over, and she left her Paris hospital. In 1915 she became war correspondent in Italy for *Le Matin*. That July her work as a journalist took her to Rome. She had a surfeit of historic churches, but found a hundred things to enchant her.[23] She met Gabriele d'Annunzio, who had the next apartment to hers at the Albergo Regina, in the Via Vittorio Veneto. She met Joseph Primoli: the remarkable dilettante, half Bonaparte, half Italian, who had been the confidant of his aunt Princess Mathilde, and had known Flaubert and Gautier, the Goncourts and Sainte-Beuve. More recently he had entertained Sarah Bernhardt, and had fallen briefly in love with Eleonora Duse. He invited Colette to his *palazzo* ('a terrible lunch,' she wrote, ungratefully, 'eight courses and as many wines'[24]). She also went, one afternoon, to the Protestant Cemetery, where she failed to see the grave of Keats, but found the pomegranates about to bloom. It seemed as if a thousand birds were singing. She continued her journey to Venice. Life in Italy was dreamlike and undisturbed. Italy had just entered the war; yet at times she felt that the country had been forgotten by the conflict.

In 1916 she returned to Rome, this time to supervise the making of a film based on *La Vagabonde* – a project which was abandoned through lack of money. She also published *La Paix chez les bêtes*: a collection of impressions of animals. Some had already appeared in print; but she gathered them, now, 'as if in an enclosure where *I want there to be no war*'.[25] 'La Chienne jalouse' already suggests the kind of *ménage à trois* which she was to describe, with extraordinary skill, in *La Chatte*.

Early in 1916 Léautaud, always ready to write scandal, had noted that 'apparently the Colette-Henry de Jouvenel marriage is no longer going very well ... He still has a great literary admiration for her, but passion is spent, and he no longer hesitates to find distractions elsewhere.'[26]

There is no confirmation of the statement. Possibly the Jouvenel marriage, like countless others, suffered from the strains of the war; but, whatever Sidi's feelings, Colette remained deeply in love with him. In September 1916 she stayed with her brother-in-law on Lake Como. 'They still don't give Sidi back to me and I long for him,' she confessed to Hamel. 'Robert is a charming young man to live with, but he is only the brother of his brother.'[27]

Sidi continued his military service. According to his biographer, he remained in the front line almost continually for four years. He also found time to write regularly for *Le Matin*, and he spent his leaves behind his desk. Once, too – in January 1917 – he went on a mission to Rome for Poincaré.[28] Renaud de Jouvenel took a less exalted view of his father's life. 'My father did not have such a heroic military career ... He was certainly at Verdun, but his friends arranged for him to come back and edit *Le Matin*, then a functionary sent him back on service, but to a territorial unit. It seems that in 1917 he and his cousin Joseph Caillaux favoured a compromise peace with Germany. He never talked about it, *as far as I know*, but the violence of his attacks on Clemenceau is public knowledge.'[29]

In the summer of 1918 Sidi found himself in southern Picardy, where there was bitter fighting. Colette found it difficult to work, she confessed to Carco in July. Her husband had just had five days' leave, he had come out of a terrible corner, survived Matz, Orvilliers and Roye, and shown much bravery. Now he had gone back to the Front, and she was suffering from the inevitable cowardice.[30] On 9 August, writing again to Carco, she added that Sidi had been with her for a week. He was leaving, once again, without knowing where he was going.[31]

A few months later, the war was over. Sidi was demobilised, and he returned to his desk at *Le Matin*. In 1919 he made Colette literary editor of the paper; he installed her in an office of her own. Maurice Martin du Gard remembered that her desk was constantly cluttered with manuscripts and boxes of sweets. 'Sometimes, from under a pile of letters, she would unearth a splendid pair of tortoiseshell spectacles which made her look like a young doctor in a play; then she would pick up the proof of a story. She wrote, telephoned, sucked chocolates gluttonously, dictated, distributed orders and laughter in all directions.'[32]

The year 1919 brought the first novel that she herself had published for six years. She had not lost her touch. The final chapter of *Mitsou*, lost in the Métro, had to be rewritten while the presses waited, and it was to move Proust to tears.

Mitsou is a novella, rather than a novel. Like *La Vagabonde*, it is inspired by the world of the music-hall; and, like *La Vagabonde*, it records a love-affair that fails. Mitsou is a music-hall artiste; she is twenty-four, and she has her protector of fifty. Into her dressing-room, one evening, a colleague brings two young subalterns on leave. Mitsou falls in love with the one in the blue uniform, *le lieutenant bleu*. She corresponds with him at the Front. She is determined to have a love-affair, perhaps the love-affair of her life. The blue lieutenant remembers the vision in the dressing-room, the velvet and the gauze; he arrives at last, and finds a young woman, dressed in black, over-eager and without enchantment. He overcomes his disappointment and his reluctance, and, for a single night, he becomes her lover. Next day he finds a pretext to depart. For him she has been just another conquest; or, rather, she has been the embryo of his ideal. She herself has grown, overnight, into a woman of sensibility; and, in an ill-spelt letter, she acknowledges her place. He had been enamoured of an illusion, of the virtues which he himself had given her. She will try, now, to be his illusion; but she knows, already, that she must fail.

Mitsou is poignant, lyrical and stern. As Violet Trefusis was to write, Colette plays on the heartstrings with the fearful familiarity of a Kreisler. Her male figures are, as usual, one-dimensional; but Mitsou remains in the flesh: sensitive to every nuance of emotion, perceptive yet not over-articulate. Despite her way of life, she keeps a curious innocence and dignity.

Abel Hermant, the novelist, recognised that *Mitsou* was slight; but no-one, he said, should call it insignificant.

I should be obliged to answer, as Racine answered the detractors of *Bérénice*, that to create is precisely to make something out of nothing.

I am not comparing Colette and Racine, though this civility is now a commonplace; nor does she have that tormented way of writing which people used to call artistic writing. She has, instinctively, the word which makes us feel what she feels, see through her eyes. She never has two words where she needs only one. Few words, many pictures; and these pictures are so clear that, if one illustrated *Mitsou* (which God forbid), the artists themselves could not disfigure her. It would be a unique phenomenon.

It is perhaps for this reason, among others, little Mitsou, that Colette made a ravishing book out of your non-existent history, a *tour de force* which one must never challenge her to perform.³³

Late in 1916 the Jouvenels had moved from the rue Cortambert to 69 boulevard Suchet, near the Bois de Boulogne. Renaud - or Kid, as she called him - used to stay there during his school holidays. Renaud went to a number of schools, in Paris and the provinces, and for two years he went to an English school at Tenterden. He was widely read, he was already observant and sophisticated. He remembered his strange and sombre room in the boulevard Suchet. It was furnished in the Chinese style which was then in fashion, with a divan-bed covered in black velvet. In the drawing-room, which was equally sombre, there was a piano, on which his stepmother played, and a painting which she had done.³⁴ Colette was too energetic and too versatile to be content with one form of expression. Mme de Polignac owned her *Branche de fuchsia*, and Claude Chauvière owned her self-portrait.

Claude Chauvière, who was to publish one of the earliest books about Colette, was to recall the visitors at the boulevard Suchet with vivid clarity, if not, perhaps, with a strict regard for fact.

I saw them pass through the salon there, . . . Japanese, Americans, Greeks, autograph-hunters, managers, authors, artists, musicians, characters of ill repute and of high renown. I saw them all there, from Aragon, breathing fire from his surrealist nostrils, to Pierre Benoit, who is now an Academician . . . There I saw the stylish Fresnay rehearse Chéri, and the cubic Madeline Guitty, and the groaning Liane de Pougy . . . There were politicians, now in oblivion, and courtiers who were almost princes, and a couple of women who were fearfully affectionate and raddled, ... and the eclectic Princess [Edmond] de Polignac, Mme Anna de Noailles, in a tailored suit and silver shoes, ... and the voluble and incisive Germaine Beaumont ...[35]

Germaine Beaumont's mother was an old friend of Colette's. As Annie de Pène, she had made her literary début in 1908 with fantasies in dialogue, *Pantins modernes*. Her best book was probably *Confidences de femmes*, which had been published in 1914. She had died four years later, during the epidemic of Spanish influenza.

She had inspired her daughter with her own admiration for Colette. One day, when Germaine was in her teens, her mother had asked her to take a letter to the rue Cortambert.

I still remember the fever which came over me [recalled Germaine some forty years later]. Should I be worthy of this mission? ...
I rang a doorbell, went under an arch, and down the side of a garden to a rather Swiss-looking house in a tangle of creepers. On the doorstep, bathed in the light reflected from the trees, was Colette. She took the letter I handed her, read it, enveloped me with a searching look, and said simply: 'Annie's daughter, you've come at the right moment. You can help me finish stringing some French beans.' ...
That was the end of my schoolgirl lyricism ... I didn't feel disconcerted, or humiliated, or disappointed, or frustrated. I felt like someone who until then had looked at life through badly focussed binoculars, and had suddenly seen clearly, because a hand had found the proper angle of vision.[36]

Germaine continued to learn wisdom, and to get understanding, from her mother's friend.[37] Late in August 1919 she was staying at Rozven. It was, perhaps, during this visit that they went on to a friend's house in Paramé. Colette accompanied a young singer on the piano. And then, Germaine recorded,

she went on playing alone in a deep silence which seemed to embrace everything beyond the banality of the house, the little garden and the street, beyond the town, beyond the sea ...
She went on for a very long time, until she woke up from her dream, and, with amiable abruptness, returned among us. No-one said a word, as if we had witnessed a spectacle which had not been meant

for us ... But I knew enough to understand one of the secrets of Colette's style, her musical infallibility. Perhaps it is also the pursuit of an inner cadence, the recommencement of a certain phrase as haunting as the sonata of Vinteuil.[38]

     ■——■

Germaine was one of the few who wrote of Colette's generosity: her constant willingness to help her friends. The same names always seemed, she said, to echo round Colette, and the dead were still alive for her; but she gave her compassion and her help to the survivors. 'How many letters,' said Germaine, 'written before my eyes, how many telephone calls, how many recommendations!...'[39]

Colette often helped Claude Chauvière, who succeeded Germaine as her secretary at *Le Matin*. An enemy of the established order, an atheist who was suddenly converted, Claude led a strange and difficult life. 'With a light and kindly hand Colette guided this boat, which was borne by conflicting currents and constantly adrift.' Colette also gave encouragement to *le petit corsaire*: to Renée Hamon who, like herself, led a vagabond existence. Renée was to die of cancer in 1943, leaving two books on Tahiti and the Marquesas which owed much to Colette's goodwill and influence. As for the poet Hélène Picard, she could not adapt herself to everyday life. Had it not been for Colette, she would have lived in poverty and solitude. Colette found her an apartment, settled her in and watched over her with a solicitude which was apparently amused, but constant and effective. 'For nine months,' she wrote to Fernand Vandérem, 'Hélène Picard has been immobilised as the result of a fall. In the meanwhile, however, she has written a fine book on poetry *Pour un mauvais garçon*. Where could you place the poem I'm sending you? Where would it be properly paid for, which is of the utmost urgency?'[40] Thanks to the tutelary friendship of Colette, Hélène was able to lead her strange poet's life, her cruel invalid's life, and to make her way gently towards her end.

     ■——■

Meanwhile, in August 1919, Germaine was staying at Rozven for precious hours, and unforgettable days of holiday'.[41] The description came from Colette. She was always to cultivate intense and emotional friendships with women. Her letters to Marguerite and to Hélène Picard, even her references to the wives of friends, sometimes seem so urgent and so sensually aware that they suggest an ambivalent nature. She had, observed her stepson, Renaud, 'almost exclusively feminine friendships, and it is clear that she was, at the very least, intellectually lesbian'.[42] Missy, 'with her short, greying hair, the appearance of an attentive, kindly priest',[43] belonged, now, to the past; but Colette was to keep her friendships with a number of known lesbians. She knew Natalie Barney and Princess Edmond de Polignac. She knew the increasingly masculine Élisabeth de Gramont, the boyish Lucie Delarue-Mardrus ('she sculpts, rides horses, loves first one woman, then another, then yet another').[44] She was one day to know Violet Trefusis, Lady Troubridge and Radclyffe Hall. Her admiration of Proust, her own writing about human relationships, make it clear that she was fascinated by homosexuality.

There was, however, nothing homosexual about the novel which she began in the summer of 1919. 'Just imagine that my play is going to be a novel,' she wrote to Carco, from Rozven, late in August. '... And I've written forty-three pages!'[45]

II

Colette was one day to recall the origins of Chéri: the most convincing male character in her work.

Chéri? To begin with, he was a little red-haired fellow, slightly crooked in one shoulder, with pink eyelashes, a weak right eye, and sniffling from a chronic cold in the head. He looked like a poor man's son, but he touched fifteen hundred thousand francs allowance...

And so the first humiliated form of Chéri was born, one day when I had great need of him for my weekly stories in *Le Matin*...[1]

Clouk, as he was called in this early incarnation, was an adequate character for the series of short stories which appeared in 1911. But he lacked the stature of the hero of a novel. One day, Colette explained, when he was having supper with his mistress, Lulu,

he noticed four mature women at a nearby table. There was not a
single man with them, they were drinking *demi-sec* champagne, eating
crayfish, *foie-gras*, sugary puddings, and they were laughing and talking
about their past. Clouk had a glimpse of his destiny, which was to die
and to be born again beloved, in other words handsome.

Langorously, as if I had dosed him with a powerful narcotic from the
South, Clouk lost colour and consciousness, plunged into oblivion, and
awoke in the arms of Léa, who called him Chéri.

I gave Chéri good measure at once: he was twenty-six, brown-haired,
white-skinned, as glossy as a tom-cat six months old. Sometimes
I stepped back, to study him. I never tired of beautifying him ...

He joined the generation of those who were in their twenties when
I was in my forties.[2]

Colette was often to be asked if Chéri existed. Auguste Hériot
seems to have given him many features. In 1921, after *Chéri* had
been published, the novelist Pierre Drieu La Rochelle spoke freely
to Maurice Martin du Gard.

Her gigolo has no interest at all. And the model has his interest, I know
him ... Splendid people, a wonderful family! Fancy turning this great
hard-working bourgeois milieu into a lot of old tarts, aunts, and shady
boxers, you think that's right? The mother went astray, I agree, but to
be Colonel Marchand's mistress, that's a different kettle of fish! ...
Chéri, the real one, the model, is still ready to be given presents, not
because of the money they represent, because he's got a lot of it, that
fellow, but because of the pleasure of receiving ...[3]

This unattractive trait was to be emphasised by Polaire, who had
been Hériot's mistress.

H[ériot] did not only avoid giving the smallest presents, he took
a slightly sadistic pleasure in having them given to him. He was
a multi-millionaire, and he was very proud to show a little tiepin,
a trinket, a knick-knack, and say: 'Mme X—— gave me that!' Perhaps
it was just because I never asked for anything, that he was especially
generous to me ...

For a long time [this in 1933] I have hardly had any news of what
H[ériot] was doing. I think he's living in Vienna; one of his friends, who
met him there, told me that I was the only one who gave him the
illusion that I wasn't simply after his fortune ...[4]

Colette, said Drieu La Rochelle, 'had thought she had done
something clever in falling for the handsome —— ... Then one

day our hero (he's a hero: masses of palms on his Croix de Guerre) settled for a real woman, the Panther, ... the baronne [sic] who was the mistress of Henry de Jouvenel. There was an exchange of places.'[5] It had happened in the summer of 1911.

Renaud de Jouvenel – the Panther's son – remembered:

Hériot – Toto to me – was not an idiot, but a very rich man, a regular warrior, brave to the point of temerity, who fought like a lion in the First World War and led an adventurer's life. He was certainly not very stable. After the 1914–1918 war, it is said that he wanted to stir up an insurrection against the English in the Near East, but that the French Government refused him any help. Out of spite – and I know it because I knew him well, and much admired him, and indeed loved him – he gave his secretary orders to send the entire contents of his house in Paris to Vienna, and even had the telephone wires torn out ... I well remember his apartment, which was full of parrots and tigerskins.[6]

Hériot's liaison with Mme de Comminges seems to have lasted for at least two years. To quote Renaud again:

At six or seven years old, perhaps until I was eight, Hériot appeared to me like the hero on the Épinal prints, his breast covered with decorations. I don't remember his face, but I recall his sumptuous presents and his Mercedes with swivelling flap-seats. Everything else I know about his life comes to me from my mother's confidences and from her letters. He was an extravagant man and I think he died mad in a hospital in Vienna ...

Toto was not a man to get married. I know nothing of his affair with Polaire and I only learned about his liaison with Colette, which was probably stormy, from Mrs Mitchell and other biographers. Perhaps he had taken her for a real woman!!![7]

Chéri – the doomed young Chéri – had owed much, one suspects, to the rich and handsome Hériot: the young man who, as she had seen, could never be happy. Chéri, like Auguste, was built on a foundation of sadness. Yet characters in fiction are rarely based on a single person in real life; and no doubt Colette had known several models for the most celebrated of her heroes.

The first time that I settled down to study Chéri, he was sitting on the edge of a chaise-longue in sky-blue damask, and he was playing with his mistress's little dog. The shadow of his eyelashes moved on the cheeks of a twenty-two-year-old, warm and rosy by the ears, as they are on youthful skins which have been caressed by the sun since childhood. He came from a small country seat in the provinces, and claimed to be making a career in Paris. In fact he did, but that is another story... His mistress, with her authority, her solid brilliance, her equable humour, was exactly like the woman who ruled Chéri; and I read on her face a leonine love...

'Now take Miki into the garden, it's a lovely day,' she said to the charming young man...

She was silent, and she remained leaning against the window-sill, crushing her breasts, to look at him. She was silent, not because of a surge of passion, but out of pure dreamy and contemplative enchantment.[8]

Colette herself never identified Chéri more precisely.

One could perhaps identify Léa. Maurice Goudeket was to write that, in about 1911, Colette had simply looked around her; 'and the blonde Léa, buxom and dissolute in a homely way, ... who attracted her attention, was called Suzanne Derval'.[9] She was an actress and *demi-mondaine*, and she was known for her performances with Lucien Guitry. Yet she was not, one suspects, the only model for Léa. Colette had once had an older woman in mind. In the early drafts of passages from the Clouk stories, Léa was florid and white-haired.[10] This Léa seemed like a grandmother, not the seductive maternal woman whom Chéri demanded. Colette transformed her, and she made her closer to her own image. Much of her own emotions went into this archetypal figure. 'Léa owes much to Colette herself,' Renaud confirmed. 'In fact, a good many of her female characters derive from her.'[11]

She was still writing *Chéri* when, on 1 January 1920, the first instalment appeared in *La Vie Parisienne*. She wrote not only against the pressure of the serial story but against the pressure of her work on *Le Matin*, and the constant demands of family life. On about 25 March she went to Castel-Novel. Claire Boas de Jouvenel had nearly come with them, for she and Colette had suddenly established a close friendship.

It had been established through Bertrand de Jouvenel.[12] The son of Claire and Sidi, he was now sixteen and a half. Claire herself had sent him on a delicate mission to Colette. He was to ask the new Baronne de Jouvenel to let his mother continue to use the name – a practice which Sidi meant to forbid her. Claire's political activities were independent of his own, but as a politician he claimed to find it an embarrassment. Bertrand was only to learn, years later, how vigorously Colette herself had urged Sidi to take this hurtful decision.

In the spring of 1920, ignorant of the facts, ignorant of the ways of the world, the studious young boy, preparing for his *baccalauréat*, arrived with a bunch of flowers at the boulevard Suchet. He was, he recalls, so shy that he hid behind the piano in the darkest corner of the salon. Suddenly, almost violently, the door burst open, and Colette walked briskly across the room. It was apparently empty. She blinked and murmured: 'But where *is* the child?' Then she turned round and caught sight of him. She was small, intensely energetic. 'My only impression,' Bertrand wrote, 'was one of strength, a strength of which the impact was gentle to me ... I really think that, at the first glance, I surrendered to Colette's protection, and that her first glance promised it to me.'[13]

Early in June, from Castel-Novel, Colette wrote to Hélène Picard that she was working intensely at *Chéri*; it must not only be finished, but finished off.[14] Soon afterwards she wrote the last page, and read the novel to Sidi, who approved. On 5 June the last instalment was published in *La Vie Parisienne*. Colette celebrated her new-found freedom by weeding rose-beds and uprooting thistles; her arms and hands were still covered with scratches when she returned to her desk at *Le Matin*.[15]

Colette was later to recall her confidence in *Chéri*, her inner conviction of its quality. In the summer of 1920, as she awaited its publication, she felt, in fact, distinctly apprehensive. Writing to Proust in June, she told him that they were still printing and sewing the book. She was anxious about his opinion, and impatient enough to send him a set of uncorrected proofs. It was a novel, she confessed, that she had never written before. She had written the others once or twice, the '*vagabondes*' and '*entraves*' had always vaguely had something of the Claudines about them.[16] Proust does not seem to have given his opinion of the proofs; she later sent him a copy of the book inscribed: 'To Marcel Proust, with anxiety (what is he going to think of *Chéri*?), and with affection.'[17] Her lack of confidence remained remarkable. Years later, Maurice Goudeket found her 'timid, ill assured, so unconvinced of her merit, indeed so modest that it verged on an inferiority complex.'[18] Colette, he said, 'was like a maker of musical instruments in the provinces, who, unknown to herself, made Stradivarius violins.'[19]

Chéri was printed and distributed with remarkable speed. It was published on 2 July 1920. It may be read, simply, as the account of a love-affair between a courtesan and a gigolo in the early twentieth century. It belongs to Paris in the years before the First World War. It belongs, more precisely, to a certain well-defined *milieu* in the sometimes louche *demi-monde*, where love was generally bought and sold, and all perversions were possible. In this brilliant, corrupt society, lesbians live in aggressive partnership, and old, decaying prostitutes batten on rich and innocent young men, just as they had done on the *petits crevés* of the Second Empire. The world of *Chéri* is a world where life is spent in trading sex, in machinations, gossip and gambling, in living a luxurious and superficial existence between the extremes of frenetic activity and idleness.

Among the most successful of these retired courtesans is Charlotte Peloux, who lives in vulgar opulence with an illegitimate son whom she has alternately pampered and neglected. Fred Peloux, known as Chéri, is above all in need of a mother; he finds the strong maternal figure and the perfect mistress in his mother's friend, the courtesan Léa de Lonval. She herself finds in him not only a satisfying lover, but the child whom she has never known. Their love-affair lifts the novel to another plane: makes it the account of a relationship with profound complexities. As Cocteau said, they speak with 'phrases torn up from the depths, with their roots, the earth and all.'[20] Their love-affair is not merely a matter of physical attraction, but of the primal needs of the heart.

One may doubt, in the early chapters, whether Chéri has a heart at all. He is beautiful and rich, accustomed to being spoilt; he has no intellectual depth and no moral purpose. His background and upbringing have left him unstable and unhappy, unable to accept the responsibilities of manhood. In his twenties, he is still self-absorbed and immature.

Léa pampers him and charms him. After a liaison which has lasted for five years, he decides, abruptly, to marry. Perhaps it would be more true to say that his mother finds a wife for him and Chéri is too weak to refuse her. He accepts the prospect of marriage without enthusiasm; Léa accepts it as the natural course of events. Only when he has gone does she understand that this has not been an affair like the rest. It has been the love of her life. She shuts her *hôtel*, and leaves Paris in order to alleviate her loneliness.

Six months later she returns to face her solitude, the slow and sombre onset of old age. She finds it hard to fill her days; she is drawn, still, to Chéri. His marriage has already failed, and he wants only to return to her. The final chapters of *Chéri* suggest with beautiful precision, with extraordinary tact, the inescapable longing of a man and a woman for each other; no novelist has understood better than Colette the workings of a woman's mind, the urgent power of her instincts, the difficult control of her emotions when her emotions have taken hold. At the moment when she most longs for him, Chéri returns, predictably, to Léa. She wants, as Colette observes, 'to play her part to perfection'.[21] And so she does. That night, in the great bed which has been the scene of her triumphs, she hears the beating of his heart.

'He is there,' Léa said to herself. And a blind security swept over her. 'He is there for ever,' she cried inside herself. Her clear-sighted prudence, her maturity, her renunciations, everything receded and vanished before the tumultuous brutality of love.[22]

She presumes too much. Perhaps Colette overplays her presumption. Next morning Chéri wakes to find her planning their departure. She means to take him away from Paris, this time for ever. She has lost her tact; she has also begun to lose her looks. Chéri becomes aware, unforgettably, of her ageing hands. Suddenly, she recognises that she herself must give him his freedom. Léa is the true hero of the novel. She shows her strength and the depth of her love by telling him to go. 'My poor Chéri,' she had reflected. 'How strange to think that when you lost your worn old mistress, and I lost my scandalous young lover, we both lost the most honourable thing we had on earth ...'[23]

Colette was later to publish her early drafts of passages from *Chéri*. The first version began – like the actual novel – with Chéri putting on Léa's pearls; it also began with the abrupt announcement of his marriage. This beginning is much inferior to the final version. Colette had also drafted the scene of Chéri's return. It carried none of the conviction of the published pages. Much more significant than these drafts is the alternative ending to the novel. Chéri had returned to Léa, and Léa had not dismissed him. They had gone together to Tunis; and there, one day, he had chanced to look at her neck and at her pearls.

It was on this neck that Chéri's glance rested, fixedly, as if he were seeing it for the first time. His mistress was sitting reading, with bowed head. Under her chin there were two folds of rather yellow flesh, and her neck was enveloped by a slack skin, which was also yellow, more yellow because of the pearls... Suddenly he closed his eyes, and his whole body relaxed, as if it were permitted to rest... Instead of Léa's neck, instead of the three ropes of irisated pearls, Chéri had seen a young neck, the colour of amber, intact, bowed with grief...[24]

Léa had kept Chéri, but she had lost her nobility, and he had lost his dream. He was ready, now, for marriage. When Colette discarded these early versions of *Chéri*, she showed her literary tact, her psychological perception.

There remain weaknesses in the published novel. Léa, for example, is only fifty, yet she thinks of her imminent old age, and her hands – which disillusion Chéri – are those of a woman in her seventies. Colette sometimes overplays herself, and sometimes she reveals the clumsy mechanism of the novel. Chéri's marriage is hardly introduced, and it is unconvincing. His mother and her grotesque acquaintances from the *demi-monde* are blatantly out of scale with the central figures.

Chéri and his mistress are described with delicate assurance. The *hôtel* in the avenue Bugeaud is a self-contained, convincing world. Its heart is the vast and vulgar bed of wrought iron and copper; but, as Cocteau wrote:

> It isn't Léa's bed which counts, it is that Colette has painted it, and cast it beyond fashion, space and time. It is that she picks up our poor human clay and makes it into iridescent soap-bubbles, it is that her wand transforms an ageing courtesan into a white cat in a fairy-tale and a gigolo, a tabby-cat from the gutter, into that terrible little wild animal which Anglo-Indians call a golden cat.[25]

In Léa's bedroom the rose-coloured curtains filter a pink light, the walls are hung with pink, the lampshades are pink and white. The colour proclaims not only the pleasures of the flesh, but perhaps a return to the womb. It proclaims not only the courtesan, with her love of dated finery, but the mother-figure who will always safeguard and control. Like the faithful maidservant – naturally called Rose – like the well-run household, the carefully chosen food and wine, the warm flesh tint suggests security. The necklace – forty-nine pearls, says Léa – which Chéri covets as the novel opens, which Léa does not wear, at night, since it draws attention to her ageing neck – the string of pearls becomes a symbol of her existence. When his marriage has failed and he returns to her, it is her pearls and scent which assure him that he has found her again. It is with these touches that Colette suggests the depth of a long relationship. She writes directly, and yet it is often with oblique observation, with suggestion rather than fact, that she creates her potent atmosphere. She does not waste emotion on descriptions of the sexual act. More powerful and more delicate, she records Chéri's repeated returns, after his marriage, to the empty street; she records his overwhelming relief when, at last, he finds the lamps are lit at Léa's *hôtel*. Colette records Léa's desperate longing, her anxiety to dress well in case she should meet him, her obsession that every male figure in the distance, every man who approaches her on her walks, must be Chéri. Such behaviour is poignant in its authenticity.

When *Chéri* was published, Colette was forty-seven. She was recognised as one of the most distinguished novelists writing in France. Fernand Vandérem declared in *La Revue de Paris* that 'Mme Colette's novel combines the most profound study of emotions and one of the most precise, most vivid paintings that we have yet been given of certain regions of the *demi-monde* ... How futile they seem after such a book, the literary classifications, the quarrels over literary schools, and all the nonsense that goes with them! ... One simply knows that this is a great novelist, a great artist, a great writer.'[26]

Some critics passed a moral judgment on a literary work. Jean de Pierrefeu, writing in *Le Journal des Débats*, suggested that 'it was time she changed her characters; she certainly possesses too much talent to continue to degrade it.'[27] Colette was bewildered. 'I have concerned myself with the pitiful – and Léa, and Chéri even more, are the most pitiful of the pitiful. Is it so vile? ... I really think I have never written anything as moral as *Chéri*.'[28]

In July and August she was at Rozven. 'It is excessively Breton and very mild ... How mild everything is – even me! I am coming to life again, in the sea and sand. My old nascent strength is awakening. It is still quite considerable.'[29]

Colette was writing to Hélène Picard. There was something ceremonious about their relationship. Colette protected Hélène, but she showed her the deference which she felt to be due to a writer of poetry. Hélène had a cult for Colette and hoarded every scrap of her writing. She lived in the rue d'Alleray, in a fourth-floor apartment, where she kept blue parrots and a collection of blue glass, and created herself a small ethereal world.

Hélène Picard and Germaine Beaumont were at Rozven when, this summer, Bertrand de Jouvenel came to stay. Sidi had been obliged to return unexpectedly to Paris, and the intended family visit became, instead, a visit to Colette.

Bertrand was his mother's only child, still shy, still anxious to lose himself among his books.[30] He had a horror of staying with people, of finding himself obliged to conform to their alien ways.

He was also depressed, this summer, by the results of his examinations. He had always had problems with his French dissertation, he had done less well in mathematics than he had hoped, and he had failed in philosophy. Colette was well aware of her own scant formal education. She proved herself remarkably understanding. She persuaded him to swim (which he had never done before); she took him to the antique-dealers in Saint Malo, to the pools in the rocks where shrimps were found. She roused his love of life, his sensibility. 'My sensibility was in a way a parasite of hers, it fed on what Colette relished. It is,' he has written, recently, 'impossible to say what I owe to her, for feeding me like this. The revelation she brought me attached her to me: I became her adopted son; it is rare for natural maternity to give such satisfactions.'[31] She also gave him the freedom of her books, among them the most recent work of Proust. 'Her book, *Chéri*, had just appeared,' Bertrand remembers. 'She gave me a copy, with an inscription round the title which read: "To my son CHÉRI Bertrand de Jouvenel". It was, in a way, a premonition of a legend which is a long time dying.'[32]

Bertrand had not been Chéri. Yet, as Colette often said to him: 'What I write comes to pass.'[33] There has long been a tradition in France that young men are initiated by their mother's friends. It is said that Germaine Beaumont, at Rozven, offered to educate the stepson of Colette. She failed, and Colette herself undertook the task. Claire Boas de Jouvenel had entrusted her with Bertrand; Sidi had trusted her with his son. Bertrand himself had trusted Colette from the first. In the house which Missy had given her, she became Bertrand's mistress. Colette was la Dame en blanc, Mme Dalleray, the ruthless older woman whom she was to portray in *Le Blé en herbe*.[34]

Bertrand returned to Paris evidently changed. As he had written: 'The impression made on me by my stay at Rozven alarmed my mother; she told my father that her son was being changed, he was being corrupted. For a year I hardly saw Colette at all.'[35] Claire Boas de Jouvenel was not unperceptive; but she could scarcely have brought herself even to imagine that Sidi's second wife had ensnared her son.

Early in September, Colette reported to Francis Carco that the sales of *Chéri* were remarkable, and that she hoped for a reprint in November.[36] On 25 September she was appointed Chevalier de la Légion-d'honneur. The news apparently reached her at Castel-Novel. Renaud counted the letters of congratulation: more than four hundred in forty-eight hours. Each of them demanded an answer. So did the telegram from Sarah Bernhardt.[37] 'I am proud,' wrote Proust, 'to have the cross at the same time as the author of the wonderfully clever *Chéri*.'[38]

Madame [wrote Gide],
I am quite astonished to be writing to you, quite astonished by the very great pleasure that I have found in reading you. I have devoured *Chéri* at one sitting. What a wonderful subject you had got hold of! And what intelligence, what mastery, what understanding of the least admitted secrets of the flesh! ... From one end of the book to the other, not a weakness, not a redundancy, not a commonplace ...
I already want to read it again, and I am frightened: supposing I were to find it less good! ...[39]

Chéri was not merely a love-story; it was also an impression of an age. André Foucault, the literary editor of *Les Œuvres libres*, declared that 'Chéri is the pre-war citizen and Léa is his customary France'.[40] Colette had created two characters so general yet so recognisable that readers were often to tell her that they had found the real Chéri. Men were highly critical of Chéri, especially older men, but women felt profoundly understood.

For the first time in my life [wrote Colette], I felt inwardly sure that I had written a novel which I should not have to blush for, or to question, a novel which, when it was born, massed partisans and adversaries around it.
And if I had had my reward from women alone, at the time of the success of *Chéri*, I could carry my head high. How I recall the phalanx of Léas, fighting in disguise, still invincible ... They had an indescribable way of recognising each other, applauding me and becoming my friends, they put their confession in a look, in the pressure of a hand ...[41]

Twenty-five years later, when she had written the sequel to *Chéri*, and many other books, Colette confessed: 'I talk about Chéri with an authority which I do not mistake for infallibility ... When people ask me about Chéri and about his end, or about Sido, I show competence and obliging compliance. I know where to find my best work as a writer.'[42]

III

In 1920, the year of *Chéri*, Colette gathered enough pieces – published and unpublished – for a book, *La Chambre éclairée*. The room in question was Bel-Gazou's bedroom at Castel-Novel, lit at night by the songs and laughter of the little girl, now seven years old. Colette also continued to serve as dramatic critic and literary editor of *Le Matin*. It was in the latter capacity that she approached Henry Barbusse. His novel, *Le Feu*, had been among the most famous novels of the 1914–18 war. '*Le Matin* entrusts me with the task of recruiting "popular novelists". So it must have some Barbusse contributions. Please come and see me soon.'[1] He asked what she had in mind. 'But, *cher Monsieur*, all I want is some chaste and stunning Barbusse ... What do you mean by brilliant offers? I am offering you a modest three hundred francs for each short story.'[2]

As literary editor, Colette was also to publish some of Simenon's earliest work.

One day [he remembered] I was told: 'Madame Colette would like to see you', and there she was, marvellous to behold in her editorial chair, suddenly addressing me as *Mon petit Sim* ... 'You know,' she said, 'I've read your last story. I ought to have sent it back weeks ago. It isn't right. It's almost right. It almost works. But not quite. You're too literary. Cut out all the literature and it will work ...' That was the most useful advice I have ever had in my life, and I owe a grateful candle to Colette for having given it to me.[3]

■ ▬ ■

The Jouvenel marriage continued on its remarkable way. Late in 1920 Sidi went to Corrèze to campaign for his election to the Senate. Renaud maintains that the physical separation of husband and wife must have occurred very early, as Sidi took him on his campaign.⁴ 'I should wager a good deal,' he adds, 'that the physical separation occurred before 1923.'⁵ Colette remained in Paris, as Bohemian as ever. She sent her husband a photograph of herself and Ba-tou, a panther from Chad, which had been given to her by Philippe Berthelot, secretary-general of the Ministère des Affaires Étrangères.⁶ Renaud reported that his father took no pleasure in the panther, or in the squirrel which jumped on his shoulder as he was coming out of the bathroom. It gave him a terrible fright, although he was a veteran of Verdun. There was even a snake which wandered over the table during meals. It probably did not stay in the house for long.⁷

In these early post-war years, Sidi pursued many different activities.⁸ He founded the Federal Union of Veterans; he organised a 'States-General of Veterans'. In November 1920 he led a successful press campaign for the burial of the Unknown Soldier beneath the Arc de Triomphe. On 9 January 1921 he was elected Senator for Corrèze. He was to keep the seat until his death. He used every means at his disposal to give the region proper roads, electricity, even an airport near Varetz, and he drew on his personal fortune, whenever he had one, to round out the local budget. His devotion was repaid by his constituents. The local schoolmaster wrote that he was idolised.

Some said that Colette 'adapted herself, with perfect ease, to her new existence as the wife of a politician in a fair way to becoming the President of the Republic.'⁹ The truth appears to have been rather different. Sidi's way of life was diverging ever further from her own. Natalie Barney had long felt apprehensive about the marriage. 'This tall, dark man, in the prime of life, intelligent and vain, was highly attractive to women – who greatly attracted him. How could he remain tied for ever to a single woman, even if she was Colette – a Colette who offered him not only her total love [sic], but her original mind, and a whole new milieu?'¹⁰ Renaud wrote more harshly: 'No-one could live with a wife who was indifferent to what interests you in life, and a wife who was perhaps sexually passive.'¹¹

There were frequent reminders that Colette was not the only woman in his life. One day, recorded Renaud, 'Henry arrived at Castel-Novel to find three women: Colette, Claire Boas de Jouvenel, Bertrand's mother, and Meg Villars, one of Henry's mistresses. Henry was furious, and rushed into the house without a word.'[12] Meg Villars, who remained a lifelong friend of Colette's, had also been the mistress and the second wife of Willy.

・――・

Early in March 1921, from the Hôtel de la Méditerranée, on the Promenade des Anglais, in Nice, Colette sent a business note to Hélène. She was keeping an eye on *Le Matin* from a comfortable distance. Writing to Marguerite on about 10 March, she seemed both relaxed and slightly bored. Her balcony looked over the sea, the flower market was enchanting, and Sidi had paid her a brief visit. Despite it all, four days of the South of France were enough.[13] In April she was at Castel-Novel, where the walls were crackling with lizards and blond with bees, and the lilac gave a fragrance to the mornings.[14] Early in May, she was back in Paris, where the success of *Chéri* continued. On 2 June she scribbled to Lucie Saglio: 'Forgive *Chéri* for making you weep, and let its author take you in her arms.'[15]

Lucie Saglio, the literary hostess, was the wife of Charles Saglio, the editor of *La Vie Parisienne* and editor-in-chief of *L'Œuvre*. They had been friends of Colette's for years. A more illustrious friendship, now, was her continuing friendship with Proust. It was based on her intense admiration of his work. She took an eager pleasure in his conversation, and felt concern about his failing health. 'I never go for long without thinking of you,' she confessed. '... Oh! if only I could be lucky enough for a Marcel Proust to be published for my holidays – That and the sea together, what a bathe!'[16] Early in July she wrote again:

My dear friend, if instead of describing competitions at the Conservatoire, attending banquets round Limoges and reading short stories for *Le Matin*, I led a life of luxury, ... I should have given myself the delight of writing to you a long time ago, because of your last book. If I told you that I delve into it every night before I go to sleep you would think it a clumsy and idiotic compliment, and yet every night Jouvenel – who is accustomed to it – gently removes your book and my spectacles from me. 'I am jealous, but resigned,' he says. The beginning of Sodom dazzled him. *No-one in the world* has written pages like that about the Homosexual, no-one! ... I swear that nobody after you, other than yourself, will be able to add anything to what you have written ... How I admire you, and how I wish that you were well and happy. But if you were well - would the clumsy padding of good health take the edge off those exquisitely delicate senses? I feel that for you I should go as far as the most murderous egotism. If [only] I had the good fortune to see you, before I leave for Brittany, - I'm leaving on the 12th, with a motley family of Jouvenel children, a daughter of my own, two sons who came to me from elsewhere and are charming. I feel I've so much to say to you. I embrace you with all my heart.

   COLETTE DE JOUVENEL.[17]

July found her, happily, at Rozven. She loved the very wildness of the landscape, the dunes, the changing moods of the sea. She had loved Rozven since the days of Missy; she loved it, now, when it was alive with husband and children, and with visitors.

As far as I can remember Rozven [Renaud was to write], it was a pretty little bourgeois house, quite a long way from the nearest village and 50 or 100 yards from the sea. I have a very clear recollection of the huge green waves (witness Courbet), and of my father reproaching me for being afraid of them, of my walks among the rocks in search of crabs and shrimps, of my longing to follow the seashore as far as the nearest town, and perhaps I saw it. Children always want to make discoveries.[18]

 Early in August Colette herself wrote to Marguerite that she had a terrible horde around her. Sidi and his brother Robert were playing with the dogs, shouting and leaping about. For the past year she had hardly seen Bertrand; but Claire Boas de Jouvenel had now overcome her alarm and apprehension, and entrusted her, once again, with her son, and Colette was giving him massage, and cramming him with food, and tanning him in the sun.[19] She also summoned Léopold Marchand, the playwright and biblio-phile, to come and help her dramatise *La Vagabonde*. Maurice Sachs, who saw them together, remembered that Colette 'had become fat and rotund, but her eyes shone with the same profound charm which must have made her so beautiful when she was slim. And how light, how elegant she was when she spoke! Her language was the language you suspect in flowers and birds, there was a wonderful poetry in her words ... And over and above all this grace and sweetness, she had an almost masculine strength.'[20]

This summer she was in no mood for writing. She had done a few short stories, and she had dried up, she told Marguerite in mid August. She snarled at blank sheets of paper. Marchand was busy adapting *La Vagabonde*, and she rewarded him with grunts and blasphemies. She wanted an open-air summer life.[21] Bertrand, understandably, felt less at ease with her than he had done the previous summer; but, little by little, their contact was re-established. He observed her with touching sensibility.

If you would know her [he wrote, years later], think of a garden in Brittany by the sea. It is early morning and she has been awakened by the melancholy two-note whistling of those birds we call *courlis:* she has come down carefully by-passing a small stack of sleeping cats, and the bulldog has followed her silently. She sits in delightful loneliness on the damp and salty grass and her hand enjoys the roughness of the herbs. The sound of the waves fills her mind, she looks now at them, now at the flowers, which are moving faintly upwards as the weight of the dew dissolves.

The earthly paradise is here: it is not lost for her; others merely fail to see it, indeed shut themselves out from it. From the still silent house, will by and by emerge a husband weighed down by the cares of State, a bookish foster-son, a friend obsessed by the recapture of a lost lover, another whose mind is on the obtaining of a given professional position. Either selfishly or unselfishly their concern is with the world of men; to all of them, the newspapers, the mail, are a life-line to what matters. Not to Colette. She is completely unconscious of political events, wholly devoid of any ambition; indeed she is incapable of any planning or scheming in any realm, even to gain or retain any human affection.

With those others she modestly disagrees as to who and what matters. What matters to her is the rapidly changing colour of the sky, the increasing roar of the incoming sea, the polish of a pebble which she has now picked up and, venturing further, the prompt dartings of a shrimp which feels that the tide will liberate it from its narrow pool. It is also the gait of her husband when he comes out: she will watch whether it is lightened by the enjoyment of the crisp air. I have seen her made happy because a new friend, as his bare feet experienced the cool firm sand, sprang up in a little dance of joy ...

She never was happier than when she could bring someone to share her delight in the things of Creation. If some other eye converged with hers in kindred appreciation of the flashing of scales in a fisherman's net, this would make her happy.

When her small daughter, long ago, suddenly stopped in her jumping, having become conscious of the perfume of the flowering troënes, Colette's hands went out in an instinctive hushing gesture: something important to her had happened and she drank in this graceful picture of awareness.[22]

She was observed by both her stepsons. Renaud maintained that the succulence of her descriptions, the extraordinary vivid perfection of her style, gave a good idea of the vivacity of her mind, of that kind of truculent vitality, the vitality of a peasant woman, which she always kept.[23] Colette herself considered Renaud with affection and sympathy. One of her lasting memories, she confessed, years later, was that of a child who was ill-treated in every way, so ill-treated that she felt a criminal that she was powerless to put it right.[24]

Renaud was Sidi's natural son; but, if he was ill-treated, it was presumably by his mother, Mme de Comminges. 'I don't wish a mother like that on anyone,' he wrote. 'It's enough to traumatise any child, and for life. She spoke perfect English, and German, read widely, was cultivated, a lover of music, wrote excellent and very vivid French, and she was certainly not lacking in intelligence, but she was terrifyingly cold.'[25] Sidi himself was devoted to Renaud, though he could not bring himself to say so. 'He was very secret,' Renaud writes, 'unable to confide in anyone ... All in all, he was an exceptional person, but he had no real friends; he made himself too feared.'[26]

There were times when Renaud was clearly happy at Castel-Novel; but, recollecting his childhood recently, he confessed that, as a boy of twelve and a half, he had found the grown-ups at Castel-Novel vexing and demanding. The only person who attracted him had been his younger sister. ' "My Caulette", the former Bel-Gazou, was nearer to me than anyone, so much so that she became my shadow for years.'[27] He felt as if he had been cast in a mediocre play; he had not written it, and he refused to act the part which had been given him. He and his sister remained so much in the margin of the family that force of circumstance threw them together.[28]

On 13 December 1921 *Chéri*, a four-act play by Colette and Léopold Marchand, was first performed at the Théâtre Michel in Paris. It was, considered Vandérem, 'a triumph, in spite of everything that was scabrous about the novel – and might be more scabrous still in the theatre.' Vandérem, it must be said, took a strangely puritan view. 'The French audience,' he explained, 'must be respected and it is already a great deal that so much spice and piquancy and truth have been slipped into the dialogue.'[29]

In the summer of 1922 the Jouvenels were once again at Rozven. Colette had known enough solitude to welcome family life. Now that she was no longer young, she was afraid of solitude, she confessed to Lucie Delarue-Mardrus, and she was now accustomed to children.[30] Lucie was forty-two. In 1900 she had married Dr Mardrus, an Orientalist twelve years her senior. Since her divorce in 1914, she had followed her lesbian inclinations. Colette understood such inclinations better than most. But, even at Rozven, Missy must have seemed a world away. 'If you could only see Sidi bathing,' Colette wrote to Marguerite, 'Sidi-Neptune surrounded by his little tritons, Bertrand, Renaud, Colette, and his stout triton – me... It is a very touching mythological spectacle.'[31] After four days at Rozven, Bertrand was obliged to go back to Paris. 'My leopard cub is going to-morrow,' Colette told Hélène on 10 July. 'Look after him between his examinations.'[32]

Sidi had nearly three weeks' holiday, and went back to Paris. Bertrand returned to Rozven; and Colette stayed on, until the end of August, with her daughter and her 'great greyhound of a boy'.[33]

Whatever she had intended, her initiation of Bertrand had not been an isolated episode.[34] He had entrusted himself to her increasingly. In Paris, she had made a habit of taking him to the dress-rehearsals which she attended as a dramatic critic; often she would bring him back to the boulevard Suchet where, in the early hours of the morning, he watched her as she wrote her article. In May they had gone together to Algeria. Now, in the absence of his father, their love-affair continued. 'When a woman of a certain age has a liaison with a very young man, she runs less risk than he does of remaining marked by it for life.' So Colette was one day to tell Frédéric Lefèvre. 'As for him, whatever he does, through all the liaisons which follow, he will constantly recall the memory of his old mistress.'[35] Colette, who had created Léa and Chéri, was well aware that she herself could survive the love-affair, but that Bertrand would be marked for life. Yet – unlike Léa – she allowed the relationship to continue; and this love-affair with her stepson must have created endless emotional problems, endless conflicts of loyalty, for him. There was no-one in whom he could confide, no-one to whom he could turn except Colette; and Colette he found overwhelming. His father was already having an affair with the Paris *couturière*, Germaine Patat, and she was a friend of Colette's. It was a world in which there seemed no codes of behaviour.

Sidi's political ambitions were taking him further and further from his wife. He was not only a Senator. He was appointed a French representative at the League of Nations. Lord Robert Cecil, one of the English delegates, recalled that Henry de Jouvenel was his greatest ally, and was considered one of the coming men in French politics. In September 1922 he was in Geneva, leading the French delegation to the disarmament commission. On 22 September *Le Matin* reported: 'Historic session at the League of Nations. M. Henry de Jouvenel's proposals for disarmament, reparations and inter-allied debts are approved by the delegates of all 44 countries.' 'What do you think of Sidi?' Colette asked Léo Marchand. 'After that, they should make him King of France.'[36] 'He is made to be President of the Republic,' said Drieu La Rochelle. 'But do you see Colette at the Élysée?'[37]

The year 1922 saw the publication of *Le Voyage égoïste*; the book included Colette's unpublished writing of 1912 and 1913. It is clear that, even then, in the year of her marriage to Sidi, the year of the birth of Bel-Gazou, she was returning in thought to Saint-Sauveur. She recalled not only the Sundays of her childhood, the fruit and flowers and trees of her paradise; she recorded, too, the 'Jardins prisonniers', some of the hidden gardens she had known: geraniums of an indescribable violet, mallows with their chandelier of corollas, and a dilapidated arbour which had been rounded to take crinolines. *Le Voyage égoïste* includes some of her most felicitous descriptions of nature.

In the summer of 1922, at Rozven, Colette had also been finishing *La Maison de Claudine*. She had written it at Bertrand's suggestion. He had asked her why she drew characters which seemed uninteresting to him, when she was so eager to talk about Sido and her childhood. One day, at his request, they went together to Saint-Sauveur. 'That vision of the child in the garden, reassured by her mother's light in the window: she told me about it long before she wrote it.'[38] *La Maison de Claudine* contained no mention of Claudine; there were instead more recollections of the countryside, the hills in springtime covered with the white smoke of the plum-trees, and the familiar house, alive with its children, its dogs and cats and birds, its rambling garden, and the beloved presence of Sido. Sometimes it seemed strange to Colette that she had known so little of her father; but she had been concerned only with Sido, and she had rarely cast a glance elsewhere. Now, ten years after her death, Sido remained the tutelary genius of Colette, the person who was loved beyond compare. *La Maison de Claudine* was the first of the books of time remembered. It reflected the immense nostalgia which filled Colette's mind, and most of her work, nearly all her life.

La Maison de Claudine was published in 1922. At the same time, by a curious coincidence, the house at Saint-Sauveur – sold by auction long ago – was once again offered for sale. It was bought by a silk manufacturer, M. Ducharne. He had a plaque set on the façade, on which were engraved the words 'Colette was born here'. Then, so Colette told Frédéric Lefèvre, 'he sent me word that the house was at my disposal, if I wanted to live in it some day'.³⁹ She herself attended the unveiling of the plaque, but she refused to enter the house. She preferred to live with her memories.

· ———— ·

In February 1923 *La Vagabonde* was first performed at the Théâtre de la Renaissance. Colette herself played the title part. Albert Flament, who watched a rehearsal, expressed his admiration in *La Revue de Paris*. Mme Colette, he declared,

has remained as she was, at her beginnings in the world of literature, not only in her character, but in her face, which has kept the same piquant, sprightly and happy side, this almost continual and almost always natural gaiety... 'I can have vexations of every kind,' she says, rubbing her hands, 'but I never let myself be discouraged. Oh, I'll never do that!' she adds, looking up and showing a mouth which seems to have received the kiss of spring. 'Life is too short!...'...

We talk about sleep. 'Oh, personally, I sleep very well... I mean a good average of seven hours...'

'A good average', a temperament of iron, a Burgundian whose face suggests a Lorenzaccio who had lived in Beaune, instead of Florence... 'And then, don't forget that I can sleep for five minutes whenever I want. At *Le Matin*, for instance, ... I sometimes have a nap in my chair for a moment or two... And I wake up with such an appetite! I gobble like an ogre!' she said, laughing. '... Oh, but after *La Vagabonde*, I must take a nice little slimming course!'⁴⁰

She needed to do so. The 'stout triton' who had bathed with Sidi at Rozven had for months weighed nearly thirteen stone. 'Poor, poor Colette,' wrote Liane de Pougy, 'swollen up with fat, puffed up with bitterness...'⁴¹ Colette made no secret of her love of food and wine; but perhaps the food and wine had come to be the classic consolation. Colette, who was so savagely unfaithful to Sidi, still found it hard to accept the advent of Princess Marthe Bibesco: Mamita's candidate as Sidi's mistress.

· ———— ·

Colette spent some of the spring of 1923 at Castel-Novel, no doubt aware of the impending storm. 'Sidi still isn't there [in Paris],' she reported to Hélène. 'But I learned that he had just gone away for a week, come back to Paris, and left again ... Germaine [Patat] is coming on Wednesday, she's written me a letter of delightful affection and touching delicacy.'[42] Wife and mistress went for a long walk near Varetz, and came home with armfuls of wild orchids. Colette remained attached to Germaine, and concerned about her health; Germaine eventually left with a bunch of dewy roses, picked for her by Colette in the early morning. That summer she returned to Castel-Novel. The relationship anticipated the bond between wife and mistress in *La Seconde*. It was as complex as any in fiction. Renaud de Jouvenel believes that Colette 'took pleasure in pushing la Patat into Henry's arms, to prevent or break up the Bibesco-Henry de Jouvenel love-affair.'[43]

At one time [Renaud explains], my father had an affair with a couturière, Germaine Patat, a woman of taste, who liked painting and frequented people like Francis Carco and Pierre Benoit. But Patat, whom my sister and I called 'Feathers', no doubt because of an excessive taste for plumage, did not please Mamita, who had a candidate, Princess Marthe Bibesco, an equally remarkable woman whom I knew very well. The Princess considered me as a friend, an intimate, she often received me, and I had numerous conversations with her ... As long as the Mamita-Henry-Marthe intrigue continued, I acted as intermediary between the Princess and my father and discreetly delivered little notes that she sent to him at home, but we never talked about it. I have a photo of her with a dedication, signed 'la modiste' in opposition to 'la couturière.' Who finally triumphed.

People have questioned the Princess's love for my father, but I have two letters from her whose passionate lyricism scarcely leaves room for doubt. The thesis of the Princess's friends in the last two years of her life is that it was a platonic love. Perhaps. But she went to Castel-Novel, took pictures of it, and what happens when a man and a woman are alone in a pretty castle? Perhaps they get tired of talking some time or other! Anyway, I continued to see her long after a rupture of whose echoes I was not aware.[44]

Meanwhile, in the summer of 1923, Colette was working on the novel which was finally called *Le Blé en herbe*. She wasted no experience. The book was the fictionalised account of her initiation of Bertrand.[45] 'I have finished *Le Seuil* (or so I think),' she reported to Marguerite in May or early June. 'Not without torments! The last page, to be precise, cost me the whole of my first day at Castel-Novel – and I defy you to suspect that when you read it ... It's the *proportion* which gave me the trouble. I have such a horror of the grandiloquent ending.'[46]

The book was hurried through the press. In Paris, at the end of June, she signed the complimentary copies. The early chapters of the novel had appeared in *Le Matin*, but when it became clear that the adolescent hero and heroine were in fact to consummate their love, there had been a barrage of protest from readers, and the serialisation had abruptly ended. The adolescent love-affair had been inspired by Bertrand's love for the youthful Pamela Paramythioti; that relationship, he writes himself, had been entirely innocent.[47] The readers of *Le Matin* fortunately failed to identify Phil and Mme Dalleray.

Those who can now identify them must find a sinister atmosphere about the book. Phil is sixteen and a half – the age of Bertrand when Colette first met him. On holiday in Brittany, he is drawn to the adolescent Vinca; and then, by chance, he encounters Mme Dalleray. Her name recalls the rue d'Alleray, in the fifteenth *arrondissement*, where Hélène Picard had her apartment, and Bertrand used occasionally to stay. Phil is drawn to Mme Dalleray, and, at the same time, he is deeply afraid of her. In her isolated house he has a sense of nightmare, of an arbitrary arrest, an equivocal abduction. Her voice is gentle, but – like that of Colette – it is virile. She is passionately implacable. She destroys his innocence; and it is clear that long after the end of the novel, whatever his relationship with Vinca, Phil will return to her, ineluctably.

Le Blé en herbe was published, and Vandérem acclaimed it in *La Revue de Paris*.

Since the death of Loti, Mme Colette is, without any doubt, the pre-eminent prose writer of our age, perhaps of many others, and, in *Le Blé en herbe*, her style seems to have gained still further in perfection. Rich with pictures, laden with colours, with the newest and the most modern turn of phrase, one feels in it the firmness, the solidity, the grain of the purest classic ...

I could not tell you all the art there is in *Le Blé en herbe,* or more precisely all the art which is concealed in it. Feelings, sensations, desires, sufferings, reticences, they are all noted with a precision which is equalled only by delicacy.[48]

In July 1923, once again with Léo Marchand and his wife, Colette set out for Rozven. 'I admired you in Paris, for being so yourself, and so active,' she told Marguerite, 'while I was sinking in a spiritual and physical bitumen.'[49] Sidi was travelling in the Balkans. He attended the conference of the Petite Entente at Sinaïa, in Roumania. On 31 July Colette announced: 'Sidi telegraphs from Sofia that all is going well.'[50] He came back by way of Prague with President Beneš. On 18 August she reported: 'Sidi came for three days on his return from the Balkans, rejuvenated, alert, stunning and charming. I hope to have him for another three or four days ... And that will be all.'[51] On 30 August: 'Sidi leaves on Saturday, the day after to-morrow, for Geneva [as French delegate to the League of Nations]. I am not trying to cut my week short to see him again, I should see him again for five minutes. His wise and loving letters dissuade me from doing so.'[52] 'Our Sidi-in-chief is in Geneva, as you know,' she wrote, some time afterwards to Renaud, 'and I've only had the briefest news of him myself, for the last month.'[53]

Colette was perfectly aware of her husband's infidelities. In October, from Castel-Novel, she explained to Marguerite: 'Sidi made me set off in a hurry because he wanted to arrive before us, and he hasn't even appeared. But this post tells me that he left Paris soon after we did ... Love, love, amour, amour ... Anagram of amour: rouma. Add "nia" and you will find at the end a lady who lays two-volume novels.' It was a bitter allusion to Princess Bibesco. 'He has no luck, our Sidi,' continued Colette. 'I expect him from hour to hour, from day to day, from one week to the next ...'[54] Her state of mind defies explanation. She was genuinely in love with Sidi; she was undeniably jealous of his relationship with Marthe Bibesco. And yet she herself continued the liaison which, she must have known, would have wounded him beyond belief.

She had planned to go on a lecture tour of the South of France in November. In mid October, at Castel-Novel, she was struggling with her work. The weather tempted her outside; the subject she had chosen seemed to be the last on which she felt inclined to speak. 'I have painfully delivered myself of thirty pages of my lecture on *The Problem of life for two*,' she told Marguerite on 20 October, 'and I see that I must not touch on it, for the moment, for many reasons ...'[55] She decided to talk instead, about the theatre. On 9 November she set out.

You see how little I write to you [this to Marguerite, from Marseilles, on the 23rd]! I had no idea how much this tour would take up my time – and it doesn't look anything ...

Today I am granting myself 24 hours of slippers, dressing-gown and reading. I certainly need it – there is more than one reason why I need it. A thousand things to tell you? Naturally. And what am I going to find back there? Of course I know.[56]

She returned to Paris for a while, and set off, once again, on tour. On 14 December, from Bordeaux, she reported to her usual correspondent:

Everything is going well, dearest ... Bordeaux is literally covering me with flowers. I am catching up in the train on the sleep which too often escapes me in Paris. The more I travel, the more I sleep, just imagine. To-morrow I leave for St Sebastien, but I shan't be talking there till Monday. On Tuesday it's Bayonne, and Wednesday I come home. Bordeaux is a fine town, full of grub and tipple. I am announced there as *Mademoiselle* Colette de Jouvenel. It's a way of keeping everybody happy.[57]

She herself could hardly be happy. That month Sidi left her. According to Maître Aujol, who was one of his secretaries on *Le Matin* before he took up an advocate's career, 'Jouvenel left the boulevard Suchet in all haste to go and live with his mother, Mamita, and he left everything behind in his hurry.'[58] Colette heard that he was considering divorce in order to marry Princess

Bibesco. On 6 January, in a letter to Mme Georges Wague, she confessed: 'I have been alone for a month. He left without a word while I was on a lecture tour. I am divorcing.'[59]

That was her own account of events; but it left much unsaid. Sidi had at last, it seems, discovered her affair with his son. There had been a violent confrontation. 'I was terrified to see myself, or believe myself, the reason for this drama,' so Bertrand de Jouvenel has written. 'But I found myself so accustomed to living in the shadow of Colette that I could not conceive detaching myself from her.'[60]

IV

Bertrand's unshakable, increasing devotion to Colette must finally have aroused suspicion; Sidi, so one must surmise, had become aware, at last, of the truth. If in fact he had, there could have been no discovery more wounding to his heart and to his pride. All that remained to him would have been divorce. However, Renaud de Jouvenel writes: 'The real reason for the divorce is that my father grew tired of a lady who was only interested in herself and in her animals. So indifferent, so foreign to his political and diplomatic career that it must have been unbearable. But no proof of this exists, and ... the judgment that was given certainly makes no reference to adultery.'[1] The reasons for the breakdown of the marriage were doubtless complicated, but the marriage ended with exceptional bitterness.

It is true enough [wrote Bertrand himself, when Colette had died] that, in her most vital days, she eagerly picked the fruits of the earth, without discriminating those which were forbidden – but this is only the lesser part of the story.

Love has two faces, *agape* and *eros*, a deep understanding and appreciation of the lovable and a petulant wilfulness to seize it. It is not easy to divorce them: Colette was immensely rich in the former and therein resides her greatness; for the latter, she suffered ample retribution.[2]

When Sidi left Colette, no doubt his family were told about her seduction of Bertrand; and they became violently hostile. Natalie Barney did not, presumably, know about the background to the divorce; she was entirely in sympathy with Colette. 'Despite her apparent pluck,' she wrote, 'Colette took a long time to recover ... Her little girl's increasing resemblance to the detested husband may have put Colette's maternal love to the test. Nonetheless, she brought up her daughter with the greatest care, and as she herself had been brought up by her mother, Sido.'[3]

Such comments on Colette as a mother were too generous. As a small child, remembered Renaud, Bel-Gazou had been left at Castel-Novel, 'barefoot, since her mother only allowed sandals – in Greek style – and she must have gone to the communal school in the village (Varetz) under the vigilant eye of the horrible Miss Draper. She was brought to Paris, where she was certainly not a worse pupil than I was. If you change schools and teachers and friends too often, you finally grow interested in something else, and you can pass for a dunce.'[4] In October 1922 Bel-Gazou had become a boarder at the Lycée Saint-Germain. She was to stay there until July 1924; she later went to school at Versailles. She was uncertain of herself, she felt lost and abandoned, and presumably she became difficult, for both schools expelled her. Eventually she was sent to a boarding-school near Bristol; this time, at least, she was not asked to leave. She stayed there for a mere six months, but her stay was brief, wrote Renaud, 'because she learned English much quicker than me'.[5] Bel-Gazou never understood her father, and he was equally awkward with her; she gained little sympathy from her mother. She felt acutely the division between her parents – both of whom were intent on their own lives.

Colette had expressed no longing for children of her own. She was to write of Bel-Gazou with fascination, with admiration for her beauty, her toughness and originality: but she showed no sense of motherhood, no constant concern for the child's well-being. Bel-Gazou was to look on Colette with undoubted awe; Cocteau maintained that she was too intimidated to write to her. 'I always saw mother and daughter calling one another from a distance, groping for one another as if in a loving game of Blind Man's Buff, or hide-and-seek.'[6] 'Cocteau was right,' confirms Renaud de

Jouvenel. 'Their relationship remained formal. The mother never actually felt maternal feelings – and, besides, the girl was very independent.'[7] Love, to Colette, meant the physical love of one adult for another. She was too self-absorbed to be a second Sido.

The breakdown of her second marriage did not leave Colette in isolation. Even she had rarely been so feverishly busy. On 12 January 1924, from the boulevard Suchet, she wrote to the faithful Hélène Picard that she was working from 8.30 a.m. until 1 o'clock the next morning. She was exhausted, but the work was necessary. That morning she had been at her table at half-past eight, drawing up a scenario which she left with Léo Marchand. Then she had had two hours' discussion with him. At three o'clock, she had called on the director of *Le Journal*. He was founding a weekly and wanted her to contribute to it. At five o'clock she had called on the publisher Armand Colin, to whom she had just sent the result of half a night of work. He had been enchanted, but the book had to be delivered by July. At 6.30 she had been at the Maison de Blanc, trying on a woollen culotte costume for the snow. She was just off to the Hôtel Royal, at Gstaad.[8]

The scenario was, apparently, lost. The book for Armand Colin was to be a children's book; Colette wrote only the preface, which is still unpublished. But, since she was alone, she needed more financial security. The end of her marriage had brought the end of her connection with *Le Matin*. In 1923, wrote Renaud, Jouvenel left the paper. Colette herself did not leave it willingly, but perhaps her husband's friends made her work impossible for her.[9]

However, for the moment she escaped the pressures of Paris, and settled with Bertrand at Gstaad, where she took her first lessons in skiing, and skated and tobogganed like a madwoman.[10]

On 5 February she returned to Paris.[11] Three days later she gave a lecture on the theatre; on 19 February she signed a contract for illustrated editions of *Sept Dialogues de bêtes* and *La Retraite sentimentale*. Next day, when matters with *Le Journal* seemed to be settled, she returned to Switzerland: this time to Les Avants, near Montreux. Bertrand was with her, once again.[12] 'People are quite entitled to think it monstrous,' he admitted, 'that I continued to frequent the boulevard Suchet after my father had left it. I justified myself by saying, as I did to my uncle Robert, that having been the cause of a break between my father and Colette, I could no longer abandon her.'[13]

Sidi himself continued his increasingly distinguished career. On 29 March he was appointed Minister of Public Instruction and the Fine Arts. At the League of Nations, with the British Foreign Secretary, Arthur Henderson, Lord Robert Cecil, Paul-Boncour and Édouard Beneš, he worked out the now famous Geneva Protocol.[14]

His political triumphs contrasted sadly with events in his family life. Robert de Jouvenel, handsome, blond and elegant, had long been suffering from a heart condition. He had borne it serenely, even though he had always known how it would end. On 3 July he died, at the age of forty-three. Colette sent a note of condolence which she did not expect the family to read. Sidi – so she told Marguerite – had been at his brother's bedside day and night. Robert had been the only great love, the only deep love of his life.[15]

As usual, she lost herself in work. Her financial situation would not let her rest; nor would her unsettled state of mind. Soon afterwards, she wrote to Renaud that she did not want to involve him in adult bitterness. She asked him to think of her, sometimes, with affection. It would be exactly the same as if he were a believer, and prayed for her.[16]

On 10 July she reported to Marguerite that she was taking Bel-Gazou to Rozven.[17] By the end of the month Bertrand had joined them. On 12 August, in good spirits, Colette told her usual correspondent that she was working badly and swimming well. She was playing Léa in Monte-Carlo for three days in December.[18] On 30 August, still at Rozven, she announced that she was leaving next day, alone, for Mont St Michel. Bertrand would arrive there some hours before her.[19]

On Christmas Day, just back from Monte-Carlo and Marseilles, she reported happily that *Chéri* was to be revived again in Paris. Three days later she confessed that she was working at her novel with desperate courage.[20] The novel was perhaps *La Fin de Chéri*. It was, one suspects, her own life which drew her back, at this particular moment, to record the end of the affair.

'For a very long time,' writes Renaud de Jouvenel, 'Bertrand was forbidden to stay at Castel-Novel ... My father transferred his affection to me for years, as if he no longer counted on the other two children.'[21] Sidi was incurably wounded by the affair, and by its continuation. Claire Boas de Jouvenel could bear the thought of it no longer. She had finally asked Sidi to break it. Sidi had done so by placing Bertrand as an apprentice with a political master. He sent him to Prague as secretary to Édouard Beneš.[22] 'The pleasures that Colette gave me,' Bertrand explains, 'were all the pleasures that one gains from the opening up of the world, and I owe them entirely to her. None the less, the climate of scandal about us was eventually to separate us.'[23]

He was rarely to see Colette again. He paid her, perhaps, one brief visit in ten years.[24] In December 1925 he married Marcelle Prat; after her death he was to marry for a second time. He became the father of four children. Yet Phil remained in love with Mme Dalleray, Chéri remained enamoured of Léa; and Renaud writes: 'When I talked about this episode, some years ago, to Martha Gellhorn, his ex-mistress, who was to marry Hemingway and to divorce him two years later, she said to me: "He still loves her. He is still in love with her." '[25] In his eightieth year he still speaks of Colette with loving admiration.[26]

■━━■

In 1924 *La Fin de Chéri* was not Colette's sole occupation. The year had seen the publication of *La Femme cachée*. Here, for the first time, she appeared under her maiden surname alone.

La Femme cachée is a collection of twenty-two short stories. Most of them are inspired by small events with an unforeseeable effect, an effect which could change the course of a life. A husband, supposed to be visiting Nogent, goes instead to the masked ball at the Opéra, and recognises his wife; she, too, is in disguise, and seeking compensation for their marriage. A young wife lies awake in bed, admiring her sleeping husband, until she chances to look at his hand: its fleshy palm, its tendons, its crab-like fingers. Her unthinking love has gone; henceforward she must control her fear and begin her life of duplicity and resignation. *La Femme cachée* is a brilliant anthology of miniature dramas; sinister, pathetic, desperate, sometimes coloured with black humour, always aware of the sadness of the human condition, the frailty of love, the impediments of age.

Colette was not only writing short stories. She continued to give lectures on animals, on the music-hall, even on rejuvenation. On 26 October a writer in *Le Journal* recorded her at the Théâtre Caumartin. She told her audience how Dr Jaworski had injected his serum into animals at the Jardin d'acclimatation, and had given them new life. 'And then, without hesitation, with remarkable trust and courage, she said: "Since I haven't been able to bring my animal here, I'm going to introduce another who has also had this treatment: I mean myself." '[27]

Bold, original and versatile, Colette was also collaborating with Maurice Ravel. Mme de Saint-Marceaux' salon had long been an informal meeting-place for the most distinguished composers and performers; it was in about 1914, at one of her Fridays, that Colette had met Ravel for the first time.[28] Three years later, she had given him the manuscript originally called *Ballet pour ma fille*. At his request it had been considerably altered, and given a different title – the one which it has kept. In 1920, after a delay of three years, he had finally set to work. The project had still dragged on and, in the summer of 1924, she had asked pointedly: 'When, oh when, shall I have the *Divertissement pour ma . . . petite-fille*?'[29] Before the year was out, Ravel had submitted the promised score to the director of the Opéra at Monte-Carlo. The first performance of *L'Enfant et les sortilèges* was given there in March 1925.

On 5 February 1925 *Chéri* was revived at the Théâtre Daunou in Paris. It was to run until 13 March. Colette herself played Léa. One of those who most admired her performance was Gérard d'Houville. This masculine pseudonym disguised a distinguished woman of letters. Gérard d'Houville was not only a poet and a novelist but the daughter of the poet Heredia, and the wife of the poet and novelist Henri de Régnier. On 15 April, in *La Revue de Paris*, she declared that

> those who have not seen Colette act in *Chéri* have deprived themselves of enormous pleasure, and also of really understanding that celebrated work...
>
> Colette, on stage, is a great and wonderful artist. Her very accent gives the words she utters something hard and rugged, which befits her part, and in which the woman seems to recall primitive times... But, in this work which is both moving and entertaining, like life itself, we are not only subjugated by the direct power, the plenitude of the dialogue, by the story of love and confused maternity... We are also moved to see the conflict of two generations and the certain triumph of youth; however harsh and pitiless it may be, this youth which remains unsure of itself, and does not really know its own mind or its own heart, it still contains the future, it is the force of life...[30]

By the time that this appreciation appeared in April 1925, a miracle had happened to Colette. She had met the man who was finally to set her life in order.

THE DARK YOUNG MAN
1925-35

I

Maurice Goudeket was Jewish. The son of a French mother and a Dutch father, he had been born in Paris on 3 August 1889.[1] When he was three, his father's business as a diamond-broker obliged the family to move to Holland. Maurice and his brother had begun their schooling in Amsterdam. In 1900 the Goudekets had returned to Paris; and Maurice was sent to the Lycée Condorcet. When he was fifteen or sixteen, he discovered the work of Colette. It delighted him instinctively; and, with the pride and fantasy of an adolescent, he announced to his parents: 'I shall marry this woman, she is the only one who can understand me.'[2] In later life, he did not claim this as a prophecy; but, as he wrote, if we realise one of our thousand childhood wishes, we are apt to call it premonition.

At the age of thirty-five he was still unmarried. His controlled manner still concealed a boyish idealism. He had always been quick to break off relationships with women, because he was still keeping himself for the one, all-absorbing passion in which, deep down, he had ceased to believe. He could not bring himself to make a sensible marriage; every day he retreated further into his corner. He had published a book of poems, which had been well received. He was quite successful in business, and comfortably off, but his life appeared to lack a purpose.

From time to time he used to dine with some friends, Bernard and Andrée Bloch-Levallois, and there he made the acquaintance of Marguerite Moreno. One evening, in the winter of 1924-5, he found that she had come with Colette.

Colette was wearing a print dress, and lying flat on her face on a sofa
... She looked like a big cat stretching itself out. I had never met her
[he recalled], never heard her bronze voice, rolling the Burgundian rs.
I don't know why, I remember that Léon Blum [the critic and
politician] was also there. Colette had hardly sat down before she
snatched an apple from a basket of fruit in front of her, and tore it to
pieces with her teeth. I imagined that she was playing the part of
Colette, and this increased my mistrust; but I couldn't take my eyes off
that extraordinary profile ... I poured out her drink, she seemed
surprised and gave me a midnight blue glance, ironic and piercing, but
somehow with a trace of nostalgia. Something rustic and healthy
emanated from her.

I talked banalities to her, she answered with a naturalness which once
again I took to be a pose ... The evening dragged on. She didn't enjoy
herself much, and nor did I. A month later I saw her, briefly, in the
wings of the Théâtre de la Renaissance, where she was playing Léa.[3]

She was playing the part which, perhaps, she best understood: that of the older woman in love with the younger man. Willy had been her senior by some fourteen years; he had dominated her by his experience, his knowledge of the world. Sidi had been three years younger than herself, but he had had the prestige of his superior social standing and his own distinguished career. Colette was not made to take a secondary part; in any relationship with a man, she had, now, to be the dominant figure. Her affair with Bertrand had taught her that she needed a man who was younger than herself, a man whose career was manifestly second to her own, a man who would devote himself entirely to her service. Now, at the age of fifty-two, she had encountered a man of thirty-five who was more drawn to her than he knew.

■——■

At Easter 1925 Maurice Goudeket decided to join the Bloch-Levallois, who were staying at the Eden Hotel at Cap-d'Ail. His chauffeur drove him down with Marguerite. Soon after they arrived, she announced that Colette was to come next day. 'Oh!' he said, apprehensively. 'We were so peaceful!'[4]

Colette arrived. During the day she wrote in her own room. In the evening they all assembled for dinner and for a tedious card-game, taminti. Colette was happy and vivacious. Maurice grew increasingly reserved.

The situation was resolved when he was recalled to Paris. He decided to leave at once by train. Since everyone else was about to go, he offered his car to Colette, and she accepted. He left with a suspicion of regret, but much relief. There was not a free seat on the train. He returned, much embarrassed, to Cap-d'Ail, and asked Colette if he might drive back with her. She had already surmised her future. 'I'm going to make a wonderful return by car,' she scribbled to Hélène on 14 April. 'How much tumult there still is in my blessed life!'[5]

On her return to the boulevard Suchet, she sent Maurice a copy of *La Vagabonde* 'in memory of a thousand kilometres of vagabondage'. She also sent an invitation to lunch.

How accessible she was [he recalled]! How clear and transparent everything became in her presence! A word or a sentence from her, and I felt my inhibitions gradually disappear, I no longer even dared to give them that barbaric name. For the world that she restored to me was a real world, the world of everyday poetry, the world which was to be our domain.[6]

Again and again Maurice returned to the boulevard Suchet. He was overwhelmed by Colette. On 7 May she told Marguerite: 'I had a very long conversation with this young man last night, he appears to his very best advantage when he lets himself go a little. My dearest, how I should like to talk to you! ... And how I should like to burst out with confidences and conjectures!'[7]

The confidences did not need to be stated; the conjectures were evident. For want of Marguerite's presence, Colette turned to letter-writing. Four days later, she added: 'I have long chats with our friend Goudeket, preferably at night ... There's my life. It's very pleasant, I must confess, and my novel is the only thing to suffer. I shall pick it up by the scruff of its neck one evening ... Write to me, for the love of God.'[8]

Marguerite answered at once, and advised her to be sensible.

Yes, I am being sensible [came the answer]! ... Last night Goudeket and I had another of those conversations which begin at ten to twelve and end at 4.25 in the morning ...

Isn't everything going to grow light at once? There is a long blue dawn which leaves me singularly assuaged and optimistic.[9]

Colette was about the same age as Léa in *Chéri*; she had fallen in love as deeply as Léa and, perhaps, with a physical passion which was even stronger. She was all the more ardent as she had not expected, now, the intense devotion which Maurice gave her. Léa had controlled her emotions, even when she felt them most urgently. Colette found it hard to disguise her exuberance and her physical, almost animal, longing.

How I love your letters [this to Marguerite, on 18 May]! And how many secrets! The heat is already pernicious. A satyr is waiting, dare I say it, behind every leaf, and there's no longer a way to sleep on the earth, in the shade. I console myself by rowing on the lake. Exercise, exercise, dispel the thoughts (again if I dare say so) which stir a lusty woman like me, a woman who breathes fire through her nostrils because of the season ... You see how sensible I am. I am expecting my nightly story-teller ... Ssh! He is having lunch here, don't say a word ...[10]

Her relationship with Maurice could hardly, now, be secret; and her lyrical mood continued. Early in June Marguerite received a postcard of the Vallée Jolie du Cousin, near Avalon. 'Acacias, acacias, and more acacias, and roses, and swift streams, and hours swifter than streams.'[11] On 11 June, back in Paris, Colette sent a more complete account of her travels.

What am I doing? Well, I'm spinning. And I use that word as a planet would use it. Yes, I'm spinning. I have seen roses, honeysuckle, forty degrees of dazzling heat, moonlight, the ancient wistaria enlaced round the iron gate of my house at Saint-Sauveur, night over Fontainebleau as we passed. I'm spinning, I tell you. Beside me, a dark young man sat at the wheel. Here I am back in Paris, but am I immobile? The dark young man, beside me, still sits at the wheel. How strange it all is! How sensible I am, how surprised I am, how much wise improvidence in my behaviour! Oh yes, I'm spinning!

You see, you mustn't worry about me. From time to time I'm anxious about it, start up, prick up my ears, and cry out: 'But ...!' and then I try not to think ...[12]

The woman who was so elated by her love-affair, so tempted to follow impulse, so afraid of error, remained the author of *Chéri*: the novelist who seemed, to her readers, an infallible adviser on human problems. Claude Chauvière recalled: 'I have seen young girls running after her car, throwing her kisses and flowers; I have seen adults, after her lecture, confiding in her their secret drama: the one event of their little life . . .'[13] On 16 June, a few days after her last euphoric letter to Marguerite, Paul Léautaud noted in his diary:

This evening, at 6 o'clock, a visit from Colette . . . She said to me: 'Léautaud, I must have a private word with you. I've come about . . . Can you guess?' A— had in fact told me, last time I saw her, that she had been to ask advice from Colette. She had gone back to her, she had persuaded her on the telephone to beg her to intercede with me . . . I told Colette how surprised I was to see her bother about such things. She told me that she does nothing but receive visits or letters like this . . .
'It's ridiculous,' I said to her. 'I'm ashamed of it. Making you waste your time like this. I've told this girl a hundred times: there's nothing to be done. Look: she is 23, and I am 53! I don't do such stupid things. I have told her so time and time again. It's unheard of to have gone in search of you.'
When I mentioned my age, Colette replied: 'You say 53? You're a year older than I am. I'm 52.' . . .
In fact she is still very pretty; and pretty isn't the word. What I should say is that she radiates physical pleasure, love and passion and sensuality . . .
We came back to the subject of A—. 'There's nothing to be done,' I said to her. 'This young lady is as I found her. No demands to be made. Let her leave me in peace.' . . .
At this she said: 'Oh yes, how right you are! It's peace you want, isn't it? Just like me. You know that I'm divorced from my second husband. I'm living, alone, in my little house in Auteuil. When the bell rings, the idea of seeing anyone, man or woman . . . How right you are!'[14]

Colette was disingenuous. The bell continued to ring at the boulevard Suchet, and she awaited it eagerly.

Oh la la, and again la la! And never la la enough [this to Marguerite on 21 June]! She's a fine one, your friend, let me tell you! She's got herself into a fine old fix, up to the eyes, up to the lips, up to further than that!

Oh! these diabolical quiet people – I'm thinking of that lad Maurice. – Do you want to know what the lad Maurice is? He's a rotter, and he's this and that, and he's really a good chap, and he has a satin skin. That's the point I've reached. My dearest, I embrace you. And I embrace you again.[15]

Marguerite answered with affection and asperity:
Now just be sensible at once, . . . and control yourself! . . .
    I have a good many things to tell you, but I shan't tell you till I get a letter which has the appearance of reason. Until then, I cannot consider you as a lucid being. You've fallen in at the deep end! That's all there is to it! All the same, I forgive you. And I congratulate myself on seeing you like this, one doesn't have the chance of a fine love-affair and perhaps 'something more' than a fine love-affair at every street corner! The 'something more' depends on you . . .[16]

On 6 April Colette and Sidi had been divorced. She was free for 'something more', perhaps for a third marriage.

In the meantime she continued to live with breathtaking intensity. Her love-affair did not keep her from acting or writing. She was planning to go on tour with *Chéri*, and she was trying to persuade Marguerite to go with her. Marguerite had reached a difficult period in her career. The theatre would not give her serious rôles, and she was reduced to provincial tours. Colette was now almost the only person who could give her opportunities. Marguerite retired to her estate at Touzac, where she wrote her memoirs. Colette set off on tour with *Chéri*. On 15 August, at Royat, she played Léa once again. 'A town a day,' she reported to Mme de Noailles, 'four acts an evening, 200 kilometres yesterday, 300 tomorrow. I have the soul of a meter. But all is going well.'[17]

    She was not only acting in *Chéri*; she was still doggedly writing the sequel to her most celebrated novel.

My dearest [this to Marguerite on 14 September], I am working [on *La Fin de Chéri*], and I am silent. You are silent, too; you are working? . . . Tell the people round you that I'm virtue itself. My daughter has been with me for a week, she's leaving for the country the day after tomorrow, adorned with a touching physical splendour. She does crosswords with Maurice!!! I don't know if I ought to say that Maurice is working ... Ssh! But, my God, how 'lovable' he is, in the most etymological sense of the word ...[18]

A fortnight later, still from the boulevard Suchet, Colette wrote again:

My dearest, if I don't write it's because I'm working. This *Fin de Chéri* will be the end of me, it bu—— bores me so. But I am working at it with a vengeance. Maurice is Maurice, often silent, full of activity and nonchalance, and I so love him to rest here, in the evening ...

I'm leaving for Brussels on 5 October [to act in *Chéri*], and I'm returning on the 17th. Will you be back? After that, I have Marseilles during 'les fêtes.' And then, from 9 January, on tour again with *Chéri*. You can imagine I want you to come ...[19]

Marguerite continued to consider the prospect of a tour. Colette rehearsed Roger Tréville, who was to play Chéri with her in Brussels; she interviewed Labruyère, the manager of the Marseilles theatre. She continued to work at her novel.

As far as Marseilles is concerned, you must come [this to Marguerite on 1 October] ... I'm sending you this letter at once, so that you can think it over. Personally, I haven't got time to think things over; I am in a hurry. The sunshine, the mild weather, the late summer are desolating – for those who are in Paris.

Maurice has been in London, since Monday – but he's coming back this evening. What with going on tour, Brussels, Marseilles, my daughter leaving for England the day after to-morrow, *Fin de Chéri*, and all the etc., etc. – I'm exhausted. And I'm rehearsing Tréville, who is charming, but hasn't yet done anything marvellous.[20]

Marguerite sent congratulations on the choice of an English boarding-school for Bel-Gazou.[21] As for Marseilles, she was tempted, but unbusinesslike. A fortnight later, from Brussels, Colette reminded her that she must write to Labruyère, otherwise he would engage someone else.

Back in Paris, Colette settled down once again to her novel. 'I must now finish *La Fin de Chéri*,' she announced on 22 October. 'My God! How difficult it is! I have 240 pages of it in my own handwriting. It's a good deal, but it isn't everything. If I don't write to you in the next few days, you will know that I'm working hard and with desolation ...'[22] She continued to work, with despair. 'I sweat blood and ink to create characters other than myself.'²³ Writing to Hélène on 18 November, she said that she did little but work. 'Oh! – *La Fin de Chéri*! I wish he'd kick the bucket!'²⁴ She longed to be free of Chéri and perhaps, now, of her own past.

Max Fischer, of Flammarion, recalled that, when Colette was writing a book, she was generally more nervous than usual. One afternoon she came into his office, 'absolutely radiant. "Well, Colette, may I ask for news of Chéri? I don't know why, I think it must be good . . ." "Good!" she cried, happily. "It's excellent! . . . All's well that ends well. I've got rid of him. I've just killed him." '²⁵

In mid December, writing from Rozven to Hélène, Colette announced that she had finished her novel, and that she was leaving that evening for Marseilles, to act in *Chéri*.²⁶ Two and a half days of rehearsals exhausted her, but the play was much applauded, and Marguerite was with her, and 'Maurice Satan' arrived at Christmas, and she was spellbound by the South of France.²⁷ Her father had been born in Toulon, and he had never ceased to be a Provençal. She had inherited his lyricism, and she had fallen in love with Provence on sight. *La vagabonde* had not arrived, she had returned. She had rediscovered a country she had lost. She decided at once to sell Rozven, and to buy a house near Saint-Tropez.²⁸

On 5 January she returned to Paris, with Maurice, to correct the proofs of her novel; then she went back to the South.

My Hélène, I'm on tour [she explained, from Nice, about a fortnight later]. Will you believe me if I say that I didn't have *a moment* to embrace you? At seven o'clock in the evening, I was correcting 247 pages of proofs, at 7.50 I was leaving, I nearly missed my train. The journey, Tarascon, St Raphaël, was an unbroken nightmare of cold. I can't tell you! . . . At Nice, it's quite different. My room is full of sun, two little parrots which I rescued yesterday from martyrdom are running about on the carpet – do you want them? I'll give them to you – and yesterday, in a nice warm theatre, I had a great success. All the people in Paris whom I'd like never to see are here . . .²⁹

Among them was Claire Boas de Jouvenel. She continued sadly, still, to bear her former husband's name. An American journalist now wrote to ask her for an interview, which (said Colette) was happily granted. He arrived at the Negresco, and cried: 'Oh, but you're not Colette!' and left at once.[30]

Since his divorce from Colette, Sidi himself had continued his successful political career. In 1925 he had been appointed High Commissioner in Syria. Colette was untouched, now, by his distinction. Maurice, in Paris, was sending her letters 'full of the most youthful love. What a cannibal I am to accept it!'[31] She was elated by his love, by the sunshine, by her visit to Nice.

On 29 January, after a visit to Menton, she was back in Paris. Writing to Hélène, a month later, she announced that she was recovering from bronchitis, and that she was working on the publicity for her novel. She was also rehearsing, yet again, for *Chéri*. On 22 February it was revived at the Théâtre Michel. 'One cannot say that she acted in her play,' remembered Madeleine Jacob. 'She did not act, she was Colette.'[32] *Chéri* ran for a week. On the last night, Albert Flament visited Colette in her dressing-room. He found her at her dressing-table, a sturdy figure from a Renoir painting.

She rubs the stick of greasepaint across her lips, and peers in the mirror to see that her eyelids have lost none of the violence of their Algerian blue. Then she runs the comb through her frothy hair, and every time someone knocks at the door, she shouts: 'Come in!' ...

She introduces them to each other, happily: these disparate people who are found in actresses' dressing-rooms ... And she laughs. Her gaiety has some of the vital savour of her body. Her laughter is full of vitamins ...

'Morocco ... I'm leaving for Morocco ... Yes, come to-morrow ... The Glaouï! ... What I'm going to eat, at Marrakesh! ... Apparently the Glaouï has got a wonderful cook ... No, to-morrow is impossible ... M. Legrand ... But of course, come in! Oh, I must sign these books, for Besnard. Have you got a fountain-pen?'[33]

Colette's versatility remained astonishing. On 1 March an audience of subscribers at the Opéra-Comique saw a new production of *L'Enfant et les sortilèges*. Writing again in *La Revue de Paris*, Flament warned his readers of the inept production.[34] Whatever its reception that evening, the general public were to be delighted. Soon afterwards, in *Le Mercure de France*, a critic wrote that a matinée audience 'seemed as enchanted as the music-lovers perched up in the gods, and it was a brilliant success'.[35]

In the month which brought *L'Enfant et les sortilèges* to the Opéra-Comique, Flammarion published *La Fin de Chéri*: the novel which, Maurice declared, years later, had still to be discovered. On 15 March, in *La Revue de Paris*, Vandérem declared that it kept him reading 'like a magic philter'.[36]

II

It has been claimed, repeatedly, that *Chéri* is Colette's masterpiece. *La Fin de Chéri* is a dismal sequel. The First World War is over; it had, perhaps, given Chéri a sense of purpose. Now he returns to the vacuum of post-war Paris. His wife, in charge of a hospital, is lost in a love-affair. His mother is in uniform: occupied with official duties, with political intrigues and financial speculations. Chéri returns to a world in which the rôles of the sexes seem to have been reversed. His womenfolk have a masculine sense of purpose, and they are the masters in the house. He himself no longer has a place. No cause demands him and no woman loves him. He is exhausted by depression and inactivity, bored by his wealth, disillusioned by society. Finally, his mother telephones Léa.

Marriage has not cured Chéri of his love for Léa; absence has not lessened his need of her. Now, at the age of thirty, he returns to her. It is five years since she had given him his freedom. He asks, now, only to relinquish it. But, despite his marriage, his experience as a soldier, Chéri has not learned to be a man; and Léa has lost the will to be a woman. She is sixty, now: obese, unkempt, a massive, sexless figure in whom he longs, with desperation, to see the elegant woman he had known. Léa is crude and earthy, she has kept no particular love for him. Her eyes seem small in her flaccid face; there is no aura of perfume around her. Only the familiar string of pearls recalls the distant love-affair. The sight of her horrifies Chéri and sends him back, at last, into the past. In the squalid room of La Copine, a louche old prostitute who had once known her, he loses himself among the photographs of the young Léa. In an alien world, he finally takes refuge among these relics: he returns to the womb, to the unchanged past, to the all-embracing comfort of Léa's presence. The last of the Clouk stories had ended, long ago, with the night when Clouk was drunk enough, 'resting his head against the welcoming shoulder of the gentle, insipid Copine – to abandon himself to his purest and most agonising memory, to his hidden, incurable love for Lulu.'[1] Now, at La Copine's, among the changeless relics of Léa, Chéri makes his one positive decision: he shoots himself.

La Fin de Chéri lacks the distinction of its predecessor; but it has the virtue of inevitability. When Léa gave her young lover his freedom, it was already clear that he would be unable to use it. He was incapable of reaching maturity, incapable of accepting life without her. He was a hollow man – hollow, except for his one persistent dream, his lifelong need. It was, after all, the basic human need to give love and receive it, and Léa alone had shown him that it was possible.

... In his nostalgia for the time when he was the lover of Léa, this sad Prince Charming never ceases to move us, almost to excite our sympathy [wrote the critic in *Le Mercure de France*]. His deep sense of his uselessness confers a soul upon him ... Undoubtedly, Chéri remains an egotist to the last ... It is an animal which Colette shows us once again, but an animal so desperate in his fierce isolation, that one's heart stands still when a lament escapes from him ... There is, of course, no repentance whatever on the part of Chéri, nor a humble self-analysis. Everyone is at fault, and so is the very ageing of Léa. He alone is right, he who has only lived for material things, and his suicide is the supreme negation of the spirit ... The final pages of *Chéri* are probably among the finest that Colette has written. We may reproach this prestigious writer ... for her indifference to the loftier preoccupations of humanity; but here she attains the salvation of anxiety, in her passionate curiosity about the physical world. For it is very true that we never go to the end of a road which life opens before us (even that of the pursuit of the most animal sensations) without finding the truth.[2]

La Fin de Chéri, like its predecessor, is a novel with two characters. The central section describes the last encounter between Léa and Chéri. All the rest is introduction or postscript. This central chapter is written on a different scale from the rest of the novel. It is Colette's account of the failure of a dream, the destruction of a man by one consuming, all-important experience. It is a brutal, clear-eyed picture of a woman who has lost her femininity. It is also an affirmation of the transience of beauty, of physical attraction, of the transience of love which depends on sex alone. For Léa has been cured of her love for Chéri; her placidity is proof enough of this. Chéri dies not because Léa has grown old, but because she in turn has cured him.

In March 1926, when Flammarion published *La Fin de Chéri*, Colette was interviewed by Frédéric Lefèvre, the editor-in-chief of *Les Nouvelles littéraires*, and she talked to him with abandon. 'In the first place, I have no literary vocation ... What is a vocation? It's something one finds it hard to resist, isn't it? Well, personally, I have never wanted to write ... But if I don't have the passion, I do feel the honour of my profession. I never work easily, I cross out a lot, I delete and add. I don't correct very much on the proofs ...'[3] Colette touched, ineluctably, on *Chéri* and *La Fin de Chéri*.[4] Then, with enthusiasm and relief, she turned to Proust.

One of the greatest writers of to-day is undoubtedly Marcel Proust. The publication of one of his books is a real event for me. I am not a literary critic, but I confess that I find it hard to explain how some people can still fail to recognise him.

The last time I saw him, it was at the Ritz, at one of those soirées where he invited his friends at the last minute, when his health allowed him to get up for a few hours. He was in evening dress; I often recall him in my imagination, with his tie coming undone, his cloak, his hat pushed too far back, that kind of youth which emanated from him, the look of a slightly tipsy best man ...

I had met him for the first time 28 or 30 years ago, at Mme Arman de Caillavet's, where he dined quite frequently. I have kept a memory of those first meetings: the memory of a charming young man, troubled about many things and a little sad. I was living on the Left Bank in those days. I saw few people, I was extremely unsociable.

All the same, he hadn't forgotten me. And when the first volume of *À la recherche du temps perdu* appeared before the War, he sent me a copy. I soon became passionately attached to it.

From that moment we began to write to one another.[5]

Proust and Balzac were the authors whom Colette never tired

of reading.⁶ She liked novels of action, set at sea or in some exotic ambience; she had read all Conrad and all Kipling in translation. But when a new volume of Proust appeared, she set aside her work and began to read immediately.

The twenty volumes of Balzac were always within her reach; she would pick out a volume at random and lose herself in a familiar world. As for Proust, she read him about every other year, read his work in its entirety, and abandoned herself to the experience.

■━━■

Colette, insisted Germaine Beaumont, 'is a nomad ... This is something that I feel profoundly ... Apart from the essential and a little of the superfluous, Colette acquires very little. Her house has never been cluttered ... She has often talked about migrations. I have seen her follow the free birds with her eyes ... To remain sitting in front of her work causes her the mortal impatience of anyone who cherishes activity.'⁷ Now, as a middle-aged woman, she continued to lead her vagabond existence. Violet Trefusis, who met her at a Paris party, thought that 'she looked as though she should be standing on the steps of a caravan surrounded by pots and pans and half-mended chairs. The mystery of the caravan was hers, beautifully bullied by the weather, here today, gone tomorrow, creaking over the Earth's wrinkled palm.'⁸

April 1926 found her, with Maurice, in Marrakesh, where they were again the guests of the Pasha. 'Wonderful journey, wonderful journey!' she wrote to Marguerite from Meknès.⁹ 'We've arrived in Rabat' – this to Hélène, later in the month – '... We have just lived for several days in Fez, in the depths of a palace lent by the Pasha of Marrakesh, alone, with only a retinue of slaves ...'¹⁰

■━━■

She returned to Paris, and to her profession. One critic, at least, was determined that it should not be the stage. On 1 June, in *Le Mercure de France*, André Rouveyre made savage comments on her recent performance as Léa, and even on her days as a dancer. No doubt the article contained considerable truth, but the truth was set down with venom. It was a curious article from someone who had long been a friend.

We have recently [he wrote] had a brief revival of *Chéri*, ... a revival in which the part of Léa was played by Colette herself ... I had not seen Colette on stage for about twenty years. She had then been in pantomime, and she had danced naked. A sad exhibition. For, if Colette already had her spiritual wings, she did not succeed in lending them to her body in the theatre ... Her bare feet came down heavily every time she jumped, with a dull thud, the smack of the heel and the ball of the foot on the cold boards ... It all showed a great deal of ignorance and presumption about the art of dancing ...

Even to-day, the woman who lacerates us with the pen is inert for us on the stage. In her stubborn attempts at acting, we see her absolutely inferior to herself ...

She would seem infantile in the presence of an intelligent professional actress ... She has no spontaneous means, she has no disposition, she has no art to express, as an actress, the drama which she carries within her ...

Let Mme Colette make no mistake: the spectator comes out of curiosity about her, personally, as a writer. It is the legitimate response to her fantasy for exhibition.[11]

In June 1926 Colette was changing the décor of her life. She wanted to let her *hôtel* in the boulevard Suchet: 'to find a lighter ship, and one that is easier to manage. Maurice was afraid that I should feel melancholy at such a change, how wrong he is [she remarked to Marguerite]! He doesn't know how much creatures like us enrich themselves every time that they can change country, change house, change skin, provided that they take ... the essential, *their* essential, with them.'[12] She was not only hoping to move from the boulevard Suchet (which Jouvenel had generously left her), she was trying to sell Rozven, because she had to pay for La Treille Muscate, her new house at Saint-Tropez. Renaud writes sharply: 'Not only had Jouvenel assured her comfort, material security, success, etc. But she made a financial profit from him.'[13] Rozven had been a present from Missy.

In 1926, after differences of opinion with the French Government, Henry de Jouvenel resigned his post as High Commissioner in Syria, and he came back to his seat in the Senate. Colette recorded his return to France, but she made no comment.[14] She was free of him, creating a new décor with Maurice; and Maurice was happy to discard his preferences and adopt her own. In mid July, from Paris, she reported to Hélène:

I came back at 8 o'clock yesterday evening from Rozven, where I had to arrange for moving house. That's why you haven't heard anything of me. I am moving heaven and earth to clear up my financial situation a little. After my thousand kilometres in 3 days, meetings with carriers, etc., I have spent my day with purchasers and adaptors [sic] of films, to try and sell them *Chéri* for the cinema. Then I must send my daughter off to her father in Limousin. After that I shall sigh with relief – a very little sigh, because I shall leave for St. Tropez, in wretched conditions, the furniture hasn't arrived, there's nothing to be booked in the local hotels ... I feel like a boat in a whirlpool. But what can I do? That's the way one lives. And I can't complain, because I have such a nice companion. But oh, how I want to sell Rozven, and no-one wants to buy it.[15]

At last Alba Crosbie, a practical friend and admirer, found 'an honest American (yes, really!) who *may* rent the bd. Suchet', and was willing to pay three months' rent until he could decide. 'This saves me,' wrote Colette, triumphantly.[16] Within the week, she and Maurice arrived at La Treille Muscate. It was desolate. There was no bed, no oven, no running water. 'I very nearly gave it all up and went away again,' Colette told Hélène. 'And then I consoled myself, and began to drive the workmen as they used to drive convict galleys. Just imagine, it worked. A wave of the wand. Not only were the windows narrowed, but the shutters, the patio-courtyard, the pink-washed walls, the electric light, everything worked, and then I thought I'd add flowers to it all. And one evening, from six o'clock till ten, oleanders, pelargoniums streaming from the earthenware jars, geraniums, everything was planted. It's ravishing. How nice it is to ruin oneself!'[17] Like Edmée in *La Fin de Chéri*, Colette had recovered 'her resilient determination, the will to live, the prodigious and female aptitude for happiness.'[18]

August was idyllic at La Treille Muscate.

There is nothing [she assured Hélène] like this gulf, these happy lands, their effortless green. The figs are already bursting and the grapes are sweet. What a climate! The one around Nice seems like the climate of another world...
   I told you about my house at its beginnings, and all the pleasure I have in becoming a gardener once again, and a labourer, a fish in the sea, even something of a cook. You will hear it all from me in person, because I am coming back on 1 September, I'm leaving again on the 2nd, for Bordeaux, I'm performing *Chéri* there for three days, and I'm coming back to Paris to move house.[19]

   She came back to a Paris which was shimmering with heat. She was planning more theatrical performances, and planning her move from the boulevard Suchet to an *entresol* at 9 rue de Beaujolais, overlooking the gardens of the Palais-Royal. This 'tunnel', as she called it, had been sub-let to her, from November, by the ever-provident Alba Crosbie, who lived at No. 7. Colette, too, was provident. 'Have you got a woman in your part of the world who would make me some *confit d'oie et de porc*, a good quantity (and especially a good quality)?' so she asked Marguerite in mid September. 'I should like to have some for this winter ... I must have provisions at home for everyday use and special occasions. I shall also have a good cellar, oh the delight!'[20] Maurice watched the preparations with loving understanding. Colette, he wrote, 'was French to her fingertips, and, above all, provincial ... She was provincial in the art of living, the economical recipes, the tidy cupboards, the provisions, she was provincial in her punctuality, her proverbs, in boxwood and lily-of-the-valley, in *galette des rois*, mulled wine, log fires, chestnuts, and slow cooking under the ashes.'[21]
   Colette had always delighted in food; but she was now in love, and she had no intention of sinking into obesity, like Léa. Her cult of health, said Violet Trefusis, could almost be described as fanatical.[22] Maurice went swimming and boxing; and Colette, now fifty-three, went rowing in the morning on the lake in the Bois de Boulogne. She caught a chill, and early in October she had bronchitis. She was confined to the *hôtel* in the boulevard Suchet, which

she had, after all, been unable to rent or sell, and there were still no bidders for Rozven.

- - -

It was, apparently, about now that she recalled her duties as a mother, and wrote to Bel-Gazou, at boarding-school. For all the vagaries of her own rather public private life, she showed a middle-class commonsense.

My darling, you have got a detention . . . It isn't serious, except that your detentions and other punishments reflect a state of mind: your own. You tend to treat your mistresses casually, and your schoolfellows, too. You feel a young demon inside yourself which, from the height of your thirteen years, judges, appreciates, esteems or condemns . . . Your failing, sweetheart, is your assurance. It is nice - and it is dangerous. It leads to checks, which are always deserved. I could easily have fallen into this weakness of self-satisfaction, for I was brought up in a village like Varetz, surrounded by little peasant girls who were slow of understanding. A sort of scruple saved me from believing that I was superior, from thinking that I was extraordinary. I owe it to this scruple, darling, that I have made myself a name in literature. You tend to say 'it's quite good enough as it is'. If you have too much contempt for difficult things, you will fail in easy competitions.
    I kiss you, darling, with all my heart . . . And with all my heart I am
your mother and your friend
COLETTE.[23]

Bel-Gazou continued to have her problems; she began to smoke in secret. Colette discovered it, and recalled how Captain Colette and Henry de Jouvenel had been enslaved by smoking.

My darling, don't be sad [she wrote]. If it was a painful shock for me to find that you were smoking in secret, that is above all because I know the force of a habit, even if it is anodine . . .
    I have such ambition for you, darling! Not an ambition for situation, but an ambition for character. Do you understand me? I can no longer blossom except through you . . .
    To smoke alone, to drink by oneself, are two weaknesses which lead you far astray. That's all. Darling, I'm glad that you wrote to me. Struggle a little with yourself, it's the best form of gymnastics. It gives you pain and a good deal of pleasure.

The letters were touching, and they were well written, but they were not wholly sincere; their moral tone was suspect, coming as it did from the woman who had been Bertrand's mistress.

Maurice was often to reflect on the relationship between Colette and Bel-Gazou; but Maurice was unable to criticise Colette, unable – if he saw it – to record the truth. He was convinced, or so he said, that, when Bel-Gazou was small, Colette had been the most attentive mother. However, she had come to think that, after a certain age, parents and children should not live together; she also felt (and here, no doubt, Maurice touched the heart of the matter) that, if Bel-Gazou remained with her, she would have to choose between her daughter and her career. His advent in the life of Colette had, he said, made no difference to these feelings, though Bel-Gazou had probably thought otherwise. Every time he saw Colette and her daughter together, they were delighted by each other's company, but they found it hard to express their feelings.[24]

Children, like adults, recognise genuine affection; and Bel-Gazou was in fact perturbed by her mother's lack of love. She detested Maurice, whom she called 'the crocodile'.[25] She was forced into uneasy independence, and she continued to suffer from the vicissitudes of her parents' lives. Colette was naturally selfish, and her liaison with Maurice made her even more self-centred. Bel-Gazou was beautiful, intelligent and original, but she belonged to the Jouvenel past.

In the autumn of 1926 Colette was beset by financial problems, and she was frustrated by her work. Her bronchitis had obliged her to postpone a theatre tour. At last, on 5 November, from the Palace Hotel in Brussels, she wrote triumphantly to Hélène: 'Here I am, I'm playing *La Vagabonde*.'[26] On 29 November she lectured at Neuchâtel on the theatre and the music-hall. Next day, still from Neuchâtel, she announced: 'Here I am, still touring, my Hélène! I'm coming back to Paris on Sunday... If you write to me in Paris, I'm living at 9, rue de Beaujolais, and I am *Louvre 68-56*.'[27]

She returned, briefly, to Paris. On 22 December she was once again on tour, this time at Menton; and Christmas found her at La Treille Muscate. It was about now, recalled Maurice, on their way to Saint-Tropez, that they spent a night at a small hotel in Valescure, a suburb of Saint-Raphael. It was kept by two sisters who had had a Parisian past. They talked for a long while to Colette and Maurice – the only visitors at the hotel. Above all they talked about their niece. She had recently made a marriage which had astounded the *demi-monde*. The conversation was stored away as safely as the *confit d'oie*. Fifteen years later it became the basis for *Gigi*.[28]

Meanwhile, late in 1926, Colette performed in *La Vagabonde* at Monte-Carlo, with Paul Poiret, the couturier, who from time to time took to the stage. On 5 January 1927 she appeared again in the play, this time at the Théâtre de l'Avenue in Paris. The revival was to run for three weeks.

Among those who saw her was a young schoolboy, Robert Brasillach. On 26 January, in a letter to his mother, he suggested the mixed feelings which she inspired.

I can't say that she disappointed me [so he explained]: I had heard so many bad things about her ... And it's true that she's fat, with no grace whatsoever. She's much too heavy. When she walks, she is disastrous: they tell her, you know, that she moves her behind like a mare. Well, alas, that's true! But when she is sitting facing you (not in profile), you don't see her body any more, and, with her open collar, you can easily imagine the Claudine of former days. And then, she's an actress of very great talent. She has an extraordinary voice; one feels it would be capable of vulgarities and the crudest words, but, in spite of everything, it's completely captivating ... I like her voice very much, and her acting, which is very natural, extremely *nuancé*.[29]

·────·

In the intervals of acting, Colette was still trying to sell the *hôtel* in the boulevard Suchet and the house at Rozven. She was dreaming of La Treille Muscate, its old rose-laurels and mimosa trees, her bedroom terrace with its view of the Var and the Mediterranean sea.

Her new apartment in the rue de Beaujolais had fewer evident attractions. It was very close to the street. André Billy, the critic and literary historian, called on her, and exclaimed, inadvertently: 'But you're almost on the pavement!' Luckily, she did not notice it.[30]

It was the first of many visits to the *entresol*. Billy delightedly recorded them.

> The Spanish wine is sparkling in the glasses. I am sitting on a corner of the divan, in front of Colette's table. Through her spectacles she fixes on you a fine and penetrating gaze in which the glass seems to concentrate a still more burning fire. I shan't give you her portrait, since you have seen her photograph everywhere ... But what the photographs do not catch is the feline movement of the eyes, the warm mattness of the complexion, the gentle and, it seems, rounded voice, its minor tone which is so strange, so nostalgic, the tone which is suddenly broken by a burst of laughter or anger; it is also this impression of muscular strength, of solidity, of physical density, which emanates from her whole person. It makes one feel that she is endowed not only with literary genius, but with the genius of flesh and blood, a privilege of almost animal indestructibility ... The hour is warm and intimate, suffused with the aroma of flowers and wine, and cakes. The brilliance of the lamps is dimmed, the cats are purring, the bulldog bitch and the *brabançonne* are dreaming in their corners; under the arcades of the Palais-Royal, only a few feet below the arched window, the wind is whistling, and the pedestrians hurrying along. You hear the clatter of the shops being shut up, the car horns being sounded at the corner of the rue Vivienne and the rue des Petits-Champs, the cry of an old woman selling *L'Intran[sigeant]* ...[31]

A journalist in *L'Action Française* added his appreciation. The apartment, he explained,

> is one of those delightful and irregular apartments which look over the former gardens of the Ducs d'Orléans. The ceiling is elliptical, like the lid of a box, and this doll's apartment is, in fact, a box lined with cretonne and full of superannuated and rococo trinkets which Colette collected long before the world took notice of them. It was she, with the charming Annie de Pène, who started the craze for crystal balls among the snobs of the last fashion but one; they are now sold by antique-dealers for their weight in gold. It was Colette who launched Spanish furniture incrusted with mother-of-pearl, and hangings with a

black ground, and the whole Devéria side of the present style of decoration: good, solid mahogany furniture, artificial flowers in glass cases, etc. It is piquant to see the daughter of captain of zouaves Colette coming round like this to her provincial origins, the key to all her sensibility as a woman and artist, the fundamental theme of all her work.[32]

III

Colette had cast her second marriage, and Rozven, and the boulevard Suchet, behind her. She had found intense happiness with Maurice, and she had created new settings for her new life. She had also established herself, with *Chéri* and *La Fin de Chéri*, as a novelist of consequence. Her standing was made manifest when, on 4 February, at the Société des Conférences, François Mauriac discussed her in a lecture on the modern novel.

You already perceive [he said] in what direction the historian of modern society may widen his horizon. Even if he is absolutely devoid of religious feeling, he still describes, whether he will or no, what Pascal called the wretchedness of man without God.

No one has succeeded better in this than a great living writer, a woman writer – and one, unless I am much mistaken, who is quite indifferent to religious questions. I am talking about Colette. A great many of you have read her last two books, *Chéri* and *La Fin de Chéri*. If you have read them, you know that it is difficult to imagine poorer, more deprived, more squalid people than the ones we find there ... And yet it is not enough to say that these two wonderful books do not abase us, do not soil us; the last page does not leave us with anything like the nausea, the impoverishment which we suffer when we read licentious books. With her old courtesans, her handsome, animal, miserable young man, Colette moves us to our very depths. She shows us to the point of horror the ephemeral miracle of youth, obliges us to feel the tragedy of the poor lives which stake everything upon a love as perishable, as corruptible, as its very object: the flesh. So it is that these books recall the sewers of great cities which still flow unto the river and mingle with its waters, and reach the sea. This pagan, this woman of the flesh, leads us irresistibly to God.[1]

The summer of 1927 found the author of *Chéri* at La Treille Muscate. Three days after she arrived, she was already the colour of terracotta.[2] She wrote in the green afternoon shade. All she could hear was the cicadas as they rattled their tiny cleavers. It was too hot to cross the beach barefoot. None the less, she was working on a book. It was to be illustrated by Mathurin Méheut, known for his pictures of the flora and fauna of the sea. She liked him so much that she was prepared to earn relatively little for the work.[3]

Colette had always been aware of the value of money. She remembered Sido's diligent economies, and the Captain's unhappy speculations. She had not forgotten how her family had known financial ruin, how they had been compelled to leave Saint-Sauveur, how the house and furniture had been sold at public auction. She remembered Willy's febrile, unremitting search for money, and the mornings when he had locked her into the salon to write. In her music-hall years, she had understood the meaning of poverty. Even in the days of Sidi, who had had no business sense, she had continued to work for her living. Now, remarked Renaud de Jouvenel, 'Goudeket put order into Colette's affairs, and did her the inestimable service of getting interesting contracts.'[4] But there were to be many stories of her own toughness with her publishers. Max Fischer, of Flammarion, had once observed: 'You love money, don't you, Colette?' 'Me?' she had answered. 'I have a horror of it! And it's because I abominate it that I want to shut up as much of it as possible, imprison it in my drawer.'[5] The answer was disingenuous. She had international standing, and she intended to be paid accordingly. She had 'a terrible love of money'.[6] Yet she was well aware that money did not buy contentment. 'I have never had a fortune,' she wrote to Marguerite, 'there is no probability that I shall ever have one. For me, being rich means possessing – apart from the affection of my loved one and my friends – a bit of ground, a car that works, health, and the freedom not to write when I don't want to write, or can't.'[7]

At the end of August, in an ebullient letter, she announced that electricity had been installed at La Treille Muscate.

I've got it! I've got it! *It* arrived when I wasn't thinking about it, and in two days it has taken its place in the house, laid on a little haphazardly, but *it* is there ... You've guessed that I'm talking about electricity ... What a pleasure! We had had enough of rambling around with candles and spirit-lamps. My dearest, all is well here.

The days go by so fast that I hear them rustle in my ears. The weather is ineffable. After a few days of mistral, there is a blue and gold stillness so precious that I already regret it, especially when I think that Maurice is leaving in a week. My daughter is living like a little animal, bathing, sunshine, figs, honey, sleep and walks ...

And the work? Page 27, my dearest, that's where I've got to. It's terrible.[8]

Maurice left for Paris, Bel-Gazou left for Limousin, and the faithful Pauline took twelve days' holiday. Colette did the housework, and Louise, the local maid, did the shopping and the cooking. La Treille Muscate still had its distractions, and even in such isolation it seemed impossible to write *La Naissance du jour*. On 14 September, over a fortnight later, Colette reported that she had written ten more pages. She was in despair.[9]

She returned to Paris. October found her in Belgium with Maurice. On 23 December, from La Croix, near Saint-Tropez, she confessed to Marguerite that she was tormented by her novel, and could not clearly see what she was doing.[10] Four days later she reported: 'I am working with incredible loathing, and with meritorious persistence.'[11] On 5 January 1928, still from the Kensington Hotel at La Croix, she announced that she was working 'with a rigour which, if it does not produce abundant results, keeps me a sort of self-esteem.'[12] 'I haven't finished my novel, far from it,' she added, six days later. 'But I think I've got through the most difficult part of it here ...'[13] She returned to Paris; but the *entresol* in the rue de Beaujolais seemed unbearably claustrophobic. Soon afterwards she set off for St Moritz, to revel in 'an extravagant sun on a frenzy of blue and white.'[14]

However, she had earned her holiday. *La Naissance du jour* was now at last with the printer. On 1 March *La Revue de Paris* ended the serial publication. Late that month, in her publisher's office, she signed the complimentary copies of the novel. They bore a printed note: 'Both legally and familiarly, as well as in my books, I now have only one name, which is my own.'

La Naissance du jour is not a novel, properly speaking. It is a celebration of the South of France, of La Treille Muscate, of the flowers and vines, the sun and sea, the indolent summer life. Several familiar friends at Saint-Tropez make their appearance, dancing at Pastecchi's, by the harbour, or revelling in an alfresco supper. Yet the reflection in these pages is not entirely accurate. The middle-aged Colette in the book bids farewell to love. She discourages a young admirer; she has, she implies, reached the age of wisdom, the age of renunciation. Yet the love of Vial for Colette is almost irrelevant; indeed, the episode seems a means of concealing her actual life. 'One can hide nothing from your perspicacity,' she herself wrote to André Billy. 'You sensed that the novel didn't exist in that novel.'[15]

Some critics were less perceptive. They took the book too seriously and praised it, perhaps, beyond its just deserts. 'It is one of the most grievously human works that a woman has ever written,' declared Charles-Henry Hirsch, in *Le Mercure de France*. '... The sincerity of these pages recalls the most moving pages of Jean-Jacques in the *Confessions*.'[16]

This book [wrote Eugène Marsan] is still described as a novel on the cover, and it is a novel, but it is also a confession. Not an autobiography, under the more or less transparent veil of the characters: a real confession in the old manner ...

In *La Naissance du jour*, the author tells us of her autumn, and how she could be loved by a young man. She rejects him, ... like a superior woman to whom age (it is her own word, I shouldn't allow myself to use it) finally reveals the secrets of life. You can begin to imagine the difficulty of such a subject. Colette has raised it to a sort of cosmic reverie.[17]

There are certain books by Colette which appear to relate episodes in her life, when in fact they precede them. *Chéri* had preceded her love-affair with Bertrand and her encounter with Maurice. *La Naissance du jour* described the renunciation of love at a time when she and Maurice were ardent lovers. Colette did not mention Maurice, in print, for another twenty years, and then he appeared in the guise of her best friend. He himself recorded that she was not only sensual, but austere. It was she who decided, in time, that the moment had come to transform their love into friendship.

'My next novel? Page 57. I am stagnating.'[18] Colette was writing to Marguerite on 25 March 1928. On 4 April, with Maurice, she set out once again for Saint-Tropez.

My Hélène, I didn't know the spring in this South of France [she continued about ten days later]. It comes armed with everything that pleases me. A real spring, Hélène, tender and sweet-smelling, heavy with quince-trees in flower, lilac, iris, wistaria, stocks, ... it is so sweet! And the toads are singing, the frogs are barking. We snatch a bathe, in an icy sea, but the sand is already so hot, and the sun, that your skin tingles with excitement ...[19]

On 17 April Maurice left for Paris and his apartment at 34 avenue du Président Wilson. Strangely enough, they still respected this convention. Since they were not married, they each kept their separate Paris addresses. Colette remained at La Treille Muscate. As usual, she was full of good intentions. By 15 June, at the latest, she intended to give her next novel to Pierre Brisson, the editor of the fortnightly *Les Annales*. She had also made arrangements with the publisher Ferenczi, who was counting on the novel at the end of September.[20] *La Seconde* was not to be delivered in time. La Treille Muscate was again too distracting.[21]

Colette spent June in Paris. She attended the sale in aid of the Écrivains combattants, and herself sold copies of her books. She alone raised 5000 francs. She dined with Léon Barthou and his brother, Louis, vice-president of the Conseil des ministres – one day to be assassinated with the King of Yugoslavia at Marseilles. She also called on Princess Edmond de Polignac. The former Winaretta Singer, Mme de Polignac had inherited an American fortune through the family sewing-machines, and acquired a title through judicious marriage. Her husband had long since died, and she discreetly indulged her lesbian inclinations. On 18 June Colette visited Mme de Polignac's friend Violet Trefusis – who had been the mistress of Vita Sackville-West. Next day she had *déjeuner* with another notable Sapphist, Élisabeth de Gramont, now the Duchesse de Clermont-Tonnerre.

Élisabeth de Gramont was among her warmest admirers.

If Colette were transported to a negro village [she wrote in her memoirs], she would guess its secret life by observing gestures, and she would give an exact and striking picture of it. She has profound understanding of the ritual, knows the material gestures which men have made since they inhabited the earth ...

There are three similar love-stories set at different points in literary space: *Moll Flanders, Manon Lescaut, Chéri*. The last one, signed Colette, is the most human, the most grievous ...

Chéri is the greatest novel about love in our time.

If I am a little morose, I re-read a book by Colette ... Through these stories of dizzying diversity there circulates the *leit-motiv* which goes from Claudine to Léa by way of *La Vagabonde*: all human tenderness, passion, love and compassionate friendship. Colette expresses those needs of affection which force human beings to lean towards each other, and she knows the distress of isolation ... Her characters live without romanticism. They are hot-blooded but they are also brave, and they accept life and its inflexible laws with a jest which is a form of modesty.

Colette had arranged to have alterations made at La Treille Muscate. She planned to return there on 7 July. At the last minute she received a telegram, asking her to postpone her visit for a fortnight. Undeterred, with dogs, cats and daughter, she left for Saint-Tropez, where she found La Treille Muscate in chaos. All the work had been begun, and no room was habitable. The beds were unmade, the oven had been left in the garage, where Louise, in tears, cooked fish for them over a spirit lamp. Next morning, early, the contractor was summoned. Ten days later, inspired by the frantic activity of Colette and the fifteen-year-old Bel-Gazou, the workmen confessed that they had never managed so much. Mother and daughter slept on the terrace. Early one morning they walked along the shore; the tamarisks were still covered with the salt crystals brought by the dew. Colette and Bel-Gazou bathed in the tranquil Mediterranean, which was still rose-coloured from the sunrise.[23]

Paul Géraldy, the playwright, who lived nearby, at Beauvallon, was to remember Colette in her summer setting.

... She likes good health. She likes everything she likes rather too much, as children do. She has a child's curiosity, appetite and modesty.

At the tavern in the old port she eats aioli, and asks for onions and garlic. They bring her strings of them. She takes large bites out of them and stuffs the rest into her pocket, for the road. In summer she sleeps on her roof, in the open air.

It is impossible to talk to her about herself or any of her novels. She escapes at once, summons her cats and harangues them indefinitely. It is her defence ...

'But don't you like glory?' asked Madame de Noailles.

No, she doesn't like glory. Or at least she only likes it from a great distance, safely sheltered in her house at the far end of the world, in the midst of her personal comfort, which consists of silence, netting to keep off the flies, fruit salads, flat cakes, basins full of hot wine with cinnamon, thick walls, the peaceful activity of her servants, and a barrier impassable for visitors.

She doesn't like work, either. She loves the earth, and animals and trees and smells. She writes to earn the right to enjoy them more and better. With stubborn determination she imposes on herself the work which has suddenly become essential because she has spent the money from *La Fin de Chéri*, or from *La Naissance du jour*, on reroofing the house, replanting the vine, and because she is dying now to buy the corner of the wood, – or else, if she is in Paris, because she has spent too much in the best shops. In fact, the poem of luxury tempts her as much as the poem of the countryside ...[24]

Late in August, still at La Treille Muscate, Colette sent an apology to Hélène. It needed courage to write letters there; it needed still more courage to work. A sentimental September was already making its appearance, morning and evening, over the vineyards and the sea. The grapes were sweet, the figs were bursting in their skins, the stillness of the nights was miraculous. Perhaps *La Seconde* would turn into the lowest kind of romantic serial.[25]

While she was writing to Hélène, Colette was also sitting for her portrait to Dunoyer de Segonzac. His etching of her was one of his illustrations for her book, *La Treille Muscate*. He, too, recorded these days in print.

In her discreet house, veiled with mimosa, I did a series of etchings in the poetic atmosphere which she creates around her.

In the early hours of the morning, she liked to work in the garden, cultivating flowers, vegetables and fruit . . .

At about noon, we used to meet again on the beach at Les Salins (she liked its transparent water in tones of aquamarine). We used to meet friends there: Luc-Albert Moreau and his dear Hélène, and often the Jouvet family, Thérèse Dorny, Pierre Renoir and Valentine Tessier.

After the bathe, Colette often used to ask me to lunch while we were waiting for the afternoon pose. The table was laid on the terrace, in the shade of a trellis covered with wistaria and vine. The lunch was excellent: grilled *rascasse*, all crackly, mother Lamponi's ravioli, all washed down by a fresh rosé from Saint-Tropez.

Colette summoned her cats; just as the *muezzin* calls the faithful to prayer, so Colette called her animals for their walk. 'The Cat's Walk!' This melody, musically scanned, decided the cats at the top of the mulberry tree to come down the tree trunk on the tips of their claws; they followed Colette in procession along the pathways bordered with purslane and amaryllis.

Then Colette went upstairs to have a siesta.

I waited for her in the ground-floor room where she used to work every day, she wrote on a little Provençal writing-desk . . . She had moved this piece of furniture to face the corner of the room, so much so that the two walls isolated her like blinkers: she was a voluntary prisoner.

When she began to work, she felt a sort of need to procrastinate: rather as if Claudine were trying to prolong the recreation. She stretched out on the divan with her pug; then she squatted on the tiled floor, and removed the fleas from Soucy, her bulldog bitch . . .

Then, suddenly, and resolutely, she sat down to write. She rested her fine, strong arms on the writing-table. She stayed there, as if frozen in an immobility which lasted for several hours. She was completely absorbed, she didn't utter a word, there was absolute quietness. The total silence was only broken by the rustle of a page of text which she threw away with controlled anger.

Suddenly, at about dinner-time, she got up and said: 'That's all for today!'

She summoned Maurice, draped herself in a cape, and set off, surrounded by her animals, to meet her friends again in the port.[26]

La Seconde was making her ill, she confessed, on 10 September 1928.[27] Pierre Brisson had expected to receive it in June, and he was understandably desperate. While Saint-Tropez offered too many agreeable distractions, Paris brought intense social life. Colette needed isolation. Just before Christmas, determined to finish her novel, she set out, with Maurice, for Belgium, to stay at the Château d'Ardenne.

This former royal *château*, now a hotel, stood on a hill at the meeting-place of two rivers, the Lesse and the Yvoigne. It was massive, hideous, almost empty, and completely isolated. It was so silent that Colette understood at once why she had been warned not to go there, warned that she would find it sinister.[28]

It oppressed her from the first. Writing to Mme de Noailles, she asked her how she would bear this unnerving, unremitting silence. A gentle rain was falling, very sweet to the face and to the eyes. She was working with the diligence of a bureaucrat, and she had a horror of her book.[29] She confessed later that she had been sullen, speechless, with silences that lasted, like her working shifts, for nine consecutive hours. Maurice, she said, had been stoical.[30]

Her work bored her beyond belief, but she had found the perfect place to write in.[31] On 31 December she burst out: 'O Marguerite, how bored I am with my work! Nine hours' labour yesterday, seven the day before – what a nice job the writer's is! But I'm *going* to finish.'[32] That night, the last of 1928, just before midnight, she wrote the last sentences of *La Seconde*. 'My Marguerite,' she announced, two days later, 'I'm coming back, I've finished . . . . I hardly believe it . . . I'm coming back. We're coming back.'[33]

She came back to write an exuberant letter to Louis Barthou, now Minister of Justice in the Poincaré Government. 'O perfect friend! I clasp you to this bosom which you have adorned with a rose.'[34] The rose in question was the red rosette in her lapel. On 5 November, largely through the good offices of Barthou, she had been promoted Officier de la Légion-d'honneur.

IV

On 1 January 1929 *Les Annales* began, at last, to serialise *La Seconde*. The serialisation continued until 1 March, and later that year the book was published. 'It is a "novellish novel",' Colette confessed to André Billy, 'and I'm a little worried about it.'[1]

One wonders how much *La Seconde* owed to Henry de Jouvenel; there seems to be much of him in the dramatist Farou.

I still think [writes Renaud] that Colette continued to pursue her revenge against my father...
In some of the Burgundian woman's works, one may ascertain a sort of hatred for the nobility. In *Julie de Carneilhan* she denies my mother the title of Comtesse and speaks of the Carneilhans as minor squireens raising horses and pigs on some ruinous estate. In *Duo*, the *château* – Castel-Novel – is only a ruin, and the man, still the same man, the one we find again in *La Seconde* in the guise of a playwright, is still ridiculous, a brawler, and inconsequent. A real obsession.[2]

Fanny is married to Farou, and she is obliged to accept his constant infidelity. Gradually she comes to understand that Jane, his secretary, is also his mistress. She compels herself to be silent; when, at last, she confronts Jane, when Jane decides to go, Fanny discovers her own need of her. Farou would only replace her by another mistress. It is better for Jane to stay and give Fanny security. The burden of the novel is one familiar to Colette: the relationship between an attractive, inadequate man and a woman – or women – who are much superior to him in understanding and in moral courage. Le Grand Farou is as simple and as feckless as a child; it is the women who are strong, considerate and caring. They recognise his weakness and his selfishness; yet they are drawn to him and drawn to one another by their concern for him. *La Seconde* is a novel of resignation. It is sober and restrained, and it confirms Colette's ironic, melancholy perception.

While the first instalments of *La Seconde* were appearing in *Les Annales*, Colette caught influenza; it seems to have been a violent attack, for she was obliged to spend nearly a fortnight in bed. She was still confined to the rue de Beaujolais when she was asked to visit the École normale. It was traditional for *normaliens* to invite writers and artists to the rue d'Ulm. Robert Brasillach recalls how they used to club together to buy *petits-fours* and port for the famous. 'What a very nice invitation!' answered Colette. 'But I'm in bed ... Can I come and see you between the 6th and 9th of March? No, not the 9th, I'm going out to dinner. Anyway, you arrange that. Or telephone me ...'[3] Brasillach called at the rue de Beaujolais.

I had hardly arrived [he told his aunt] when she began the conversation by saying: 'Sit down wherever you like, but not on the cats.' She is a fat woman, over made-up, but she is very amusing, and she's kept much of the Claudine of former days ...

We wondered what we should do with Colette to make her stay, we should have danced on our heads, if necessary. We almost did. I exploited my culinary talents to concoct a little tea to please her. We took her all round the École (not on the roofs, she is too fat), and sang her the really spicy songs from the École revue. Next time she comes, she will bring her daughter with her.[4]

Brasillach long recalled that afternoon in the spring of 1929 when Colette arrived with her bulldog Souci (they tried to feed it on banana sandwiches). He remembered how she had taken a walk around the garden, 'and referred to all the trees by their names, which we didn't know, as if they were friends.' He remembered 'her thin smile, her frothy hair, and her rich, rough voice.'[5] He was not the only one to observe her animal quality, her peasant vigour. Janet Flanner, the American journalist, described her as 'a short, heavy-bodied woman with a crop of wood-coloured hair, with long grey luminous eyes and a deep alto voice, ... who still speaks French with a racy Burgundian accent.'[6] Rebecca West saw her out with her dog, and was almost frightened by her animal energy and fierceness.[7]

Colette was increasingly dissatisfied with her *entresol* in the rue de Beaujolais. In March – a strangely impractical move – she rented an unfinished ground-floor apartment near the Quai d'Orsay; when it was finished, she disliked it and refused to move in. Later that month she and Maurice paid a rapid visit to Madrid,

Seville and Algeciras, and sailed for Morocco. On Easter Monday, 1 April, from the Villa de France in Tangiers, she wrote to Hélène about the realm of the Pasha of Marrakesh, and about the cooking of Si-Kassem, which would fatten Don Quixote. She and Maurice were to leave next morning, at dawn, in a wretched cockleshell of a boat, and she wondered how they would reach Toulon.[8] The cockleshell proved, however, to be the SS *Orsova*, and on 3 April she confessed that she was delighted with it. One ate all day as one did on every comfortable English ship. She and Maurice had also met Henri de Rothschild, whose yacht was anchored off Gibraltar; he had invited them to dine on board.[9]

She returned to Paris, to find a warming review of *La Seconde* by Marcel Prévost. 'Oh, the talent of Colette! Impossible to pin it down on a page, with words; it immediately looks like a big butterfly dissected on an entomological board. It is the direct emanation of herself, it has her impassioned face, her voice with its grave sonorities, her vivacity broken by sudden lassitudes. Her books have more than an atmosphere; they have a climate.'[10] Colette was enchanted. 'I got back (yesterday evening) from Tangiers ... What a delightful friend you are! Your phrase: "Her books have more than an atmosphere ..." Ferenczi will leap at it, he has already phoned me.'[11]

Colette was back from her travels, as restless as ever; but she had a new source of pleasure: a rented house at Les Mesnuls, a hamlet near Montfort l'Amaury. She intended to teach Bel-Gazou how to furnish the house with a mere fifteen hundred francs' worth of camping equipment.[12]

She spent part of the summer at the Château de Costaérès, the Marchands' romantic island house off Ploumanech, on the coast of Brittany. The island reminded her of Le Paradou, the wild, enchanted garden which Zola had described in *Le Docteur Pascal*. It was a Paradou of four hectares, invaded by roses and wild strawberries, a forest which was almost literary, it was so fragrant and so beautiful.[13] 'Twenty-one lobsters in ten days,' she added on 23 July. 'Plus nineteen spider-crabs which are bigger than your ...

hand. Plus I don't know how many fish. Plus, this morning, two langoustes, o my Marguerite, two formidable monsters, two langoustes which, at trade price, were worth 140 francs! ... This way of life suits me terribly well. But I miss Maurice, who is coming to fetch me on Friday.'[14]

They left Costaérès for La Treille Muscate, where the patio was wreathed in flowers, and the zinnias, announced Colette, were as big as centre-tables.[15] Maurice returned to Paris, Bel-Gazou arrived for her 'ruinous and marvellous' holidays. She wore boys' shirts, swam underwater like a little shark and drove every kind of car except the Talbot, which her mother was determined to preserve. 'As for me, no news,' Colette reported on 12 September. 'Nothing except this physical life, which suits me so well.'[16] She had already gathered in the grapes. She hoped that her vines would yield some 1500 litres of wine.

＊

On 19 September she was back in the rue de Beaujolais. She had come back empty-handed and, once again, she was bowed down by the work she had left undone. As if this were not enough, *La Revue de Paris* asked her to succeed Paul Souday as dramatic critic. It was an ill-paid, exacting task, but she accepted it.[17] Marguerite had persuaded her to give a series of lectures in Berlin; she did so between 20 and 25 October. 'You couldn't imagine a warmer welcome,' went her card from the Hôtel Esplanade. 'Extremely happy, and equally tired.'[18]

Christmas found her at Saint-Tropez: a charming Saint-Tropez which, in winter, became a village once again. She and Maurice dined with Dunoyer de Segonzac. He was still working on the etchings for *La Treille Muscate*.

The book was not to be published until 1932. Colette had written it as a pretext for the illustrations. It was one of two books which were born of her affection for Saint-Tropez. The other was the edition of *La Naissance du jour* illustrated by Luc-Albert Moreau. Both books, wrote Maurice, were considered to be their illustrators' masterpieces. This was hardly surprising. There had rarely been such intimacy between the artists, the author and the setting. Segonzac and Moreau used to work at La Treille Muscate whenever they felt inclined. They were accepted as part of the household.[19] Cocteau later asked Colette why she had written a book on Saint-Tropez and its artists. 'Because I don't want to be thin like you,' she answered, 'and to be stranded in hotels.' 'And why do you write a book a year?' 'For the same reason.'[20]

In February 1930 she was once again in Berlin. This time she had been invited by Sarrasani, the manager of a famous travelling circus; and when she and Maurice arrived at the Hôtel Excelsior, they were greeted by the circus band drawn up in the foyer. 'Everything is wonderful,' she reported to Marguerite, 'the weather, the circus, the wild animals, the 21 elephants, the little new-born camel, the tiger-cubs, everything!'[21] On the last day of her visit, Sarrasani gave a dinner for her under the big top. The sixty guests were served by the snake-man, the juggler and the clowns. It was a dinner to delight *la vagabonde*.

Her vagabond existence continued. One day this spring – she never dated her letters – Colette announced to Hélène:

Tomorrow morning (unless the weather is terrible) I'm leaving for Montfort with Maurice and the animals, we shall spend ten days there – if possible. But what a cold spring ... I am working hard at my continuation of *Sido*. Yesterday, I got drunk with work: from 2 in the afternoon till midnight, taking 20 minutes for dinner. I'm mentally defective from it today, so I've done well! My address: La Gerbière, Saint-Nicolas, Montfort l'Amaury, Seine et Oise.[22]

Colette had now abandoned Les Mesnuls, and Maurice had bought La Gerbière. His financial straits were to oblige him to sell it the following year, but in the meantime Colette admired the lilies-of-the-valley, delighted in the blazing fires and the contented cats. She had also written forty-one pages.[23] *Sido* had been published the previous November. Ferenczi was to bring out the enlarged edition in May. Colette still smiled as Sido had smiled, her accent was the echo of Sido's voice. She had not lost her almost mythical love for her mother. The manuscript of *Sido* was bound in a piece of an old blue dress with white flowers which Sido had worn.

Colette herself spent part of the summer in Paris. At a fancy-dress party at Neuilly, she was gratified to see Francis Poulenc disguised as Chéri, escorted by a Colette with an English accent. Part of the summer she spent at La Gerbière. 'Today it's so July that not a leaf is trembling in the air which is both fresh and warm. There are no flowers, now, except the inexhaustible roses ...'[24] On 10 July she and Maurice left Le Havre on a month-long cruise which was to take them as far as Norway. They sailed with Henry de Rothschild on board his yacht the *Eros*. 'There are no "undesirables" (I mean no bores) on board the yacht,' Colette reported. 'The Léo [Marchands], Pierre Benoit, Marthe Régnier [of the Comédie-Française], that's all.'[25] They sailed into Danish waters, and into a storm which lasted thirty hours, and they were forced to take refuge in Kiel. On 14 July they set out for Copenhagen. Four days later, from Bergen, Colette reported: 'My Hélène, the first night without darkness is just over ... At eleven o'clock last night, we were playing bezique on the bridge, and stark naked swimmers were frolicking round the ship. What a wonderful voyage!'[26] She was enthralled by the jade-coloured water, the infernal corridors of rocks, the waterfalls, the snow, the increasing beauty of the unknown. On 10 August she ended the cruise which she recorded in *Notes de Voyage*.

•——•

After his return from Syria in 1926, Henry de Jouvenel had taken up residence with his mother.[27] Mamita had a modern house in the rue Chardon-Lagache, in the fashionable part of Auteuil. He induced her to sell it and to buy a stately old mansion in the rue de Condé, which was near the Senate. His associates called on him there. None of them felt at home.

In 1929 Mamita had died. Her legacy was not enough to let Sidi maintain Castel-Novel and its large estate. Luxury, however, had become a way of life with him, and on 4 August 1930, while Colette was cruising on the *Eros*, he married Germaine Louis-Dreyfus, the widow of an immensely wealthy banker.

Sidi's third wife was Jewish, as his first wife had been; and she was nearly his own age, like all the women he had ever loved. No doubt her fortune enhanced her other charms, and his marriage to her was so expedient that it passed for being little else. She was, wrote Renaud, 'an imperious matron, apt to dramatise, an excellent musician, whose second daughter I married, as if to complicate the situation still further. She would have been a passable mother-in-law, were it not that she spent a good half of her life ... putting herself on stage and playing a part which, unfortunately, no-one had written for her.'[28] Yet Paul Reynaud described the marriage as the happiest part of Sidi's life, and André Maurois, who found the bride 'beautiful, very beautiful', saw Sidi with her at Castel-Novel and felt 'an impression of security, of perfect understanding, of happiness keen and delicious to the point of anguish.'[29] This marriage did not only secure Sidi's estate near Varetz; it brought him a villa on the Riviera and Talleyrand's former mansion in the rue Férou in Paris.

Sidi delighted in luxury more for the sake of sharing it than for its own sake: indeed, he was wildly hospitable. However, he did not display his wealth any more than he did his other assets. He was a perfect *grand seigneur*: discriminating but not exclusive; always active, never busy; frivolous about serious matters, earnest about others, yet steadfast in everything. He impressed all comers, however differently. 'This great, strong, magnificent lord,' wrote one, 'with avid and ferocious eyes – jungle eyes – marvellously intelligent, marvellously amoral, is a man of the Renaissance, a technician of *virtù*.'[30] Whatever they thought of him, none could help loving him.

In August 1930, on their return from Norway, Colette and Maurice drove to Saint-Tropez. Once upon a time, recalled Maurice, it had been 'spared by frenzy'. He and Colette and Mistinguett had sat around a table in the *pâtisserie* Sénéquier, and Miss – who had longed to be a serious actress – had begged Colette to write a drama for her: the most poignant drama possible.[31] Now, in the high summer of 1930, Saint-Tropez was uninhabitable, 'full of the people photographed by *Vogue*'.[32] Colette – who was also photographed by *Vogue* – found the port 'barred by three rows of Hispanos and Bugattis, the "natives" in Chinese trousers, and thirty people, suddenly assembled by magic, waited for me to come out of the newsagent's with such impertinence that ... I didn't disguise what I thought of them.'[33]

All Paris was visiting Saint-Tropez. Among them were Francis Carco and his wife, and Pierre Renoir, the film director (and son of the painter). 'But my little house is peaceful, and sufficiently apart,' so Colette reported to Hélène. 'I'll write again, we are rushing off to bathe as if we were burning ... The lizards greet you, and the giant hornets, as blue as Spanish waves, and the hawk-moths, which have eyes like red beacons, at night, and fat bodies as warm as the bodies of cats.'[34]

She had never felt so averse to people and, especially, to work. Despite her literary commitments, she did nothing but revel in the sun, swim and play tennis, eat and sleep.

We are waiting for Renaud, who should be coming by car from the Pyrenees to fetch his sister [this to Marguerite on 31 August]. They will leave on the 5th or 6th for Castel-Novel. I take good care to avoid the port, where all Paris and all Montparnasse are in evidence. There are, among two hundred others, Mme de Cl[ermont]-Tonn[erre] in pyjamas, Mlle Lefranc[q] [the dramatist] as a small ship-boy, Mme Walter [the architect's wife] in workman's overalls, Daniel-Dreyfus [the banker] in shorts ... Valentine-Tessier-Pierre-Renoir have just left again. Etc., etc., etc. ... No enticement or constraint would make me dine in the port this season.[35]

Her friends came to lunch or dine with her, instead, at La Treille Muscate. André Billy arrived with Pierre Varillon.

We rang the bell [remembered Billy], and the faithful Pauline appeared.

'Madame isn't here,' she said before we had even opened our mouths.

'But Madame *is* here, Pauline, because she's expecting us.'

Pauline smiled and we went in ...

'Good morning!' cried a familiar voice, a voice robust and musical, like the actual style of Colette.

The room in which she stays in the daytime is a big cement cube, built behind the house. A few fine pieces of Breton furniture full of books, a big work table, a huge divan with its mosquito-net, and pieces of pottery of a vegetal green stand out against the walls, which are whitewashed a milky white. On the table are two piles of paper. The sheets on the right are immaculate, the ones on the left are covered with the famous writing, firm and upright. The floor is also strewn with sheets of paper, crumpled, or rolled up in a ball.

'Well, there you are, my dears, I toil and sweat. What a penance to shut oneself in here fifteen hours a day when it's so beautiful outside! Would you like to see my garden? Would you like to see my vine?'

Colette made twelve hundred bottles last year and she will make more this year.

She drags us off to the kitchen garden where clusters of tomatoes alternate sensibly with sweet onion plants and decorative artichokes.

'Oh, what trouble I've had with this kitchen garden! I dig myself, you know. It's very good for your health; before eight o'clock in the morning, of course... But you haven't seen the marvel... Come here!'

We follow Colette to the bottom of the garden, push open a gate, and stop, in speechless admiration. We are on a beach, on the most delightful beach you could possibly imagine.

'I bathe here twice a day, in absolute peace and solitude. Look, it's hardly a hundred yards away, this little sea, entirely my own. I bathe at night. Oh, what a touching pleasure it is, to bathe at night!'

We are coming back, now, towards the house. While we have been visiting the garden, Pauline has taken the bottles out of the well: the bottles which only come out to be drained. Already all the fruits of the South are waiting on the table: plump water-melons, black and white grapes, purple plums.

'This,' says Colette, 'is the basis of my diet. No meat at all, none of that horrible blue summer meat, which attracts all the flies, all the vermin in the world. Fruit, vegetables, fish, and occasionally half a young chicken delicately sprinkled with oil and grilled in the open air on embers of fennel and rosemary...'

Before we sit down, however, we all have to see the house: small, perfectly proportioned, and adorned with carefully chosen rustic furniture. Since the writer has lived here, it has been enlarged by a verandah; and that is where Colette sleeps, when she's dragged out a mattress.

'And that,' she ended, 'is my life here: work, bathing, a few visits from friends, and sometimes, in the evenings, a dance or two in the dance-halls at Saint-Tropez, with Carco or some artists...'[36]

Late in the summer of 1930 she went back to Paris, changed her suitcase and set off for La Gerbière. 'And I will try to redeem myself in my own eyes by writing,' so she assured Marguerite.[37] Pauline was away, and Colette could not live in her *entresol* with four animals unless Pauline was in Paris. On 28 September, the day Pauline came back from her holiday, she returned to the rue de Beaujolais.

She was not to live there much longer. By the first days of February 1931 she was installed at the Hôtel Claridge, in the Champs-Élysées. 'You understand,' she explained to Georges Wague, 'I am aiming at an apartment in the Palais-Royal. The one I had was charming. But just think: I lived there for 4 years in obscurity, with a lamp day and night ... If, in a year or eighteen months, I don't have the apartment I am aiming for, I'll stay here. I'm already very tempted to do so.'[38]

V

There could have been no more dramatic contrast to the *entresol* in the rue de Beaujolais than the sixth-floor apartment in the Champs-Élysées. The balconies, with their bird's-eye view of Paris, were soon transformed with flowering plants. The rooms were hung with a wallpaper sent from London, alive with a pattern of parrots and flowers. They were filled with books and Japanese prints and with Colette's collection of glass; and, lying on her grey velvet divan, resting against the plump red cushions, the *châtelaine* announced: 'My Hélène, ... I've slept at Le Claridge. If only you could see what I've done ... to this pigeon-house! Two rooms, two balconies, the sun, a wind as if you were standing on the bridge of a ship ... The cat, which is about to have kittens, is drunk with delight and refuses to come in even when it rains. You *must* come and see this bridge, this turret, this mill, this attic ...'[1]

One friend who came to see it was Adrien Fauchier-Magnan, whom she had known since the early days of her Jouvenel marriage. Fauchier-Magnan had a reputation as an historian, but he was renowned for the magnificence of his way of life. In their *hôtel* in the boulevard Haussmann, and then in their Italian *palazzo* at

Neuilly, he and his wife displayed their splendid art collection, and drew *le tout Paris* to their private theatricals and entertainments. Gabriel-Louis Pringué, a notable man-about-town, recalled the ballets and plays they had staged before the 1914 war. The Fauchier-Magnans were, he said, 'the great magicians of my time, transforming daily life into a civilised and constant fairy-tale.'[2] Yet even Fauchier-Magnan, on a visit to Colette, was impressed by the diversity of her friends. On a recent visit to Morocco he had, he explained, 'been received by the Glaouï, clad in his imposing white Arab dress, and flanked by an interpreter who translated our conversation. Then, one day, in Colette's room at the Claridge, I saw a strapping fellow come in, wearing golfing clothes, speaking perfect French, and to my extreme surprise Colette introduced me: Monsieur Fauchier-Magnan, His Highness the Glaouï.'[3]

Colette entertained the Glaouï in the Champs-Élysées. In the twenty years and more since she had left him, Willy had sunk even deeper into ill-health and poverty. In 1907, when Ernest-Charles had studied 'the Willy case', he had predicted a sombre future for him. Willy, he wrote, had created a school of licentiousness; but he himself was going downhill, and he had gone down too far ever to come back.[4] Rosny recalled that, after his separation from Colette, Willy was destroyed by his weaknesses. He was incapable of doing regular work, and he could no longer resort to expedients. His collaborators abandoned him. During the war he had found so little journalism in Paris that he had taken refuge in Switzerland, where the state had helped to support him. He had come back to France despondent, weary and embittered. His wit was no longer found amusing, people had begun to forget his former prestige. Rosny sometimes met him in this period of hardship. 'His ravaged face, with red blotches, his faded blue eyes, were pitiful. He implored more often than he attacked; the new society was interring him before his time, like other people who had better titles to remembrance.'[5]

Late in 1927, while Paul Léautaud was talking to Alfred Vallette, the editor of *Le Mercure de France*, they had had an unexpected visit from him.

> He complains [reported Léautaud] that he is suffering from arteriosclerosis and that he already has the symptoms, the staggering for example, rather like the state of a drunk man ... His mind is still intact, however ...
> When he had gone, I asked Vallette how old Willy was. He answered: 'Willy? He's the same age as I am ...' So he is 69, even older, I think [Willy was in fact 68]. Vallette said he found him 'absolutely gone to pieces'. I said: 'He must have lived it up a good deal in the past?' 'No doubt.'[6]

Léautaud recorded that Willy was taking iodine: a treatment which was medically improbable. It seems more likely that he was taking iodides, which were sometimes prescribed for syphilis.

'See that I don't die in misery,' he had begged his friends. In January 1931 he died in the arms of his son. There was much to forgive him; but: 'Discoverer of Colette! The title is not insignificant. For this reason, much will be forgiven him.'[7]

⁌――⁍

Willy belonged to a past which was so distant that his death left his former wife unmoved. She was in love with Maurice, and assured of growing fame. In the month of Willy's death, Flammarion brought out a volume of *Les Plus Belles Pages de Colette*.

She herself was, as usual, living with unflagging zest. La Gerbière, the house at Montfort, had been sold to the couturière Coco Chanel, who wanted to take immediate possession. Armies of workmen were sent from Paris and worked without remission; Colette had hurriedly to put her furniture in store. She also had to revise the scenario for *La Vagabonde*, which was being filmed; she had already been paid for it, but the money had been spent. In mid February she took a brief holiday with Hélène Jourdan-Morhange, the violinist and renowned interpreter of Ravel. With them was Hélène's future husband, Luc-Albert Moreau. 'Good morning, Marguerite! I'm completely happy!' went her card. 'Look at this snow! Just think of this blue! And a southern warmth about it all!'[8] As Germaine Beaumont was to say, one did not grow old in the company of Colette. She kept one youthful, eternally alert with interest and curiosity.[9] It was a gift which she would always keep. At the end of her long life, Jacques Chenevière said that, as soon as she was present, everything became more alive: even the wine became more aromatic, and it glowed more warmly in the glass.[10]

A fortnight after her holiday, Colette was on her way to Roumania.

What a city, my Hélène [this from Vienna]! I'm leaving for Bucharest in two hours, exhausted with tiredness. The programme for these two days has been unbearable. I can't bear them a grudge for their enthusiasm, these delightful Viennese! The French Minister at the station, with photographers and journalists, a splendid evening party – a concert 2 hours after my arrival (24 hours in the train), yesterday a luncheon-party for thirty at the Embassy, the lecture at 7.30, another evening party at 11, to-day a political-journalistic lunch, a score of interviews, people on my landing at 9 o'clock in the morning, oooh Hélène how exhausted I am! It's going to be worse at Bucharest ... I'm threatened with a royal audience and ... with a Roumanian decoration. I'm dreaming of the moment when I fall, dog-tired, into the train to come home ... How happy I shall be! And the cases to pack, and the albums to sign, and all the rest! No, I'm not made to be on show for sixteen hours out of 24.[11]

[Bucharest, 1 March 1931.]

Ah, my Marguerite, six nights on a train in a single week – not to mention the days! From to-morrow, Monday, I shan't *really* go to bed before Friday evening. Great success at Vienna. But that doesn't rest you, on the contrary. Think of me. Pity me a little.[12]

Colette was fifty-eight, and working with the intensity which she had shown in her music-hall days, nearly thirty years ago. When she finally returned to the Hôtel Claridge, she was prostrate. On 18 March, confessing her exhaustion to Hélène, she added that she was leaving to lecture in Cahors. Then she was coming back to Paris, and setting off again to lecture in Tunis, Oran, Constantine, Sfax, Bizerta and Algiers. It was a very bad year, and she and Maurice needed money.[13]

In her eyrie at the Hôtel Claridge, in the intervals of lecture tours, she struggled with the book which was finally called *Le Pur et l'impur*. *Ces Plaisirs ...*, to give it its early title, was 'about old love-affairs, it touched on homosexual love ...'[14] In the early summer of 1931 she was also correcting the proofs for an illustrated edition of Paradis terrestres. The frenetic activity continued. 'I'm waiting for telephone calls from the Société des Auteurs, Czechoslovakia, an agent, Ferenczi, a visit from a young woman agent from Roumania, and Léo Marchand.' So she explained, in another letter. 'All these lines converge on a project for a film. And I am wise enough to know that, if the project were feasible, it would already have been done. But there.'[15]

She continued her literary labours, delighted in dining on her balcony, where she was growing geraniums and wild strawberries; sometimes she slept there, in the open air. She received a visit from Missy. It was perhaps on this occasion that Fauchier-Magnan encountered 'the character who had been the subject of Parisian gossip ... I had,' he wrote, 'been struck by the extreme smallness of her feet, which contrasted with the men's clothes which she wore, but I was not struck in the least by her rather insignificant conversation. Together, we took leave of Colette, and, as we stood on the landing, waiting for our lift, Mme de Belboeuf said to me, in a gentle little voice: "When we get out of the lift, would you mind not calling me Madame? It could be embarrassing for me." '[16]

Another visitor from the past was Mme de Comminges, the ferocious Panther of years ago. Renaud de Jouvenel arranged the meeting.

As an opening shot [so he recorded], my mother said: 'Just imagine, the day Henry left me, I wanted to kill you! ...'

'Impossible!' cried Colette.

The two women then became good friends; they had at least two subjects of conversation: their mutual Jouvenel, whom Colette called the Reverend Father Jouvenel, and me.[17]

In mid July 1931 Maurice drove Colette to La Treille Muscate, and left her in solitude for three weeks. As usual, she intended to work hard; but, on 10 August, still labouring at Ces Plaisirs ..., she complained that she was at grips with difficult things.[18]

Her struggles with *Ces Plaisirs* ... did not prevent her from corresponding with Francis Poulenc. He had set some of Apollinaire's poems to music. She re-read *Quatre Poèmes,* and dreamed what might be done with them.

Dear Francis, what pretty notepaper you have! Write me more letters like that, on big sheets of paper all striped and spotted with music. Thank you. I have no piano here, but I am attentively re-reading *l'Anguille* and the other delightful *Poèmes.* Yes, I am thinking about *l'Ombre.* Do you see it as a rather short cinematographic sketch ...? Do you think one might dress this in 1880 style? Anyway, we shall talk about it together.[19]

In the meantime she laboured on at her book. 'Maurice is leaving, to look after his crumb – crust is too opulent a word.'[20] So she told Marguerite on 1 September. 'I am working like an ant; I build up something, and chuck it away, and begin again. The weather is lovely, lovely, lovely, the grapes are bursting with sugar and the dew makes them as blue as lavender.'[21]

As usual, it was impossible to work in the summer, in the South of France.

I haven't finished my book ... It's distressing [she added on 5 September]. I'm coming back at the end of week, hard up, but not at all disheartened. It's a damned nuisance, all the same, Maurice and I are going through one of those patches ... Earn a lot of money, and then you can say to hell with everyone ...

Here are the September storms. If they are frequent, they will console me a little for leaving this place ... They are harvesting the grapes this week ... Oh, all these melons, all these figs that I'm going to leave behind me![22]

She was not to leave them so soon. That day she had an accident. It was not serious in itself, but it brought the end of her exuberant good health. It was perhaps the beginning of her physical decline.

[6 September 1931]

My Marguerite,
I fractured my fibula yesterday, and I'm in plaster! Don't blame anybody, even me. A neighbour had dug little narrow ditches, very deep, at the side of a path – perhaps just out of spite? Logically, I should have broken my thigh. But how it hurts! They took me off: ambulance, hospital [at Saint-Tropez], X-ray – and plaster. But no temperature, and I'm bursting with hunger ... It could have been worse. Perhaps it's the end of the bad patch.[23]

Maurice returned to Paris, and the time seemed longer to her without his serene and equable company. By some providential chance, Dr Moreau, from Paris, paid an unexpected visit to La Treille Muscate, and he advised Colette to leave as soon as possible. The local doctor decided boldly to remove the plaster. Since it defied all surgical instruments, he attacked it with her secateurs and hedge-clippers. Wary and bandaged, she caught the train at St Raphael.

In October she could walk about a hundred yards. Maurice Martin du Gard recorded that her accident obliged her to walk henceforward on flat heels.[24] No doubt that was why she wore sandals until she was finally bedridden.

At the Hôtel Claridge, she struggled to finish *Ces Plaisirs*. . . . 'This book bores me to death,' she lamented to Hélène. '... But perhaps it will soon be finished. My life is just financial worries. Won't they ever end?'[25] She finished the book, 'as usual, in nights and days of despair.'[26]

Years later, with a curious lack of judgment, she spoke of *Ces Plaisirs* . . . as the book which might one day be recognised as her best.[27] Yet it is an incoherent collection of essays, and not all of them are new. La Chevalière is a melancholy portrait of Missy. She has the attraction that Colette often finds in someone of doubtful or hidden sex; but she has known nothing perfect in love, except for her own idea of it. La Chevalière is strangely idealistic; she is also pitiful, and – as Colette presents her – she could never experience the profound contentment of a 'marriage' like that of the Ladies of Llangollen. The most promising character in *Ces Plaisirs* . . . remains Madame Charlotte. Middle-aged, with a lover of twenty-two, she is a lesser version of Léa: a character who seems to demand a novel. Perhaps she is too like Léa for Colette to write it. As it is, *Ces Plaisirs* ... has the stuff of a novel and elements of autobiography. It reflects the author's boredom and labour. It is a disappointing 'made' book.

'I've finished my book. I haven't finished my foot,' Colette complained on 5 November.[28] She dared not go out in the wintry weather. Henri de Rothschild, munificent as ever, sent her an elegant consolation.

> My dear [she answered], you have given me very great pleasure, a livelier pleasure I know than you imagine. It isn't only the pleasure of having this charming necklace of antique silver and old coral. It's also that I terribly appreciate everything that proves affection, the continuity of affection; and this appreciation is intensified by the severe shock which I have suffered. Yes, come and see me for a moment before you go. Naturally I shall stay in Paris ...[29]

In pain, frustrated and exhausted, she found another way to earn a living. She decided to manufacture cosmetics from her own formulas. On 12 December she sent a note to Marguerite: 'My dearest, since you have kindly offered, I'd like you to steal some Max Factor for me ... It's for the laboratory, of course.'[30]

VI

The Société Colette for the manufacture and sale of beauty products – 'a baroque idea of Goudeket's,' said Renaud[1] – was established on 2 March 1932. Much of the necessary capital came from the Princesse de Polignac, the Pasha of Marrakesh and the banker Daniel-Dreyfus. The Institut de Beauté opened at 6 rue de Miromesnil on 1 June.

The opening was brilliant, reported a journalist,

> and drew a crowd of sightseers, friends and admirers, not to mention reporters, gossip-writers, photographers and cineasts ... The new temple of beauty was resplendent with whiteness and gleaming nickel ...
> More or less fantastic accounts vied with one another for the columns of the daily papers ... Other appreciations later appeared in the weekly and monthly publications; people went back to the question of principle ...

Sido's daughter – Colette at the age of five.

Colette as a schoolgirl at Saint-Sauveur. Wearing a dark dress with a large white collar, she is sitting third from the left in the front row.

The earthly paradise. Colette and her brother Léo in the garden at Saint-Sauveur.

Sido and the Captain. Colette's parents photographed at Châtillon-Coligny.

Colette at eighteen with her parents, her half-brother, Dr Achille Robineau (right), and her brother, Léo Colette.

The beginnings of a writer. Colette at work with her first husband, Willy.

Willy with the 'twins', Polaire (left) and Colette, in 1902.

Colette in her 'squirrel's cage': photographed at 193 rue de Courcelles in the early years of the century.

Rêve d'Égypte: Colette and Missy in their celebrated mime, 1903.

Colette and Missy photographed in the rue Saint-Senoch in about 1908.

'Our Pretty Actresses.' A publicity photograph of Colette, 1910.

'I have a new heart.' Colette with her second husband, Henry de Jouvenel, in the early years of their marriage.

Colette at Castel-Novel with Henry de Jouvenel and their daughter.

Colette at Rozven, photographed in about 1920 with her daughter, Bel-Gazou, and her stepson, Bertrand de Jouvenel.

Bertrand de Jouvenel.

'The dark young man': Maurice Goudeket at about the time Colette first met him.

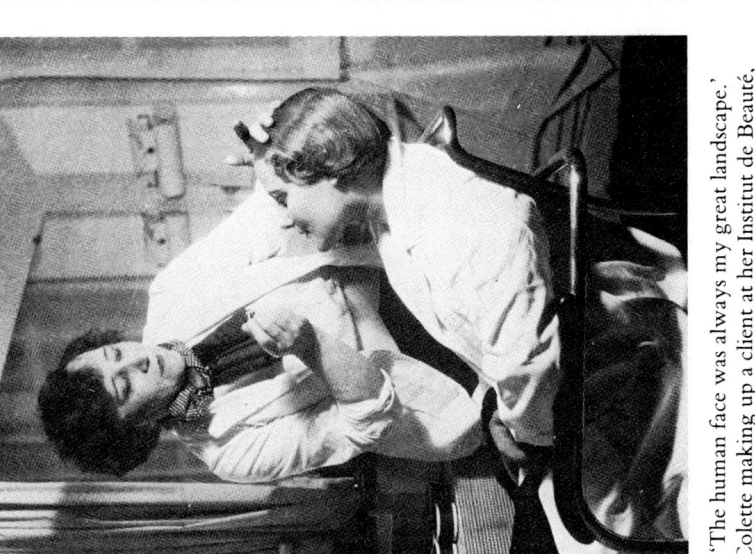

'The human face was always my great landscape.' Colette making up a client at her Institut de Beauté, in about 1932.

M. and Mme Maurice Goudeket on their honeymoon. This photograph was taken at the top of the Empire State Building, New York, in May 1935.

Dialogue de bêtes. Colette and a friend in the arcades of the Palais-Royal, in about 1938.

Colette at work on her divan in the rue de Beaujolais. The blue lamp hangs over her head; the gardens of the Palais-Royal are seen through the open window.

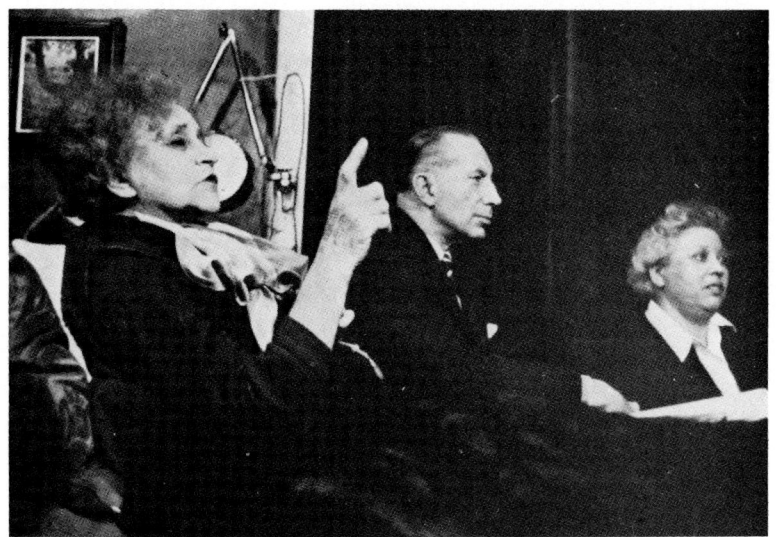

Colette, Maurice and Pauline, photographed in the rue de Beaujolais.

Colette's eightieth birthday, 28 January 1953. Watched by some of her *petits Goncourt* and by Bel-Gazou, Colette blows out the candles on her cake.

Colette in conversation with Prince Rainier. This photograph was taken in Monaco in the last years of her life.

Colette on the terrace of the Hôtel de Paris, Monte-Carlo.

As for Colette herself, she smiled, with a faintly ironic benevolence. 'But I have always made beauty products, for myself and my friends. No-one must see my Institute as a caprice.'[2]

Princess Georges Ghika recorded the opening with acerbity. Colette, so she said, had exclaimed: '"My fortune is made – here is Liane!", and she threw herself into my arms. I reeled – she is no mean weight – and let her sell me everything she wanted.'[3]

At the rue de Miromesnil – no doubt wearing her favourite scent, Corylopsis du Japon – Colette herself sold her cosmetics and gave lessons in make-up ('the human face was always my great landscape'). In June and July, though she suffered from the constant standing, she worked in the shop five afternoons a week. Late in July she returned to La Treille Muscate, and in August she opened a small shop at Saint-Tropez. 'There are two brothers, who deal in antiques,' she explained to Marguerite. 'They believe that the Colette products will do well here. I am leaving it to them.'[4]

Colette's adventures with cosmetics gave a malicious pleasure to Natalie Barney. Miss Barney was the first to appreciate feminine beauty, and she admired Bel-Gazou,

> her pretty sunburnt complexion contrasting with her hair, which was dyed platinum blonde ...
> You can imagine my surprise when, strolling one evening on the quai at Saint-Tropez, I saw a Bel-Gazou scarcely recognisable under common pink and bruise-purple make-up, ill-distributed on her pretty cheeks with high cheekbones and her young eyelids. This make-up made her look like a prostitute rather than the somewhat wild young girl, which she was. I learned that this essay in embellishment was due to the maternal hands of Colette – still far from expert in her new career as a beautician.[5]

Cécile Sorel was to perform in Sacha Guitry's *Maîtresses de Roi* at the Casino de Paris. Colette, she wrote, 'insisted on making me up herself. She created a work of art.'[6] Natalie Barney considered otherwise. 'Cécile Sorel, who wanted to help the enterprise, allowed Colette to practise on her, but Colette changed her method between one eye and the other. The result was an asymmetry which doubled the great actress's age and discouraged other volunteers.'[7]

In September 1932 Colette went to Marseilles, where she and Maurice had a stand at a cosmetics exhibition. In October she visited Geneva and Zurich. On 21 November she lectured at Tours; on the 22nd she spoke at Caen. The following afternoon she was back in Paris, where she gave a make-up demonstration at a department store, Au Printemps. On the 25th she left for Dijon and eastern France.[8] In mid December she reported that she was off to Luxembourg ('which lives entirely on beauty products'), and coming back on the 22nd, because she was talking in Belgium for three days.[9]

She returned from Luxembourg with water on the knee. However, on 7 January she set off for Amiens; on her return she duly left for Brussels. After this flying visit she hoped to go to Toulon and Cannes.[10] Then she planned to come back to Paris 'to work at my little novel, which is making hardly any progress.'[11] The 'little novel' was to be *La Chatte*.

Colette was nearly sixty now, and she was far from well; yet she lived with frightening energy and zest. On about 20 January, she announced to Hélène:

I am leaving to-day at 5 o'clock: Bordeaux, Pau, La Rochelle, Nantes, Rennes, Blois. I have been in Paris for a week, since I came back from Toulon, Cannes, etc. But every minute of this week I have had to look after a very violent cold on my chest. I am setting off again, not cured, but nearly all right. Just *nearly* ... Maurice wanted to stop me from going, but what could I do with the engagements made, the impresario, the halls already booked? And we're going through the two hardest months of the beauty products business, December and January – so I'm setting off again.[12]

She was concerned with the problems of ill-health and money; she was also, from time to time, concerned about her daughter. In 1928 or '29, remembers Renaud, Henry de Jouvenel had sent Bel-Gazou to work for his mistress, Germaine Patat, the *couturière*. 'She later made friends in the cinema and worked in it, but one can't say that she had a career in it. She almost always frequented women, just like her mother, and it was with one of them that she opened an antique shop in Paris. It didn't last any longer than anything else. I helped her a good deal, but I asked no questions. I knew her girls, she knew most of mine, but we didn't talk about them, not out of modesty or hypocrisy, but really because everything that wasn't "us" was "something else", a world apart.'[13]

On 28 December 1932 Henry de Jouvenel had been appointed French Ambassador in Rome, and – said Colette – he had wanted his daughter to go with him. However,

> my daughter refused to go to Rome [so she explained]. She maintains, and rightly, that her life should not be that of a young Embassy daughter, who wears evening dress and passes the coffee and brandy in the salons. I have nothing to say to that, but Jouvenel could not purely and simply go off and leave the girl without material means of existence. It is virtually arranged.[14]

It is hard to establish the truth. Perhaps Colette was inventing once again. Renaud de Jouvenel writes: 'Bel-Gazou did not refuse to go to Rome where none of Henry's children was invited. At that time, relations were bad between her and my father, and she was living her own life, as they say. After all, she was over twenty.' And Renaud adds: 'She never wanted to be involved in politics, in which she was right.'[15]

Whether or not she was invited, Jouvenel went to Rome without her, and she continued to lead her unsettled life.

As for Colette, in the early days of 1933, she worked at the subtitles for an American film: 'close, boring, almost mathematical work.' She also 'scratched away at a little novel, *La Chatte*.'[16] She was compelled to drive herself hard. Late in January, she explained to Hélène:

> I have accepted thirty lectures at the worst time of the year for me. What I earn eases the business, and supports us. Maurice is as he should be, he travels by Métro (2nd. class), and at the moment he is selling washing-machines very cheaply, and a fascinating tool for unblocking water-pipes and lavatories. In fact we are *fine*. I have reduced Le Claridge to unbeatable terms, and we're going ahead.[17]

She worked hard at her Salon de Beauté, but she finally abandoned the profession in which, as Natalie Barney said, she had shown determination rather than talent.

On the last day of April 1933 Colette finished *La Chatte*. 'My Hélène, I've come out of my nightmare ... These last weeks have been so hard for me that I'm ashamed of it ... Days (and nights) of eleven hours of work. More than once, last week, I saw the dawn break. My God, how unhealthy work is for me!'[18] It was unhealthy but it was essential. On 15 June she signed a contract for the scenario of *Lac aux dames*: a film based on the novel by Vicki Baum. Late that month she also signed the presentation copies of *La Chatte*. It was her first novel in four years.

Maurice wrote that her respect for every form of life, animal or vegetable, resembled religious fervour. To her the animal was equal to the human being. 'Il n'y a *qu'une* bête.'[19] *La Chatte* presents an extraordinary version of the eternal triangle, for the third protagonist is the cat itself. The novel begins with the somewhat implausible marriage between Alain and Camille. Alain is young and handsome, and an only son; he is still under the influence of his widowed mother. Camille is pretty and ambitious, highly-sexed, and socially beneath him. After the wedding, the young couple move to a ninth-floor flat. However, Alain has never been in love with his wife. His sympathy, respect and admiration, his intuitive understanding are given to Saha, his cat; and he soon brings her to live with them. At night he leaves his sleeping wife and moves to the divan, where Saha joins him. Camille, driven to despair, throws the cat from a balcony; its fall is broken by a blind, and its life is saved. Alain returns, with Saha, to his mother's house, and the three-month marriage is over.

Saha is based on the cat which Colette and Maurice had bought at a cat-show in the avenue de Wagram: La Chatte, the best-loved and most famous of all Colette's many animals. In this novel, with extraordinary deftness, she suggests the strength and intimacy of the relationship between man and beast; indeed, at times, the rôles are transposed, and, in the final sentence of the book, the cat 'humanly' watches the departure of Camille, while Alain, hand curved like a paw, plays with the fallen chestnut on the grass.

The cat is the mistress of the situation and the central character of the novel; yet this is one of the rare occasions on which Colette studies a man in depth. Like many other male figures in her fiction, Alain is a person of indeterminate sex. As Pierre Trahard was to write, the androgynous did not displease her. 'Most of the men she paints have the glance, the mouth, the body of a woman, just as her women ape the boy, and are male women ... The result is, with Colette, that the sexes are hostile, ranged against each other to the precise degree to which they tend to merge.'[20] Alain's interior monologues reveal more than his spoken words: they reveal that, like Colette herself, he sought in times of stress to return to his beginnings. His mother is no Sido; but his childhood room, his garden, are his essential and enduring dream. It is not a dream which he can share. His marriage is a predictable failure; but the earthly paradise – which Colette recalls with its luxuriant colours, its wealth of sharp and delicate and heady fragrances – remains intact.

On 4 July, in *Le Petit Parisien*, Jean Vignaud praised *La Chatte* without reserve. 'I really feel,' he added, 'that, beside Alain's mother, I saw the ghost of Sido, that unforgettable Sido, who follows, accompanies, protects Colette and awaits her, somewhere, at the gate of an enchanted garden.'[21]

My dear Jean Vignaud [came the answer], I have just read your magnificent article. And I was often compelled to blink, the praise was so brilliant ... You have [also] written a magic name, the one which honours mine, that of Sido. It is the recompense of a long life – I am sixty – that I sometimes *feel* my likeness to my mother. Everything belatedly, delectably proves it to me, she was an incomparable woman. I say 'sometimes', because I am not often equal to her.[22]

• ⸺ •

Colette spent most of July at work on the scenario of *Lac aux dames*. Finally she was obliged to seek the sun and sea at Saint-Tropez. There, late in the month, she had a visit from Jean-Pierre Aumont, who was to make his cinematic début in the film. Colette assessed him as an actor; he in turn assessed the owner of La Treille Muscate:

Robust rather than stout, with muscles developed by digging and weeding, her body heavy with every food and with every love, this solid Burgundian woman bestirred her household with the authority of a farmer's wife. She rebuked the dog and cat impatiently, like a woman who knows, this sensual peasant with the rough accent. Her eyes did not belong to her. They were piercing, lucid eyes, eyes without indulgence, eyes which revealed her subtle and incisive genius. So Colette appeared to me, reigning over the gulf of Saint-Tropez from the confines of La Treille Muscate. Had it not been for the eyes, one would readily have called her, like Catherine the Great, 'Your Solidity!'

One evening, overwhelmed by the heat, I asked Colette if I might have a shower. 'Take off your clothes and stand there,' she ordered. 'My plants need a drink.' Naked, in the midst of the vines and the bougainvilleas, I was obliged to let myself be watered by Colette.[23]

Colette was content with her summer life. 'I have a horror of writing,' she confessed, as usual, to Marguerite. 'I should like to continue the life of unbridled luxury I live here: barefoot, a faded woollen [bathing-costume], an old jacket, lots of garlic, and bathing all the time.'[24]

In the intervals of bathing, however, she kept a vigilant watch over her career. She thanked André Lang for his review of *La Chatte* in *Les Annales*: 'My dear colleague, . . . the whole article is charming. If you could only see Saha, the real one . . . She is on the table. She has been there – dare I say so? – for seven years. I think that she sends you her friendly greetings, too.'[25] Colette was concerned with gratitude, and with a favour yet to come: her promotion in the Légion-d'honneur. Writing to the critic Fernand Vandérem, she confessed:

I can't for the life of me remember the date of my rosette [as an Officier]! Monzie has affectionately busied himself about my *cravate* [as Commandeur], but . . . I don't think it's just been a question of delays. I'm assured that the Council of the Order doesn't like the fact that I make (excellent!) cosmetics. Because a French writer should only live – and on occasion die – by the pen. I am also assured – but what am I not assured? – that for certain councillors of the same Order I am still a dangerous person, a cavalcading 'creature' of the music-hall.[26]

Her theatrical connections were now more imposing. One of her neighbours in the South of France was the popular dramatist Édouard Bourdet; in 1936 he was to become Administrator-General of the Comédie-Française. Occasionally, recalled his wife,

Colette would arrive at the Villa Blanche rather out of breath, because she had climbed the last flights of steps on the terrace. 'Oh, how I regret my healthy fifties!' she used to sigh, and she immediately made efforts to please Édouard Bourdet's beloved cat. It condescended to receive her homage, slightly winking its golden eyes ... At table, she would be lavish with recipes and useful addresses. After dinner she would recall memories, witticisms and anecdotes as she alone could do. She spent a whole evening leafing through old 1900 albums; and, in the presence of Bérard, whose blue eyes turned a deeper blue with curiosity, she recalled Otéro, Liane de Pougy, Émilienne d'Alençon, Lantelme and many others. She described their dresses, the way they did their hair and made themselves up, their jewels, their loves, their griefs, she re-created their vocabulary, their exploits and their eccentricities.

Édouard Bourdet thought that *Chéri* was a masterpiece, and he would have liked to revive the play at the Comédie-Française. There was talk about it for a whole summer. But the absence of the ideal actress, and Édouard Bourdet's desire that Colette should touch up the last act, made Colette herself unenthusiastic, and the project came to nothing.[27]

In 1934 Colette became the dramatic critic of *Le Journal*. Her weekly column was one of the two in Paris with authority – the other one appeared in *Le Temps*. She was to keep the post for five years. She devoted four or five evenings a week to the theatre. Her articles appeared on Sundays, and much increased the paper's circulation.[28]

Colette had had a minimal formal education, and she was unlikely to be an informed or sympathetic critic of the classics. She brought to her task, however, her perception and lucidity, her sensuality and her lively interest in the modern stage. She knew many dramatists and actors, she had more than once written for the theatre and she had years of experience of the profession. Dancer, mime and actress, she knew more than the average critic about theatrical life and techniques.

In the four volumes of *La Jumelle noire*, her collected dramatic criticism, which appeared between 1934 and 1938, she excels in her impressions of the contemporary theatre. She records Cécile Sorel at the Casino de Paris; and – with a certain artistic licence – she describes the return of Mistinguett to the Folies-Bergère.

'During the long storm of applause, we could all see the blue of her eyes change under her tears.'[29] She gives her impression of *La Machine infernale*, by Jean Cocteau, and of *Y'avait un prisonnier*, by Jean Anouilh. She discovers Jacques Tati: 'No fête, no spectacle of art and acrobatics will be able to do without this astonishing artist. He has invented something ... He has invented being the player, the ball and the racquet together; the football and the goalkeeper, the boxer and his opponent ...'[30] As for Maurice Chevalier – who had once appeared in *La Vagabonde* – Colette pays her repeated tribute to him: 'It gave me great pleasure to rediscover, deep in his roguish blue eyes, the fierce look of a very young artist who, like myself, used to be a nomad on tour. He often used to cross my path, once upon a time: a tall, fair, rather unsociable young man. Even then, with his dancing and singing, he delighted the public.'[31]

The nostalgia for those days, the days of *La Vagabonde*, still inspired Colette. She still missed the solitude and the fraternity of the music-hall.

On a suffocating afternoon in June 1934, Paul Leroy, the journalist, made his way through the rich and cosmopolitan crowd in the foyer of the Hôtel Claridge.

White-gloved commissionaires, in search of a tip, lie in wait for the generous client. Porters size you up, and appear to assess the capacity of your wallet. Let us escape the importunate, and plunge into the lift. There we are! ... 6th floor! Apartment 609! Mme Colette! ...

I am greeted by Pauline, the maid; she has been in Colette's service for nineteen years. She is very sorry: Madame Colette is playing truant to-day: shopping in Paris, having tea, ices at Flament's.

M. Maurice, the secretary, or rather the chargé-d'affaires, receives me in the salon of the author of *La Vagabonde* ...

There are some scarlet roses in full bloom on a small chest, and they lavish a bitter fragrance in their ecstasy.

A door opens. Boudoir! Padded cell! Sanctuary! It is Colette's studio.

More roses, and enormous peonies which make a sort of bloodstain on the white runner.

Books. Japanese prints. A few watercolours of flowers.

Elegant glass cases full of glass ornaments . . .
No clock, no ephemerides: nothing to recall the inflexible rhythm of the hours and days which eat away our lives . . .
A murmur of voices. It grows louder. Colette has come back.
And there she is, in her studio!
Her first words?
'What does *The Cat* say?'
With an expansive gesture, she throws her hat on to the divan. It lands without much disturbing Soucy, the bulldog.
She is wearing a black coat and skirt, with a green scarf draped across her shoulders. She is barefoot, in slight leather sandals.
She is certainly small, and her harsh, tumultuous voice is constantly surprising.
She makes a few sallies, proclaims her anger with a tradesman, she storms about a woman she doesn't know who has just sent her a little play she has written, to have the opinion of 'the great Colette'. Then she calms down and falls, exhausted, into a deep armchair . . .
La Chatte is beside her, attentive; the bulldog Soucy is smiling broadly. Colette is in her element. 'My animals!' . . .
Colette is completely absorbed by her animals, but she doesn't lose a snatch of the conversation, which turns into cock-and-bull stories . . .
'What is your final opinion on love, Madame Colette, Love with a capital L?' . . .
'Personally, I understand love as they did in the days of the Borgias.'
'Oh, Madame Colette!'
She bursts out laughing.
'Don't go and say that, for goodness' sake! People would believe you, I've got such an awful reputation.'[32]

The year 1934 brought a novella, *Duo*. In this characteristic work, Colette describes the ending of a marriage. Michel is loving, appreciative and sensually aware. Alice is domestic, attractive and self-absorbed, and she has recently had an affair with one of his colleagues. By an unlikely accident, Michel discovers a love-letter sent to her by Ambrogio. Despite her protestations that the affair is over, neither of them can forget this aberration. Michel cannot bear the thought that she has been unfaithful. He drowns himself.

The unhappy marriage and its rapid deterioration are recorded with a delicate touch; but the story is implausible. Gabriel Marcel reviewed it in *L'Europe nouvelle*, and he found harsher criticisms to make:

Nothing but the wretched, eternal problem of the alcove. And what, for me, makes this atmosphere almost unbearable, is the author's clear connivance with her characters: the unconscious cynicism which prevents her, I don't even say from judging them, but from assessing them ...

There is, as we know, a book by Mme Colette called *L'Ingénue libertine*. That title says everything, illuminates everything; the contradiction which is displayed there lies at the heart of all her work, and gnaws away at it like a cancer.[33]

Such criticism was nowadays rare; most journalists discussed Colette with warm enthusiasm and with a certain awe, as if she were already a legend and a national institution. Robert Brasillach watched her while she herself was watching a play:

Her head was slightly tilted back, her eyes were half-closed, she seemed to be following an inner dream. From time to time, with a swift feline gesture, she caught hold of something, her opera-glasses, and confronted her dream with what she saw on stage. She chose, as a painter chooses elements in nature, a colour, a face. A few days later, we read one of those magic articles in which it was all re-created before our eyes: the subject of the play, the plot, the actors and the scenery.

In the theatre, Mme Colette seems to apply a rule which is perhaps a great rule: she believes. She believes in what she is being told, in the characters and in the story. And then she judges as she would judge real life: with her experience, with her rough, illuminating wisdom.[34]

This summer, she was also judged by the novelist and dramatist Henry de Montherlant.

Colette writes as she thinks, as she feels, as she speaks. Between what we read and what she has thought, felt, spoken, *there is nothing*. It is the natural style. I am not saying that there are no great writers without a natural style: there are exceptions. But I must say, proclaim, repeat, that the writer with a natural style is the only miracle in literature.[35]

Montherlant assessed Colette with admiration and exactitude.

The difference of *class* between Colette and Gide, is the difference of class between Saint-Simon and Anatole France.

And there is a more valid reason for the half-silence of the pundits about Colette. When you shut *Chéri*, you say: 'That's it.' Two syllables, but no other praise is equal to them ... The critic doesn't know what to do, because there is nothing to explain, nothing to criticise; one can only admire.[36]

Leroy once asked Colette what she would have liked to be, if she had not been a writer. 'Musician or painter,' she said, at once, 'labourer or sorceress, oh! especially a sorceress!'[37]

In 1935, asked to name the greatest living writer of French prose, French writers voted for Colette. Jacques-Émile Blanche, the artist, wondered if the future would ratify this judgment.[38] In the meanwhile, as Élisabeth de Gramont observed: 'Colette continues to enchant her contemporaries ... Colette is the only writer who has been able to incorporate everyday language, the language of the moment, in the rhythm of her page, no sensorial perceptions escape her, she seizes them and expresses them in words; with her, the power of instinct is intact.'[39]

Gérard Bauer agreed; one day in February, Colette was talking to him about the art of the chronicle:

She said to me: 'There are days when you have to write your article with nothing; and these are the most successful.' But that is Colette, and nothing, when she speaks about it, is everything. In other words, it is life itself, the dog which is sleeping or growling at being disturbed, the cat which is crossing the garden, wandering off on some mysterious errand, or the flower which is leaning its head out of the vase – curiosity? weariness? – or the smell of a dish, the hope of a return, the anxiety at a departure. And from this everyday matter, from these banal events, she makes something rare, through the miracle of a living style.[40]

She brought her style – Bauer called it her 'pantheist grace' – to the most everyday events. She constantly endowed reality with the prestige of a fairy-tale.[41]

Jacques-Émile Blanche insisted that, if they had changed the rules of the Institut de France, Colette would have been elected to the Académie-Française. No woman was to enter the Académie until a quarter century after Colette had died; but on 9 March 1935 she was elected a foreign member of the Académie Royale de Langue et de Littérature Françaises de Belgique. Paul Léautaud thought it 'comical, and not very exalted, ... to become a Belgian Academician';[42] but it was an honour which touched Sido's daughter.

Sending the news of her election to Hélène Picard, she wrote from a new address. The days of the Hôtel Claridge were over; she was living now in a block of flats, the Immeuble Marignan, at 33 Champs-Élysées. 'For me it isn't a very grave matter to move house,' she explained. 'I really think that this "eagle's nest" – or stork's nest – won't displease you. When, oh when can you come, Hélène? You will see all the rooftops of Paris. And I miss you ... The Belgians have given me Anna de Noailles' chair at their Académie. That's fine! But I'm already green with fear thinking of the session, the inaugural speech ...'[43]

■─────■

Before she delivered her address, there was to be a far more important event in her life.

It was now ten years since she and Maurice had embarked on their relationship. She had always been afraid that, like Léa de Lonval, she would have to let her young lover go; but she had kept her fear to herself. Maurice, too, had remained uncertain; he had felt 'infinitely favoured to hold the attention of such a woman. I thought,' he wrote, 'that I could only be a transient figure in her life.'[44] For ten years they had continued to live at separate addresses in Paris, and to spend the greater part of their lives together. For ten years they had both avoided the suggestion of marriage, in case it should damage their relationship.

Maurice had now turned to journalism; and they had both been invited, as journalists, to describe the maiden voyage of the *Normandie*. She was to sail for New York in May. Strangely enough, it was the prospect of an American visit, the question of sharing cabins and hotel rooms, which finally led Maurice to propose. 'If we got married,' he said, joking, 'there would be no problems.' Colette, he remembered, looked up at him, 'and suddenly I understood all that this strengthening of our relationship would mean to her.'[45]

Only one friend was consulted: Pauline Verine, who had been in her service since the age of thirteen, in the days of Castel-Novel. 'What do you think about the marriage?' Colette enquired. 'Well, he isn't bad,' said Pauline.[46]

We were married [Maurice recorded] on 3 April 1935, at 11 o'clock in the morning, at the *mairie* of the 8th arrondissement, which had seen my birth forty-five years earlier. It hardly took more than ten minutes. After which we took our witnesses to lunch in the country, at Les Vaux-de-Cernay, at an inn called Au Père Léopold. We liked its rustic cooking. The menu, which we had ordered, included an omelette à la crème, and shoulders of pork, plump and smooth. In our imagination we re-created the absent violinists, the screeching fiddles of a village fête.[47]

Claudine had long ago slipped out of the classroom at Montigny to collect a handful of snow. It had tasted slightly dusty, deliciously cold. Now, on their way home, reported Maurice, 'between two bright intervals, the snow began to fall, snow in large flakes, brilliantly white. Colette asked me to stop the car. She got out, with delight, to receive the impalpable manna on her face. She never remembered the date of 3 April, she generally forgot anniversaries, but she always remembered that springtime snow.'[48]

MADAME MAURICE GOUDEKET 1935-54

I

Their honeymoon, in May, was to be their visit to New York. She and Maurice sailed on the *Normandie* with some three thousand other notabilities: official personages, Academicians, actors and artists, socialites, even a peripatetic maharajah. The liner, Maurice remembered, had taken so long to build that its sumptuous decoration was already dated.[1] The crossing was monotonous, and Colette passed the time by exchanging detective novels with her old friend the novelist Claude Farrère. She was, however, enthralled by her first vision of New York.

Never shall we see that again, never shall we forget it. We are still in quarantine, but the impatient city has surged out to meet us. A flight of multicoloured aeroplanes, of gyroplanes, surrounds us, fêtes us, showers us with paper petals. The sea around us rocks as many boats as there are waves. The sirens, and the crowd of humanity which pack the bridges, mingle their cries, tatters of *La Marseillaise* flutter in the wind...[2]

Colette was still largely unknown in the United States. When the *Normandie* docked in New York she would no doubt have been safe from the Press who boarded the ship had a reporter not observed that she was barefoot, in sandals, and that she had painted her toenails scarlet. It did not hurt, wrote Maurice, mildly, that she was also an author. There was a general stampede towards her.

A few hours later, from the 24th floor of the Waldorf-Astoria, she and Maurice marvelled at the New York skyline. To her it was as romantic 'as the cities which emerged, bristling and barbed, from the dreams of Gustave Doré and Victor Hugo.'[3] Maurice was forty-five, and she herself was sixty-two; but, since they were on their honeymoon, they determined to visit New York as if they had been a young couple from Detroit. They had themselves photographed at the top of the Empire State Building, they visited the enormous Roxy cinema, and Colette made the discovery of Woolworth's. They had decided to avoid all the more or less official functions, but they did, it seems, attend one party, given by her American publisher. It was there that the novelist Glenway Wescott met her.

I remember her strong hands [he wrote] – serious writing is a manual labor! – and her fine feet in sandals, perhaps larger than most, rather like the feet of Greek goddesses. I remember her slightly frizzly hair fetched forward almost to her eyebrows ... I remember her delicate nostrils and her painted thin lips ... She gave it as her opinion that there was nothing at all surprising about skyscrapers: man having been all through the ages a mountain-climber, a tower-builder. I then expressed my pleasure in the little conversation I had had with Maurice Goudeket, her distinguished, interesting third husband. 'He is a very good friend,' she said, and she emphasised friend a little...[4]

She felt very much abroad in New York. Maurice recalled, years later, how she had seen a black cat on a window ledge. She had stopped at once. 'At last!' she said. 'Someone who speaks French!'[5]

On 11 August another marriage took place. Bel-Gazou married a Dr Dausse. Renaud de Jouvenel had disliked the man from the first.

Late one afternoon at Colette's, at the time when she usually received her friends, I saw a rather tall, bearded man, Dr Dausse, my sister's fiancé. He had brought an orange-tree in a pot and he said to Tante Colette: 'It is so like your daughter.' I found him antipathetic at once, and I felt he merely thought that he would profit by marrying the daughter of Colette and Henry de Jouvenel ... To show my disapproval, I did not attend the marriage, which took place at Castel-Novel.[6]

Nor, it seems, did Colette attend the marriage of her child. It was some measure of the bitterness of her own divorce. It was also, perhaps, some measure of her lack of love for her daughter.

Bel-Gazou's childhood had not been easy; her marriage was disastrous. Within two months she decided to divorce. 'Why?' enquired Renaud, forty years later. 'I have never known and I haven't asked her. Even now, I don't think that she would explain. Something really serious must have happened, ... since she was not a virgin, and I doubt whether she confided the real reasons to her parents.'[7] She herself remembered, long years after the event, that she had told her mother, awkwardly, of what she imagined to be her disgrace. Colette had had no time for conventions. 'I understand,' she said, brusquely. 'You've got the wrong man. It's no use being miserable any longer. You're much too young to be unhappy. Now you'd better go and tell your father.' Henry de Jouvenel, said his daughter, had shown an equal lack of convention. 'You can't be expected,' he said, 'to put up with boredom.' Bel-Gazou was, apparently, heartened by her parents' understanding. 'They didn't waste time thinking what the divorce would mean socially, or in any other way; they thought of what was best for me.'[8]

It seems an unlikely account of what happened. If her father was in fact still alive, it was improbable that she would have seen him.

I was completely unaware [wrote Renaud] that she had gone to see Henry de Jouvenel on her mother's advice. I should find it difficult to imagine because I have often pleaded my sister's cause *to* our mutual father, but without result. He wrote to me that he was sorry not to see her, and thought that she had a wrong idea of him which he attributed to the ill that Mme Colette might speak of him, which is clearly not verifiable. And I am amazed that my sister should have such a clear memory of words which were spoken forty years ago, which does not mean that she is lying.[9]

Both her parents were in fact absorbed in their own lives. That summer, from Saint-Tropez, Mme de Comminges wrote to Renaud: 'Colette is here ... She looks like a monstrous turd on wheels. With her, a horde of young beauties whom she drags off to the market, to Kismet, to the bazaars, and Maurice trots along with a distant and slightly ironic air.'[10] Colette was too preoccupied to look after Bel-Gazou. She asked Renaud if he would do so. 'You'd think,' he said, 'from her letters and her writings that she loved her daughter, but she was really inhuman.'[11]

It was therefore Renaud who looked after Bel-Gazou. He was not only her friend, the most loyal and the most constant. He was, he knew, 'her only recourse', and he behaved 'as her parents – her progenitors – would have been incapable of doing.'[12] He was discreet by nature, and careful not to offend her sensibility.

I contented myself [he remembered] with giving her moral and financial help (giving her nearly 42,000 francs, which represents some £4,200), and also probably by giving her shelter. Her mother thanked me for this, but I haven't published those parts of her letters which relate to this history, because it isn't done. Since I was determined that my sister should owe nothing to this bearded fellow, I paid Dausse's florists' bills, because, if he sent my sister flowers, he did not pay for them. This curious character went so far as to claim back the wretched diamond he had given to my sister, on the pretext that it was a family jewel, and this is something else which is not done. I had it returned to him, kept the ring itself and had another jewel set in it. The parents found it quite simple – but wasn't our father dead? – that I should replace them.[13]

At the very end of his sister's life, Renaud ventured to ask her: 'Why the devil did you marry that Dausse?' She answered, without conviction: 'Perhaps because I wanted to normalise myself.'[14] That was probably the nearest that she came to an answer. 'She must have begun very early,' writes Renaud, 'to have relations with girls or women, but ... the subject was tabu between us.'[15] Like her mother, Bel-Gazou had lesbian tendencies. Colette had damaged her more than she knew.

In 1934 Henry de Jouvenel had returned from Rome to become Minister for the Colonies. He had had no time to prove himself, for soon after his appointment the Daladier Government had resigned.[16]

He had spent the summer of 1935 in Varetz. Late in September he returned to Paris. On 3 October Italy invaded Ethiopia, and Jouvenel saw that Franco-Italian friendship, which was essential to French security, and indeed to peace, was now impossible. It was a bitter blow for a man who had worked so hard for Franco-Italian understanding.

On the morning of 5 October he tried to define his thoughts in writing. That afternoon he spent some time discussing the New Deal with Bertrand – now a political journalist – who had just returned from America. Father and son had been reconciled. In the evening he took his family to the Théâtre-Marigny. After the performance, he sent them home by car and took a stroll along the Champs-Élysées. Just before midnight, two policemen saw 'a tall, well-built gentleman collapse to the pavement, visibly in great pain.'[17] They hailed a cab and took him to hospital, but they were too late. Sidi had suffered, like his brother, from a heart condition; he had had a heart-attack, and he died that night. He was fifty-nine. As *Le Figaro* observed: 'Death spared Henry de Jouvenel the only trial he never could have borne: growing old.'[18]

Sidi had been a distinguished Ambassador to Rome, where he had helped to pave the way for the Four-Power Pact. The most prominent wreath on his hearse came from Mussolini, who assured Mme de Jouvenel that her husband's memory 'will remain indelible among us'. Sidi was buried in the cemetery at Varetz. 'I had a visit from Mme G—, who attended M. de Jouvenel's funeral,' so the Abbé Mugnier, in Paris, wrote to Princess Bibesco, in Roumania. 'All Limousin, except the clerics, accompanied him to his last resting-place.'[19] Colette professed to be unmoved by Sidi's death; yet, through her coolness, one can still discern the love that he had always inspired. 'I hadn't seen Henry de Jouvenel for twelve years,' she told Hélène Picard. 'And I certainly shouldn't have recognised him in the street, because he had greatly changed. I'm told that, when they showed me a recent photograph, I said: "Oh, he's finished." I think his wife must be desperate with grief.'[20] Perhaps Bel-Gazou's wedding photographs had reminded her of what she herself, by her own unforgivable conduct, had lost.

Now the third Mme de Jouvenel sent some of Sidi's furniture to be auctioned; Renaud took Bel-Gazou to the sale and bought her what she wanted. He also gave her Curemonte: the *château* in Corrèze which had come to him from Robert de Jouvenel.[21]

Early in 1935 Colette had told Hélène: 'Maurice has had to translate an American play, and I have had to improve the translation. It isn't certain to be performed, but, you understand, it has to be ready if the chance occurs. It's the sort of work you do in a crisis. Especially a crisis in selling books.'[22] Colette's adaptation was not used. She spoke of working on other adaptations from English, but they were not published, and perhaps they were not completed. Sometimes, in her long career, she felt obliged to write commercial journalism: publicity material for perfumes by Worth and Lelong, for wines from Legrand and Nicolas, for Rodier fabrics, for 'La Captive' watches. She also gave a talk at Lelong's, which remains unpublished.[23] The constant need for money drove her on.

She and Maurice now lived at a smart address in Paris, and they kept their house at Saint-Tropez. Maurice had no professional qualifications. He laboured on at a series of undistinguished occupations; he lacked the single-mindedness, the flair and dynamism of the successful entrepreneur. Or perhaps his enterprise was his wife's career. Louise Weiss described him, acidly, as the administrator of Colette's talent.[24] It was surprising that a writer of her international standing should have been so beset by financial worries. However, as he himself explained, she had been deprived in childhood, and these deprivations had left their traces.[25] It was not simply the love of money which impelled her to work so hard, it was partly the constant fear of lacking it.

Early in 1936 she published *Mes Apprentissages*: her memoirs of Willy and of her beginnings as a writer. She reflected, in tranquillity, on her turbulent first marriage: the marriage which had destroyed her dreams, brought her almost to the point of death, and had introduced her to Paris and to her career. She spoke with wisdom and charity of her relationship with Willy whom, even now, she could not understand. 'What must be written is the story of that man. The trouble is that no-one really knows him. Three or four women still tremble at his name: three or four I know. Since he is dead, they are gradually ceasing to tremble. When he was alive, I confess that they had reason to do so.'[26] Colette was frank about her motives for marriage, about her desperate unhappiness, and about Willy's final rejection of her. She was surprisingly generous in her assessment of this louche entrepreneur, this gifted failure, this corrupt, sophisticated, immature and repellent man to whom, she recognised, she remained indebted.

Mes Apprentissages was certain to arouse strong feelings; and, as usual, Paul Léautaud recorded the comments and the gossip. On 4 February he noted:

Auriant tells me this evening: Pierre Varenne and Deffoux, with whom he found himself yesterday, are raging against Colette's book, because of the way in which she speaks of Willy. Deffoux told him that one he found himself next to Colette at a *déjeuner*. 'That old skunk, that old drunkard, that old ——,' she said about Willy. 'What did he achieve?' Deffoux: 'What did he achieve? But you, Madame!' She promptly turned her back on him. Deffoux says she has never forgiven him ...

As for Pierre Varenne, he told Auriant that one day Willy showed him an album of photographs. Among them was one of Colette, completely naked, her hands tied to a ring fixed to the wall ...[27]

The disapproval was not unanimous.

This book, I repeat, is a bold book [insisted Robert Brasillach]. But it is a true book, a book in which there are no concessions to Romantic fashion, a book in which instinct is not described as virtue. It is an honest book, severe on its author, as it is on other people ... We know that the greatest secrets will remain concealed. It is well that this should be so. It is well that this rather rigorous book, which rejects almost everything that made the charm of Mme Colette's books, this book in which nature hardly appears at all, in which the style is stripped bare, demands its most certain enchantments from silence. We shall learn much from it.[28]

On 19 February Gide recorded that he had read it 'with very lively interest. There is much more than a gift there: a sort of genius which is particularly feminine, and a great intelligence. What choice, what discipline, what felicitous proportions, in a tale apparently so wild! What perfect tact, what courteous discretion!'[29]

On 21 January 1936 Colette had been promoted Commandeur de la Légion-d'honneur. In April she was due to become an Academician in Brussels. She was still alarmed by the prospect: 'all misanthropy and anguish, and sick inside.'[30]

On Saturday 4 April, barefoot in sandals, her toenails lacquered scarlet, her scarlet-and-silver rosette in her buttonhole, she was duly received into the Académie Royale de Langue et de Littérature Françaises de Belgique; she took the chair of Mme de Noailles, who had been the first woman to be admitted.

She was introduced by Valère Gille.

Madame, I am not the first to say that all your work is simply poetry: that it is only a fortunate overflowing of your being, the very delight of life in perpetual creation, a Dionysiac hymn ...

You are incarnated in your style. You yourself give it such intense existence that we seem to see all the words come to life, see the sentence undulate and draw itself up, like the supple spine of a cat beneath one's caress.

Your style is a perpetual creation, a perpetual pulsing of the sap of life, a perpetual sensuality. It is sensations made into words.

Your style has the gift of life, like that of Musset or of Loti has the gift of tears ...

You are at once boldly romantic and fundamentally classic.[31]

The Académie Royale does me so great an honour [replied Colette], I find it, when I measure it, so disproportionate to my merits, that for the past few months I have trembled at the idea of appearing before you ...

If only you could see me as [Valère Gille] has painted me! He has not made me so intoxicated that I have lost the one virtue on which I pride myself: I mean the virtue of having doubts. I am more circumspect every day in the presence of my work, and more uncertain that I should continue it. All that reassures me is my very fear. The writer who loses his self-doubt, who trusts himself, with age, to a sudden euphoria, to prolixity, ought to stop writing. The time has come for him to lay down his pen.[32]

According to tradition, Colette then delivered a tribute to her predecessor. It was an elegant portrait of Mme de Noailles, which contrived to say little in praise of her work.

It was now, towards the end of the 1930s, that Rosamond Lehmann saw Colette.

I met her only once [she recalls], when I was staying with Princess Edmond de Polignac (Winnie) . . .

She came in late one afternoon to have a chat with Winnie – or so I imagine, as we three were alone, and beyond shaking hands with me she took no notice of me (I was very glad of this) and sat gossiping with Winnie and discussing recipes while I listened. She was wearing a shapeless dark voluminous garment and sandals on her bare feet. At one moment she looked at me, and then murmured to W.: 'Je n'ai jamais vu un visage si bien fait' – which as you can imagine filled me with blushing surprise and delight.

When she got up to go she again shook hands with me, smiling her wonderful smile, and said I must excuse her, she hadn't read my book (Poussière?) and didn't suppose she would as she read no novels nowadays.[33]

She read no English, and perhaps she was too absorbed in her own novels to read other people's fiction.

•—•

Bella-Vista, a book of novellas, was published late in 1937. The title-story was, it seems, part fact, part fiction. Soon after she acquired La Treille Muscate, Colette had gone to supervise the builders and decorators who were working on it. She had stayed at Bella-Vista, a small hotel nearby. It was run – the story went – by a middle-aged lesbian couple; the only other guest was the inexplicably sinister Monsieur Daste. The atmosphere of Bella-Vista had become increasingly oppressive. One of the lesbians proved, in fact, to be a male transvestite, who seduced the maid at the hotel. Monsieur Daste was found to have a mania for killing and maiming birds, and left after slaughtering a cage of parrots. There is a touch of Simenon about this curious tale, but it is unworthy of Colette.

On 9 December, in *L'Action Française*, some days before the book's publication, Brasillach published a surprisingly kind review of *Bella-Vista*, and discussed its author's significance.

Where lies the charm of Mme Colette's books? The latest of them, perhaps more than all the rest, tells us how difficult it is to answer that question . . . Of course, one has the right to like other books, one has the right to know them and to prefer those which are evidently greater. But, personally, I don't know any which gratify me so completely, which give me such immediate and total satisfaction ...

Mme Colette is not the dupe of these human puppets which she presents to us. But she strips them of their varnish and disguise, she uncovers their pettiness and essential sadness. And at the same time she finds in them, beyond their vices and beyond their faults, a sort of pitiable grandeur, which is that of the human condition.[34]

She was rewarded by her admirers. Years earlier, a silk manufacturer had bought the house at Saint-Sauveur where she had been born, and he had offered it to her, in homage. Another miracle now came to pass. Late this year, Colette was interviewed by André Arnyvelde for *Paris-Midi*. He asked her why she constantly changed apartments, why she led so unsettled a life. She answered that, 'ten years ago, when I was living in the Palais-Royal, I moved heaven and earth to make them lease me the first floor in my house, and, if I'd been able to get it, I should never have moved again.'[35]

On 6 November *Paris-Midi* published 'Les Démenagements de Colette'. Next morning she received a letter: 'Madame, I read in *Paris-Midi* that you still covet the first floor of 9, rue de Beaujolais. I am living in this apartment. I'm quite ready to let you have it.'[36]

II

Early in 1938 Colette established herself in the setting which became part of her legend. Soon afterwards she announced to the Saglios:

We are very tired, but we are in the Palais-Royal! That is a blessed consolation. We also have a round basket of red tulips in the centre of a round table, a comfort to the eyes and to the soul.

My thanks and blessings to you both, dear friends. Come and see my view! Immediately, it doesn't matter when! They are never very comfortable, these apartments round the square. But what an exclusive province! Mme Massé [the restaurateur in the passage Choiseul] sends me cooked pears, the bistro opposite sends me over a couple of stuffed pancakes, the antique-dealer comes up with greetings and little joss-sticks, and the door-keeper sees me with my dog off the lead, and cries: 'Won't you ever learn?' The lampshade-maker wipes away a tear. The excellent restaurateur at the Roi Louis XIV [in the place des Victoires] says to me: 'Have you come back to find me? My wife and I were in the rue du Cherche-Midi.' Show me another quartier like this! And the coal-man in the rue Chabanais is an old acquaintance, too!

Dear Lucie and dear Charles, you must come and eat at the bistro in question. On Tuesdays there is a cassoulet fondant, and the wines are regional. Would you like Tuesday?[1]

Violet Trefusis was aware of the comfort of the rue de Beaujolais: A genius for comfort characterised Colette's dwelling-place ... She was essentially domesticated, *une femme d'intérieur*, who loved receiving in her own home. To use a word that must astonish those who did not know Colette, she was 'cosy'. She loved mixing the *sauce vinaigrette* that accompanied her home-grown salad, her kitchen was more familiar to her than her drawing-room, she adored comfort, and disdained luxury.[2]

She liked not only comfort, but familiarity. She liked the stormy sound of the pigeons in the Palais-Royal, which greeted her every morning as she woke. She was faithful to her household gods. 'Whatever her address might be,' Germaine Beaumont wrote, 'I have always known Colette in the same setting, with the same glass paperweights on the mantelpiece ... And Colette always says to me, with the same look, and the same voice: "So there you are, my child!"'[3]

Another visitor was Julien Cain, Administrator-General of the Bibliothèque Nationale. Sometimes he called at the rue de Beaujolais; often Colette went to the library, nearby, 'in search of familiar faces, and not in the least in quest of books. What books would she have looked for, there? The ones she wanted to know, the ones that had enriched her, she kept in her memory, which was unerring. Balzac, for a start, and I recall an astonishing conversation the day I took Marcel Bouteron to see her.' Bouteron, the editor of the novels and correspondence, had devoted his life to Balzac. He and Colette spurred each other on. 'Lost in their game, for hours, they brought to life the characters of *Splendeurs et misères*, and the scenes of *La Fille aux yeux d'or* . . .'⁴

▪▬▪

Part of the summer of 1938 was, as usual, spent at Saint-Tropez. On 6 September Colette returned briefly to the rue de Beaujolais. November found her in North Africa, where she was reporting the Assizes at Fez for *Paris-Soir*.⁵ On 4 December, back in Paris, she wrote to Hélène:

In the past fortnight I have to my credit not only *Paris-Soir*, but a publicity booklet for a brand of cigarettes, a text for an (enchanting) new edition of old flowers painted by Redouté, the proofs of *Le Toutonier* (you will receive it as soon as it appears) and other brushwood which helps me to kindle my fire. As for Maurice . . . But you know the refrain, and you know what virtues ornament our life.⁶

Maurice himself recorded the pressure under which she worked. She would often write an article for *Paris-Soir* while their messenger was waiting in the kitchen.⁷

▪▬▪

In February 1939 'the beloved Cat' died of old age; the following month the bulldog died. 'Maurice and I are in the depths,' Colette told Edmond Jaloux, 'especially because of the Cat.'⁸

Since she had outlived her enthusiasm for the gramophone, she had given away all her gramophone records except for 'the Cat's tune', an American tune which had brought a smile to the Cat's face. Now she smashed the record, and chose silence. She mourned the Cat as deeply as if it had been a human being. Long afterwards, a clairvoyante came to the rue de Beaujolais and saw the ghost of a cat in the apartment. 'She comes and goes and strolls about,' so she told Colette. 'She does as she likes, because she is dead.' Colette was stupefied but comforted. She took care never to recall the clairvoyante, for fear that she would hear that, this time, the Cat had left for good.⁹

Colette denied that she was superstitious, but she was fascinated by reading cards and telling fortunes, just as she was by the mysterious patterns in her glass paperweights. It was in this spirit that she allowed Edmond Bénisti to read her hand. Her hand, he wrote, was eloquent, though life had taught her not to tell her secrets. It indicated a longing for silence, even for the cloister, and yet the impossibility of total solitude. Colette denied that she had any yearning for monastic life, but she confessed that she might be drawn to a hermit's existence. The idea of God, continued Bénisti, was in her hand, but he could see no worship. There was a longing for something higher. 'That's true,' confirmed Colette, 'but I honestly confess I don't know what. I'm waiting.' Bénisti also divined remarkable powers of clairvoyance. 'It's too long to tell you about,' said Colette. 'I once thought of a subject. Before the book [*La Chatte*] had had time to appear, the drama which I had *invented* had *actually* happened.'[10]

In 1939 she published *Le Toutonier*, a sequel to *Duo*. Alice, Michel's widow, returns to the studio which she had once shared with her sisters. Bizoute is now married. Colombe is still at home – writing music for Carrine, with whom she is in love. Hermine is still enamoured of the married Monsieur Weekend. When the novella opens, Alice is the well-to-do sister; when it ends, she needs compassion. Colombe goes on tour with Carrine, Hermine hopes at last to marry Monsieur Weekend. Alice gives up the apartment which she had shared with Michel; she returns to the studio: to *le toutonier*, the big, sprawling sofa on which the sisters slept. *Le toutonier* is the constant comfort, the symbol of family closeness, of a world she needs much more than she had recognised.

'The clash between the happiness of the "nest" and the personal adventure ... I think,' wrote Robert Brasillach, 'that this is really the subject of this little book.'[11] The novella is flawed by melodrama; but it is fired, one suspects, by recollections of Saint-Sauveur, by Colette's recognition of the strength of family affections. It is amusing, original and touching.

In 1939 Colette decided to sell La Treille Muscate. It was a hard decision to make; but she had come to be overwhelmed by journalists and sightseers, by admirers who disturbed her privacy. Saint-Tropez was now too fashionable, too accessible. It was also near the Italian border, and there was increasing apprehension about the ambitions of Nazi Germany and the German–Italian alliance.

The political situation worsened rapidly. On 21 August, tired by the pressure of events, Colette wrote to Hélène from the Hôtel Métropole at Dieppe:

I've been here a week. Fatigue demanded it. La Treille Muscate has been sold, and very badly sold (because of Mussolini), but at least the mortgage is paid, and there's enough left to fit up a little house at Montfort-l'Amaury. That's the end of the South of France. Barca. I say barca to dissuade myself from having regrets...

We are coming back in a week.[12]

Before the week was over, England and France were on the verge of war with Germany. Colette was anxious to go back to Paris, Maurice begged her to stay in Dieppe. Finally, on 27 August, they returned to the rue de Beaujolais. War was declared a week later, on 3 September. 'Where are you, my very dear Winnie?' Colette wrote that day to the Princesse de Polignac. 'I am thinking of you, naturally, in the midst of all these troubles and criminal stupidities.'[13]

Winnie de Polignac was in Devon. On 10 August her youngest brother had died; on 21 August he had been buried in the family vault at Torquay. After the funeral, she had decided to stay for a while in England and take a cure. When war was declared, she was persuaded not to change her plans. So she explained to Colette.

What a good letter, my very dear Winnie [came the answer]! Good for me, although it is full of some news which saddens you, that of the death of your last brother. The last, the one that nobody can now engender or begin again. As I think of the strange old brother who remains to me, the brother whom I was relieved to despatch to the provinces the other day, I say to myself: that's my last brother. The last, with me, who bears likenesses, differences, ways of speaking, faults which are common to a family. He is 73, and has only lived for music and postage-stamps.

My dear Winnie, you talk about 'treatment'. But you're well now, aren't you? Life is calm here – while we are waiting. Seeing only a very few people cannot displease me. Maurice Goudeket, who is over fifty, is safe from mobilization – for the moment. Every life is a question of day to day, a question of which I have certainly had quite a long experience. Sometimes I pass your house, where they have very carefully stuck strips of paper over the windows...

During the brief false alert, the other morning, you would have been pleased to see a worthy passer-by in the Garden who stopped and dutifully took his gas-mask out of its case, to put it on. Thus equipped, he went on his way, and I was sorry not to see him emerge, his proboscis under his arm, in the rue des Petits-Champs, where people are rebellious and unruly, and loiter about, and ignore injunctions from policemen. Should one blame them for it? Or should one rather blame the poor lady in a taxi who put her gas-mask on so well that she could not move the catch of the mask, or call the cab-driver to help her, and passed away?

If you are well over there, and safe, and in good company, don't come back. Isn't that a sentence of disinterested love...? I embrace you, dear Winnie. Let me write to you from time to time. I lay Maurice Goudeket at your feet. He is a good man – rather disappointed that he, who was a volunteer soldier for four years, is only an involuntary civilian...[14]

What an idiotic war [she wrote to Hélène Picard, the same month]! We had already come back when it was officially declared. Maurice wanted to send me away!!! I shall go and find out if you're there. I come and go, and write anodine little articles. I'm waiting. My Hélène, tell me if you're there. At night, as I lean out of my dark window, I say to myself that perhaps you are also leaning out of yours, over your garden, between the dreams of the parrots. I embrace you, my Hélène. I should never have believed that the human race would come to this again...[15]

She was not only writing 'anodine little articles', she had begun to broadcast to America.

I go through your neighbourhood, once a week, between midnight and four in the morning, to go and talk on the American radio [she continued, later that winter]. The dawn of day is so innocent, and Paris is deserted, and still asleep... My Hélène, I think about you every day.

They are giving me treatment (X-rays) for the arthritis in my hip. I am absolutely disgusted to have arthritis in the hip! And sessions with the dentist. 'O hideous old age!' as my mother used to exclaim.[16]

Writing again to Winnie de Polignac, Colette was in less melancholy mood: indeed, she was decisive and vivacious. She had once given the Princess a painting of a fuchsia. Now she wanted a painting in return.

Very dear Winnie, thanks to the war, I dare at last to ask you for something which I very much want ... Give me something that you have painted. An unfinished portrait of a dahlia. The colour that you saw on the sea. Whatever you like. There you are, I've said it. Thank you.

Everything is designed to enchant me in your enchanting letter. All your deadpan humour is there, and it is so young. Your letter makes me very happy, except that it comes from a long way off. But you had the imprudence to tell me that you were listening to me, that was enough to make me speak timidly last Sunday, and to get stuck everywhere, because I was thinking of you. Just imagine: Maurice and I talk to North America on Monday, at three o'clock in the morning. The one who does best is Goudekets, who 'presents' the French classics and, so they say, speaks very good English. My formulas of politeness, in English (?), provide my talks with their one comic note, – or so I fear as much as I hope. But the two journeys in Paris, at 3 and 4 o'clock, are astonishing. Yesterday, there was a thick mist skirting the little blue lamps with conical dresses – a very pretty hallucination. And you would have spent a pleasant moment at the rehearsal of a sort of radio sketch (still at 3 a.m.) organised by Paris-Mondial. Charles Boyer without a wig, his wife without make-up, Mireille, Ray Ventura in shirtsleeves and braces, Philipp Holmes as he is, and ... the Comédie-Française speaking English. It was a big effort for these good people. And they all blushed, before they spoke, like children telling fibs. The rush towards the canteen also deserved to be seen ... Nothing to eat except bread, a transparent slice of salt meat, warm beer ... Dear Winnie, I'm telling you what little I can. Today, an alert at night and gunfire by day. As I had only just gone to bed at the time of the alert, I had a good reason – the bad ones are enough for me – not to leave my bed.

Are they working at your house, or are those only piles of sand? I flatter myself with the idea that you have ordered an underground music-room for your friends ... I entrust you to your friends, to music, to the benevolence of fate. But when you come back, I shall give you a great celebration with at least six people, with mulled wine and a plinth of Munster [cheese]. I embrace you with an affection which is always the same, my very dear Winnie. Maurice is respectfully yours.[17]

Colette's request was granted. Winnie de Polignac duly sent a painting from England.

Very dear Winnie [wrote the grateful recipient], the little picture has arrived. And, imagine, it is almost exactly as I 'saw' it. There are the dahlias; aren't those red salvias, on the right? And in the background that touch of blue-green which, through the grace accorded to the painter, is enough to give the presence of the sea. Dear Winnie, thank you for painting me a landscape entirely of mother-of-pearl, flowers and verdure. It will not be framed till you come back – when you have finished it with a W, which is all that's missing ...[18]

·——·

In mid February 1940, though she thought she had bidden it farewell, Colette returned to the South of France. She settled at the Hôtel Ruhl, on the Promenade des Anglais.

My very dear Winnie,
Your letter is the letter I needed on this grey 2 March in Nice (very pretty all the same). I've been here nearly a fortnight now, and I'm not allowed to come back to Paris till the 14th. Work, fatigue, a sedentary life, arthritis of the hip, white globules looking for 'hooks' (it's slang) on my red globules, – you know it all. I am quite alone here, between the flower market, the bistros which are still very good, and the sea. The strange thing is that this is enough for me.
I think of your Henri-Martin house. And it seems to me that an empty house often behaves like a child who is left alone, it turns on the gas and water, lights the fire, and cuts the electric wires. Dear Winnie, you should have a bachelor flat, whether or not it is near the big house ...
Yes, go to London often. I advise you, with my authority, to take French cooking as a panacea. 'A dessert-spoonful every two hours.' And let them prepare your safe return to Paris.[19]

Winnie de Polignac was not to return. She settled in a flat in Park Lane, and it was from here, in the next few months, that she followed the disastrous course of events and the fall of France. There could be no thought, now, of returning to Paris. On 26 November 1943, before the war was over, she died.

Meanwhile, in the early months of 1940, Colette was aware that a closer figure was to depart. In her letter to Winnie de Polignac, from Nice, she added: 'My old brother, my last relation, is still about to die at any moment, in the Yonne. His pulse rate is *26*. In other words he is not suffering, and although he is apparently still among us, he is already very far from life...'[20] He died at Bléneau on 7 March. 'No pain,' she told Hélène Picard, 'he never knew that he was dying. I shall not hear him play the piano again, with chapped fingers, which seemed all benumbed, and produced sounds of a round and sparkling quality.'[21] It was a literary comment. One wonders how deeply she was grieved. Achille, her half-brother, had died on the last day of 1913 – there was hardly a trace of him in her work. Renaud de Jouvenel maintains that, apart from Sido, she showed no love for any of her family, 'and she allowed her brother Léo to die alone, perhaps in poverty.'[22]

In June the Germans entered Paris. Colette, Maurice and Pauline escaped by car to Curemonte: the château in Corrèze which now belonged to Bel-Gazou. They spent the summer with her there. Petrol was unobtainable, and Colette sometimes wondered if she would ever leave this 'verdant tomb'.[23] In July she complained to Charles Saglio: 'We are waiting, Goudeket and I. There is no better recipe for growing old. Why didn't I stay in Paris?... Maurice was too anxious about me.'[24]

Maurice had other anxieties. He was Jewish by birth in a country under Nazi occupation. It was the time of 'the final solution'. Renaud recorded how he met Claire Boas de Jouvenel in Brive. 'She fell into my arms and complained: "Your brother resents my being Jewish!" On which she went off to be converted. So did he, but later.'[25] Religion could be changed, but the racial problem remained.

In the summer of 1940, the summer of the fall of France, Colette was unable to reach the rue de Beaujolais; yet, at this time of personal and international crisis, she thought less about it than she did about Saint-Sauveur. She thought, instinctively, inevitably, of Sido. She recalled, yet again, her enchanted childhood, the freedom of the garden and the countryside, the comfort of the house where Sido reigned, loving and vigilant, over her husband and children and animals, and waited on the doorstep for her daughter to come home. It had been a childhood without restrictions, a childhood with no sense of literary vocation.

How sweet it was, this utter absence of literary vocation! My childhood, my free and solitary adolescence were both preserved from the anxiety to express myself, they were both entirely occupied with directing their subtle antennae towards what is seen and heard and felt and breathed in ... There was no railway in the part of the country where I was born, there was no electricity, there was no college or big town nearby. In my family there was no money, but there were books. No presents, but affection. No comfort, but freedom. There was no voice which borrowed the sound of the wind and, with a little puff of cold air, slipped into my ear the advice to write, and to go on writing: to tarnish, by writing, my calm or excited perception of the world ...[26]

From Curemonte, she and Maurice and the faithful Pauline made their way at last to Lyons. It was in unoccupied France, and only through the Swedish consul did they get permits to return to Paris, which was in the occupied zone. On 11 September they were back in the Palais-Royal.

It had always been, said Colette, a little province of its own, 'graced with a kindness, a solidarity, which are lacking in the real provinces. The war turned a handful of inhabitants into a coalition of friends. Like the other districts of Paris, the Palais-Royal had its maquis. It possessed its hidden parachutists, its Englishmen sheltered at risk and in silence, its protected Jews ...'[27] She began to write a weekly chronicle of life under the Occupation.

On 25 October she also published two novellas under the title of *Chambre d'hôtel*. The story which gives the book its name suggests that Colette is a writer in decline. It is an unhappy exercise which borders on detective fiction, and often strains the reader's credulity. Like *Bella-Vista* - to which it bears certain resemblances - it is patently written to a formula. The characters are exaggerated, the story is melodramatic and unworthy of the author of *Chéri*.

She wrote too often, now, for money. The new year brought the publication of *Mes Cahiers*; it also brought *Journal à rebours*: an ill-assorted collection of essays, some of which had been written years earlier. Colette's brief comments on the state of France are strangely unmoved and unmoving.

Yet in 1941 she became increasingly aware of the deprivations brought by the war and the Occupation. 'Maurice is looking for books to buy, and for books to sell,' she reported to Renée Hamon on 24 March. 'Everyone else has plunged into bookselling, ancient and modern. The feverishness of people shut up in a city ...'[28] Food was becoming scarce. 'How do you eat?' she asked Hélène, two months later. 'Pauline and I do what we can, which isn't a great deal. The lack of meat doesn't depress me as much as I should have thought. But my poor, patient Maurice feels very deprived of his underdone meat ... My Hélène, I am finishing a novel. Again. I really have to ...'[29]

Julie de Carneilhan was serialised in *Gringoire* from 13 June to 22 August. Later this year it was published in book form by Arthème Fayard. It was the last full-length novel that Colette was to write; and some said that it was as close a reckoning with the elements of her second marriage as she allowed herself.

Anatole de Monzie, Henry de Jouvenel's closest friend, assured her that he found 'nothing in this novel which evoked the *personnage* of de Jouvenel'. Colette replied: 'If you didn't recognise him in Espivant, it's because he isn't there, and my little character is imaginary, and never aimed to be anything more – or less. No, Espivant is not de Jouvenel.'[30]

Such comments were perhaps disingenuous. Renaud de Jouvenel maintained that Colette's models 'are always taken from her immediate entourage.'[31] 'As for *Julie de Carneilhan*,' he added, 'my mother considered it as a direct attack on herself, and she was in a good position to judge, but all opinions are possible ... I interpreted the characters as being Claire Boas, Henry and Isabelle de Comminges.'[32] Mme de Comminges was frank: 'I don't like her book at all. Her story about me is idiotic, and the rest is worthless.'[33] Some thought that the third and final Mme de Jouvenel also appeared in *Julie de Carneilhan*. She was the heiress who was content to hold Espivant by her money. As for Espivant himself, Renaud found him not only like his father, but a stock character in Colette's work.

Colette did not *see*, perhaps because she didn't look at people. Let us say that she did not have the eye of the photographer or the painter ... She had only one image of a man, that of the rather stupid seducer, a brawler, sure of himself or ridiculous, self-centred, a man whom one would treat today as a phallocrat. The same type of man appears again in *Julie de Carneilhan*. So it is a kind of obsession.[34]

Renaud even sees in the book a lasting grudge against the nobility. Colette, he writes, 'denies Julie the title of Comtesse and represents the Carneilhans' home as a ruined building where they rear horses and pigs. And she does not know in the least how to make a real Comtesse talk, or to describe how she lives.'[35]

In the summer of 1941, in German-occupied Paris, Colette felt bitterly deprived of the company of her friends.[36] A German orchestra gave an evening concert in the great courtyard of the Palais-Royal; and, as they played Mozart serenades, the stormclouds shifted overhead. Life seemed unreal, and Paris seemed curiously empty. 'How beautiful Touzac must be just now [this to Marguerite on 29 July]! ... It isn't that Paris is ugly, its great deserted spaces give us relief, and I can instal myself in the Tuileries, where the flowers are beautiful, with no more neighbours than I used to have, once upon a time, in the Bois.'[37]

Colette was reassured by her notes from Marguerite. She was anxious about Hélène Picard: about her life as a recluse, about her health and her financial problems, about the parrots which Hélène could no longer feed. Perhaps the birds should be sent to Guichard, the famous parrot-keeper in the Palais-Royal.

What are you going to do with those parrots [she asked]? If, for want of provender, you resigned yourself to parting with them, how could they be transported to the parrot man in the Palais-Royal? I know from him that certain birds, if they are under-fed, don't appear to waste away, but die quite suddenly. He has some grain, himself, which he bought for its weight in gold. But he wouldn't sell some for anything in the world ...

No cars. The Métro is a torture with my arthritis. Otherwise you would often see me. I am not moving from Paris, we aren't moving.

I am working on a curious job: I am writing scenes for the coming revue at the Théâtre Michel . . .

The Garden, under my windows, is beautiful. Maurice is the best companion in the world.[38]

On Friday, 12 December, at twenty minutes past seven in the morning, the Gestapo came to arrest him.

• ━ •

'He left very calmly for some unknown place,' Colette told Hélène, 'charged with the crime of being a Jew, of having gone through the last war as a volunteer, of having been awarded a medal. I'm told he may be camping in some huts at Compiègne. Some friends are trying to do something for me.'[39] On 23 December she added: 'An elderly man who has been freed told me that Maurice was well, and in good heart. Straw on the ground to sleep on. Thirty-six to a hut. All brave.'[40]

Maurice himself faced internment with remarkable courage.

I was arrested at dawn, in December 1941, and taken with a thousand Jews to the camp at Compiègne. Our farewells were all the more agonising since Colette and I were trying to reassure one another and even to smile. I understood at once that the best way to prove my love to her was to survive, and that to do so I must . . . live the camp life as if I had known no other.[41]

III

Colette was sixty-nine. On the eve of her old age, she was suddenly alone, except for the solid presence of Pauline. The solitude in which she abruptly found herself was a solitude unlike any other she had known. It was made worse by unremitting fear. Few Jews arrested by the Gestapo were likely to escape 'the final solution'.

Colette appealed to everyone of influence she knew – and her friends were many and distinguished. Sacha Guitry was one of those who worked for the release of Maurice. Bonmariage said later that Guitry saved Maurice from certain death, and that Colette showed him base ingratitude. Gold and Fizdale, in their life of

Misia Sert, maintain that it was José-Maria Sert who saved Maurice. Sert, an exotic Spanish painter, had been a friend of Colette since he arrived in Paris at the turn of the century. He was a Catholic rightist. He also had the accommodating nature of the collaborator. Though he was violently anti-German, he had cynically come to terms with the German authorities. 'I am sure,' wrote Misia, his wife, 'that even I do not know how many people were released from prison through him, or how many he saved from being deported or an even worse fate.'[1]

On 12 January 1942 Colette herself explained to Lucie Delarue-Mardrus:

Since 12 December, [Maurice] has been about a hundred kilometres away ... Wooden huts. Coffee in the morning. Soup at 10 o'clock. After which there's only 250 grammes of bread and a cup of tea. Impossible to correspond, to reach, to exchange. I am knocking on doors. They only evacuate 'serious' invalids. I'm waiting. If I could only get him a line or something to eat ... Thank you for being worried, and for caring about my perfect companion.[2]

She herself cared so much, recorded Natalie Barney, 'that, seeing herself unexpectedly in the mirror, she could not recognise herself in the altered face.'[3]

—·—

As her immobility increased, *la vagabonde* had been obliged to learn the art of stillness; her world had begun to shrink to a single room. Had she been less brave, its red walls would have seemed a prison to her; but she learned, now, how to overcome imprisonment. Alone, in the rue de Beaujolais, in an enemy-occupied city, with no notion when the war would end, she found salvation in memory, experience and knowledge. As Germaine Beaumont said, she created a new genius for herself.

It was born, I think, during the years of Occupation, when every life might be called restricted if not that of a recluse. The enforced obscurity, the curfew, the watching behind a curtain which one does not dare to lift, the waiting behind a door for footsteps which are late in coming, footsteps one won't hear for a long time, footsteps one may never hear again; the book which falls from the hand, unfinished, broken off in the middle of a line; a tapestry which trembles so much under the fingers that one cannot put a needle through it, and the mouthful of food which stops in the throat, the bread which tastes like sand; Colette kept all that, which was the common lot, she kept every nuance, every speck, as she had kept the best part of a life which had once been happy.

The blue lantern began to shine on her brow and on her hands, to become the symbol of an essential value, persisting in spite of the universal chaos and the particular horror of the oppression...

Colette hardly stirred. She watched, she waited, she suffered, and she was burdened with other griefs... She has said little about this time, written little about it, but from time to time a phrase emerged from among other phrases, and it tore one's heart. Colette abandoned excessively complicated themes in tapestry. She re-covered a Directoire chair. 'It's for Maurice's desk, when he comes back,' she told me.[4]

Maurice himself later recorded that Colette controlled her anguish, and did not neglect her work. 'But she used to get up at night, go to my room, sit down at my work-table, and remain there, motionless, for hours.'[5]

On 31 January 1942 Marie Dormoy hurried to Léautaud's. She had come from the rue de Beaujolais, where she had had an appointment with Colette to buy one of her manuscripts for the Bibliothèque Doucet.

After a rather cool fifteen minutes [Léautaud reported], Colette was absolutely delightful to her, and, when she discreetly suggested going, twice kept her back...

She talked about love, of what men are, saying that she had always been ready to efface herself if the man she loved was in love elsewhere, because the man's happiness was more important to her than anything, ... but that men don't understand this, they take it as a proof of indifference and detachment, when it is exactly the opposite. All in all, a charming welcome. Colette is to search among her manuscripts for one which will satisfy the Bibliothèque Doucet,... and she will let her know when to come and fetch it. She told me that Colette still has quite a pleasant face, but her body is appallingly deformed...

Colette's husband, Maurice Goudeket, a Dutchman, is still incarcerated. Colette hopes that, through certain influences which she has brought to bear, she will see him freed in three days.[6]

It was, in fact, on 6 February that Maurice returned, by a miracle, to the rue de Beaujolais. Dishevelled and exhausted, he stripped himself of his clothes in the hall, and demanded a bath to rid himself of the smell of Compiègne.

I'm trying to take up the work which I found impossible in his absence [Colette confessed to Hélène a fortnight later]. His presence is not enough to make it easy ...
I find that, since Maurice has come back, I am bruised all over with tiredness ...
Maurice kisses your hands, my Hélène. He spent eight weeks in a world with no colours except dirty grey and white. Even now, he is struck with wonder by a blue lamp against a flame-coloured curtain ...
I have done an armchair in tapestry, an 1840 design, with a bunch of flowers (dahlias) on the seat, a bunch of flowers (convolvulus) on the back ... And two butterflies on each elbow-rest. All on an off-white ground. I had a career there! The profession of a writer has killed it.[7]

In the spring of 1942 Colette was given an extensive course of X-ray treatment and injections.[8] She was very tired, and she was anxious about her health. She was also apprehensive that Maurice might be re-arrested. During the summer, to relieve her anxiety, he left for the unoccupied zone and went to stay with friends in Saint-Tropez. He asked the new proprietors of La Treille Muscate if he might look round the house. He explained that he was the husband of Colette. They welcomed him warmly. 'Come in, Monsieur Willy.'[9]

Colette remained with Pauline in the rue de Beaujolais. It was in these months of anxiety, in her seventieth year, that she recalled the conversation of fifteen years ago, at the little hotel in Valescure. A provident housekeeper, she had stored the conversation on the shelves of her capacious memory. She set her story at the end of the nineteenth century, in the heyday of La Belle Otéro, Liane de Pougy, Émilienne d'Alençon, at the time when she and Willy had known the brilliance of the *demi-monde*. *Gigi*, that mordantly witty and exuberant novella, was published this autumn in *Présent*, a weekly which appeared in Unoccupied France.

On 11 November the Allies landed in North Africa, and it was announced that the Germans would now occupy all France. Their first concern would no doubt be to remove those whom they found undesirable. Maurice felt it wise to leave Saint-Tropez at once, and to make his tortuous way back to Paris.[10]

November brought not only his return to the rue de Beaujolais, but an omen of the literary future. Sacha Guitry, ever generous, proposed Colette for membership of the Académie-Goncourt. Rosny, the president, was enthusiastic. Guitry decided to sound Colette. He invited her to lunch at Drouant's, in the place Gaillon, where the Académie held their famous meetings. He arranged for them to lunch in a small room next to the Goncourt room. At the end of the meal, he showed her this, and asked: ' "Colette, would you like to join us soon?" And so, my dear colleagues,' he confessed, 'I gave you the slip, and I voted for her before you did. Your election just confirmed my own, that's all. She had her first lunch at Drouant's alone with me.'[11]

•——•

'Yes, of course I'm lazy,' wrote Colette to Marguerite on 4 February. 'I am always lazy when I'm working. You understand me, my Marguerite. I have a little job, which I'm finding quite difficult, to deliver on 15 March.'[12] The 'little job' was perhaps *Nudité*, which was published in Brussels later in the year. Colette was, however, to publish much in 1943, including *Le Képi*, another collection of novellas and assorted works of non-fiction. In the title-story she returned to a familiar theme: a love-affair between a young man and an ageing woman. In a moment of abandon, Marco coyly puts on the lieutenant's képi; then she sees his face, and knows, beyond all doubt, that this will be the end of the affair. Suddenly she becomes aware of her faded looks, her loss of dignity. Bertrand de Jouvenel, who read *Le Képi*, was struck by Colette's bitter consciousness of the chasm between youth and age.[13]

•——•

Early in 1943 the line of demarcation between the occupied and unoccupied zones of France was removed. 'Well, my Marguerite, you'll be coming and going freely, now,' Colette insisted. 'And, if you set off again, we'll be able to exchange letters, real ones. Such hopes make me patient about the fog and the return of the cold ... These three years of Paris weigh upon me.'[14]

In this spring of 1943, constantly in pain, constantly aware of the hardships and anxieties brought by the war, Colette turned to religion. 'There's no doubt that the Catholics don't like me!' she herself had remarked to Renée Hamon. 'And yet I'm a Catholic, I was baptised, I had my first communion, my confirmation, I was even married, once, in church! What do they want?'[15] She had been puzzled, for, as Edmond Bénisti had discerned, she had the idea of God and – though she was not a regular churchgoer, though Maurice wrote that she had no faith – she felt a longing for something higher. She had recently been given a prayer-book; and, as she wrote to François Mauriac: 'I have not failed to read in it every day what I promised you I'd read ... I feel a savage about many things, but without any ill-will, quite the contrary. Maurice Goudeket is beginning to understand perfectly how to light small candles at our neighbour, N. D. des Victoires ... Maurice is so worth the trouble of knowing. More than I am. But he dresses in neutral tints, so it isn't easy ...'[16]

Such praise was understated. Colette was well aware of her husband's virtues. He looked after her with a rare and unremitting devotion. 'Maurice is being patient,' she told Marguerite late in June. 'I have suffered a good deal these last few days. You see, nothing changes except vaguely ... I am still under Soulié de Morant [the acupuncture specialist], because he tells me that a lesion as old as mine can't be cured quickly ...'[17] The arthritic pain continued; in July she also had a gastric complaint, and she lost nearly two stone in nine days.[18]

She continued to be ill for the next two months. On 21 September she announced that she had abandoned acupuncture 'because I've been ill, just imagine, for two months, with what I called food poisoning. But we now know what I have, and what I once christened enteritis, poisoning, etc. I have ... a protozoan! And a tropical protozoan, if you please! Me – and I've hardly travelled at all!'¹⁹ Marguerite wrote anxiously to ask if Colette was better.

Well, no my dearest [came the answer]. I'm not cured yet. They stuff me with laudanum, exopancreine, simaruba – a pretty name! – and cresentyl ... Not to mention other things, all bitter, among them a quiracrine and a tiny little pill, which is capable of turning your skin yellow. Luckily the guests are invisible! ...
  I must stop because I feel slightly giddy. But it isn't dangerous, it's the remedial poisons ...²⁰

She faced her almost constant pain with extraordinary courage, and she refused the sedatives which would have diminished both her vitality and her work. Under the blue lamp, as blue as moonlight in a theatre, Colette continued to write.

* * *

The rhythm of her life had once been feverish; now it was not so much age as pain that obliged her to slow her pace. Her indifferent health affected her work. *Trois ... Six ... Neuf*, which appeared that year, had been written at a sitting. Three, six, nine had been the ritual figures set down in leases, for tenancies of three, six or nine years. Now Colette recorded the curious contrast in her nature: her love of home and her vagabond instinct. She recalled her *hôtels* and apartments in Paris, and the charm of La Treille Muscate. The essay had its interest for the student of her life, but it had no literary style. It was not only the quality of her work which was in decline. She found it increasingly hard to concentrate. Writing to Marguerite on 25 January, she said that a novella – probably *L'Enfant malade* – had been dragging on for more than three months. For the past week she had been living the life of a recluse, to finish the story once and for all. She had celebrated the end of her 'novella-nightmare' by going to the Théâtre-Français to see Claudel's *Le Soulier de satin*. The five-hour performance had seemed less oppressive than she had expected.²¹
  On 3 February Colette sent Marguerite some disturbing news. Misia Sert, whose husband had helped to free Maurice, had known Liszt in her childhood and Mallarmé when she was a

young woman. She had patronised the Ballets Russes, reigned over a court of writers and artists. Renoir had painted her portrait, and Cocteau had dedicated work to her. Now, elderly and nearly blind, she had been attacked in a Paris street. She said that her life had been saved by her companion, the film designer Christian Bérard. 'You see,' wrote Colette, 'the shades of Touzac are more reassuring.'[22]

Alas, they were not. Pierre Moreno, Marguerite's nephew, played an important part in the Resistance in the south-west. A fortnight later, a friend in Paris telephoned Colette to say that Pierre had been arrested for the second time. 'I wish,' she wrote to Marguerite, 'I was twenty-five years younger, and strong on my legs, and could come and help you.'[23] She found it agony to walk, but she promised that she would drag herself as far as Notre-Dame-des-Victoires, to light a candle for the absent Pierre.[24] To Renaud de Jouvenel, she lamented that she was leading a narrow life, and that she hadn't set foot beyond the Bois for three years.[25]

She needed all the strength she could find. There was a constant struggle for food in Paris; indeed, she owed much to the good offices of Tonton, the proprietor of Liberty's Bar in the place Blanche. She had a bad pain in her side, and she was ill for more than a week. 'What bears us up,' she asked Marguerite, 'except a fatalism which is content to be more and more blind?'[26] The state of illness was not unfruitful: it brought many visions. Colette, like Proust, owed something to ill-health and pain. But she knew now that her arthritis was incurable.

The La Chapelle *quartier* was bombed. 'Perhaps you have heard about the quite terrible night in Paris [this on 23 April]? You know the Palais-Royal well enough to imagine the noise and shaking which an air-raid (the first of that kind) can create in this enchanting, crumbling edifice. So I won't dwell on it. The night beginning now is crystal clear, we await it with all the fatalism we can muster.'[27] 'Our days and nights have more and more alerts,' she added, five days later. 'It's noon, we have had three air-raids since four o'clock this morning.'[28] On 1 May she reported that there was no hot water, and no light for thirteen hours a day.[29] On 9 May Mme Gaston Fournier, the collector of rare butterflies, took her for a drive in the Bois. The lakes had dried up; and, in one of them, small irises were growing.[30]

■▶━━◀■

Late in May Pierre Moreno was finally freed.[31] As she waited for the Allied landing, the liberation of Paris, Colette was finishing *Paris de ma fenêtre*. The original version, *De ma fenêtre*, had appeared in France in 1942; the more substantial version was to be published this year in Geneva. 'We do not look,' wrote Colette, 'we shall never look enough, never carefully enough, never passionately enough.'[32] She looked at the world, in miniature, as she saw it from the Palais-Royal. 'A child's call, a burst of laughter spring from the garden underneath my window, and fall on my page as vivid as a red geranium.'[33] She recorded the animals of the Palais-Royal; even now, she recalled the South of France, 'where the sun ... rouges the cherries in May',[35] and she recalled still more cherries, with transparent, red-lacquered flesh. Cocteau rightly said that she wrote in gastronomic style.[36]

'And what conditions one works in, here!' she added on 7 June. 'Yesterday, after ... a sonorous night, I think we had seven or eight alerts. Even when you don't leave your chair, it isn't comfortable. And then, yesterday, the excitement of this landing ...'[37] The Allies had landed in Normandy; the invasion had begun at last.

That evening there came news of a small and pitiful drama.

They telephoned [continued Colette] to tell me that Missy had attempted suicide – something like a harakiri, about ten days ago ... I'll try to find out. Because I've heard nothing of her for two years. With one of those childish whims (81 years old) which she always had, she had *signified* to me that she wouldn't see me again, and I took good care not to protest. Since then, she had lost her memory more and more, and always lost her bearings in Paris, even when she noted down her destination on a scrap of paper. There's nothing cheerful about the end of her life. I'm going to try to find out more about it. Maurice was full of pity and astonishment in the presence of this incomplete human being.[38]

Missy had long been incomplete; she had lost her bearings not only in Paris, but in life. In her latter days, she had had herself called the Marquis de Mora. She had continued to dress as a man, and it was easy to mistake her for one, for age sometimes makes the sexes resemble one another. But Missy had now avoided what she used to seek, and had sometimes sought protection against admirers. 'The last time I saw her,' wrote André de Fouquières, 'it was in her apartment in the rue des Eaux. She was dressed, as usual, in a black frock coat and full trousers. She lived on a small life annuity, apparently forgetting her past. She had herself called "M. le marquis", and would not tolerate anything else. Young people who had no relationship to her used to call her "Uncle".'[39] She had now hastened the end of her long and unhappy life. Her first attempt at suicide had failed; she made another, and she died on 29 June, 'in a mysterious way, asphyxiated by gas. There were,' added Fouquières, 'about ten faithful friends at her funeral at Saint-Honoré-d'Eylau. A shield with her arms was the only sign of her House ... M. Sacha Guitry was chief mourner!'[40]

Three months later, on 24 August, the Allied tanks rumbled down the avenue d'Orléans, and all the bells in Paris rang again. Colette refused to believe in the Liberation until she had visible proof. She demanded to see a Scottish officer, complete with kilt, in the rue de Beaujolais. Maurice ran to the place du Palais-Royal, and there, by great good fortune, encountered the most Scottish of majors. He invited him to lunch; and, in the rue de Beaujolais, within a few yards of Le Grand Véfour, they celebrated the Liberation with a tin of black market corned beef.[41]

IV

On 28 January 1945 Colette was seventy-two. She was resigned to being sensible about many things; but, as she assured Lucie Saglio, she was fighting every inch of the way.

She was oppressed by pain and disability, and by the disturbing aftermath of the war in Europe. On 24 January Robert Brasillach had spoken bitterly about clearing the names of alleged collaborators. 'When I think that Colette signed her letters "your old friend", and that she wrote to me: "I am glad to have seen you grow up ..." It was during the Occupation, she knew quite well what I was doing, I haven't changed since ... It's better to shrug one's shoulders!'[1] Brasillach had found an outlet in fascist and anti-Semitic papers; he had been committed to Nazi ideology. It was said that the authorities had found a photograph of him in the uniform of a German officer. Whether or not this was true, he was sentenced to death and executed on 6 February. Colette had been one of many to sign a petition for a reprieve; but General de Gaulle had refused to reprieve him.

— · —

'I embrace you, my Marguerite, and I covet the most ordinary wicker-chair, beside you, outside the Royal.'[2] So Colette confessed to her usual correspondent in the spring. She would have given much to spend a few days with her oldest friend on the Promenade des Anglais in Nice. When she wrote again, however, it was from Les Salins d'Hyères, where she and Maurice were staying briefly with Simone Berriau. A former singer, actress and theatre director, Simone had once dazzled Colette by her zest and her audacity. Now, perhaps, Colette found her energy somewhat overwhelming. To Paul Géraldy, who had been her neighbour at Saint-Tropez, she wrote: 'I am cleansing myself of five years of Paris, and the South of France has stunned me.'[3]

She was exhausted by years of ill-health, by years of confinement to the rue de Beaujolais, and by the innumerable stresses of the war; but, whatever her condition, she felt obliged to work. On 23 April, once again in Paris, she announced: 'Ferenczi has come back, he naturally wants to "bring out" a book as soon as possible. That will be managed by means of four unpublished novels. The best of the four is *Gigi*.'[4]

— · —

While Ferenczi arranged for the publication of *Gigi* in book form, and *Belles Saisons* was published by the Galerie Charpentier, Sacha Guitry's wish was belatedly realised. On 2 May Colette was elected to the Académie-Goncourt. Roland Dorgelès, the novelist, went to ask her 'if she would sit with us at the Goncourts' table ... She spun no fine-sounding phrases: she laughed and said yes, and,' he reported, 'she kissed me like a simple countrywoman. She brought us not only her glory, but her rough kindness and her honest friendship.'[5] She was only the second woman to become an Academician; the first had been Judith Gautier, the brilliant and beautiful daughter of Théophile.

Marguerite sent congratulations. 'This isn't a letter,' answered Colette, 'it's only a big thank-you, a kiss. I'm rather knocked-up, as you can imagine.'[6] She was sufficiently 'knocked-up' to send away Charles Saglio, who called twice, in vain, with his congratulations.

Dear friend [she explained on 6 May], we ask for most indulgence from the people whom we love the best ... These last three days have got the better of me, and even of the pleasure which I'd have had in telling you the details of my latest incarnation ...

Banquet (for seven), photographs, interviews - these pleasures aren't suitable at my age, and they never have been. I must admit that my gracious colleagues have done their best to spare me all vexation. None the less, these three days, not to mention my leg, have been ... let's say tiring ...[7]

Tonton, who had helped her with food during the days of the black market, sent the new Academician some coffee and an affectionate greeting, 'both of which,' she told Marguerite, 'delighted me ... I haven't got photographers or reporters round me any more. What could I give to either, anyway?'[8]

She gave one youthful journalist an answer to the inevitable question: 'Madame, did Chéri exist?'

It hardly matters [she reflected] if we establish whether, in some or other place, a very old man, now white and bent, has escaped from the suicide which I imposed on Chéri. But it is a pleasure to me that my youth of obscure origin, the melancholy which draws him, at last, towards barren purity, should have affected a large public, if only as a spice of curiosity.

Young man, I could have answered: 'Yes, I have met Chéri. We have all met Chéri, adorned with his meteoric qualities ...

'Yes, of course I have met Chéri, and I have met him more than once, just as I have met different temptations ...'[9]

Perhaps she was thinking, now, not only of Auguste Hériot, but of the stepson whom she had hardly seen for some twenty years.

Yet now she could give reporters something beyond the origins of her *histoire de diabolo*. She gave them, and their public, a symbol of everything that was most profoundly French. In an interview she said that she dreamed of 'flowers and strawberries, and living in a more tranquil universe.'[10] She recalled the simple way of life; she seemed a symbol of courage and endurance. Photographs showed her on her divan, with a fur rug over her legs. Her papers, pens and scissors and glasses were strewn on a small bridge-like table across her lap; there were a bowl of flowers at hand, and mounted butterflies on the shelves behind her. Over her left shoulder hung the extension lamp. Its shade was made from a piece of her blue writing-paper. She called it her *fanal bleu*. It was blue, wrote Germaine Beaumont, like an Egyptian night, that lamp which drew towards her so much friendship, so much admiration. Sometimes, wrote Roland Dorgelès, a belated stroller passed through the Palais-Royal, and thought that he could discern a face at a window where there was always a light. 'It was the sorceress, who was asking questions of the night, and, little by little, wresting her past from the shadows of the garden.'[11] Cocteau maintained that the ghosts in the arcades of the Palais-Royal would always respect the light of the blue beacon, and say: 'Let's disappear. Colette is working.'[12]

July brought a heat-wave to Paris. She and Maurice went, once again, to stay with Simone Berriau. Her energy was, as usual, alarming. There were never fewer than sixteen at table: indeed, for a week there were twenty-one. Colette sought escape on the terrace outside her room, with a view of salt-marshes and the sea beyond. There, in tranquillity, she worked at her book of memoirs, *L'Étoile vesper*.[13]

On 19 August, with evident relief, she and Maurice caught the train from Marseilles.[14] In Paris she found Antoine Rasimi, the impresario and the lessee of several theatres, eager to revive *Chéri* again.[15] As for Marguerite, she was preparing her part in *La Folle de Chaillot*. In the last decade or so, her fortunes had changed. She had finally agreed to play comic parts, as Colette had long advised her to do. The cinema had discovered her, and she appeared in nearly seventy films. Since the cinema had drawn attention to her, the theatre claimed her back. *La Folle de Chaillot*, directed by Louis Jouvet, was first performed at the Théâtre de l'Athénée on 19 December. It was to run until 26 May 1946, and it was to be twice revived. It was the greatest triumph of her career. Colette attended the fifth performance. 'My Marguerite, ... the end of the play, as you perform it, takes hold of our hearts ... I embrace you, with an emotion which is not yet extinct.'[16]

She herself laboured on at her memoirs: imprisoned by her work and by her increasing disability. 'I don't go out, except for the Goncourt. Maurice is busy trying to arrange a treatment in Switzerland.'[17]

In March she and Maurice left for Geneva, where they spent six weeks. 'There are so many ways of being cured,' reflected Colette. 'Perhaps I shall find a new one ...'[18] The treatment failed to improve her condition. In June she was in such pain that her doctor, Marthe Lamy, urged her to go at once to Uriage. The journey was long, and she found it agonising. She and Maurice stayed at the Hôtel Bellevue, where she was under the care of Dr Roman. 'X-rays at once, injections too,' she told Marguerite on 2 July. 'I suffer day and night. But Dr Roman – who's more than good – promises me that I shall get better in spite of the antiquity of the trouble. What more do I ask? ... The country and the weather are wonderful. Don't worry, I'm still optimistic, at the moment.'[19]

On 14 July, Bastille Day, while she was still at Uriage, *L'Étoile vesper* was published. It was the book of an ageing writer: a stream of consciousness which caught up a strange miscellany of themes: the Occupation, the German entry into Paris, the Liberation, the origins of Chéri, pregnancy and childbirth, old photographs. Yet, from this incoherent book, certain touching impressions remained. Even now, when Colette could see the end of her path, she was constantly aware of love, the love that had made her work and her life, the love, she wrote, 'that comforts me until I cease to live'.[20] One senses the presence of Maurice, his constant vigilance, his perpetual eagerness to fulfil her wishes. One senses their loving tact to each other. She is maintaining the pretence that she is not in pain, and he is pretending to believe it. But Colette talks, now, of insomnia and of the actual pleasures of illness, the chance it offers of nobility. 'One is obliged to accept that misfortune moulds us. It is better to mould misfortune to suit ourselves, and even mould it to our advantage.'[21] She is aware of love, and pain, and the closeness of death. She is aware of the landscapes she has known, in fact and in her imagination. She is also aware of literature. 'Deep down inside me, a tired mind continues its gourmet's search, wanting a better word, and better than better ...'[22]

Late in July Colette announced that she and Maurice were leaving Uriage. 'I am knocked up,' she told Marguerite, 'and it was necessary. Dr Roman didn't conceal from me that the pain wouldn't leave me for a day during the cure. Now I must wait two months for the result which he has explicitly promised me ... We shall stop for 8 or 10 days with friends near Grasse. The good thing for me, my dearest, is that I am forbidden to work at all for two months!'[23]

She and Maurice went to stay with Charles and Patat de Polignac, who had rented a country house, Les Aspres, south of Grasse. Charles was the nephew of Winnie de Polignac. On 14 August Colette returned, with Maurice, to the rue de Beaujolais. Two days later she told Marguerite:

I am overwhelmed by such morbid tiredness – or so it seems to me – that the only person I should have seen is Marguerite. They think that this exhaustion is the result of the cure, but my doctors won't be back in Paris till the day after tomorrow ... I should have come back by aeroplane, to avoid too much fatigue, but the Préfet of the A[lpes]-M[aritimes] sent the tickets too late, Maurice got us sleepers in the train with great difficulty. I made him anxious, poor man! It's because that cure at Uriage was so much more severe than it seemed at first ... I am happy here, in spite of the pain.[24]

She was well enough, when she returned to Paris, to impress Peter Quennell with 'her brilliant eyes and her huge nimbus of grizzled grey hair', by her commanding personality.[25] She was well enough to be witness at the *mairie*, and at Saint-Roch, when Pauline was married that November. She, Maurice and Bel-Gazou attended the wedding-breakfast. Pauline's sister-in-law was a baker in Clichy, and the gargantuan banquet was held in her bakehouse. Pauline – now Mme Tissandier – had refused to marry without Colette's consent; and she had insisted on remaining in her service.[26]

There were times when Colette needed solitude; there were still times when she chose company. On 23 November Gide recorded:

A most unexpected telephone call. It's Colette, who wishes me a happy birthday, and says she would like to see me again. She was touched by what I said about her in my *Journal*; which I doubted that she'd been aware of. Of course I shall answer her request; but, alas, knowing perfectly well that, once the first effusions are over, we shall find nothing to say to each other.[27]

Maurice described the visit from Gide: a touching, predictably vain attempt to adapt himself to the climate of the rue de Beaujolais.[28]

The new year opened, sadly, with the usual preoccupations. In January Colette had influenza and, for a few days, she lost her voice. She was waiting for a visit from Dr Menkes, another Swiss doctor, who was to treat her on her next stay in Geneva. She was seeing him at the urgent request of Maurice and some of her friends.

I am arranging my life as I can [this on 21 April], and Maurice is trying to make it as easy as possible for me ...

As I cannot go out and meet people, I have to give some inevitable people access here, in my mouse-trap. For the rest of my time, I'm in pain and I rest. The two are not irreconcilable – not always. And Maurice, among the other cares that he shows for me, is planning my departure for Switzerland. I can't refuse to go any longer, I'm in too much pain. He will take me there, and then come back, and leave me to Dr Menkes for – alas – six weeks. We're leaving on Friday morning. Oh, see me before then! No clinic. My address: Hôtel Richmond, Geneva. I'm sure that you'll write to me, you know that I shall write to you.[29]

She kept her word. On 1 May she sent Marguerite a picture postcard of Geneva. 'You know this view, my Marguerite. I shall contemplate it for a little while ... I am going through an attack of the wrath of God, and the treatment itself is severe. But we shall see.'[30]

On 24 June Maurice bought her back to Paris. Her treatment had done her good; she had less pain, now, day and night. Walking was, as she confessed, 'another pair of legs',[31] but she and Maurice drove to Versailles to dine with the redoubtable Lady Mendl. Elsie Mendl, wife of Sir Charles, had made interior decoration an acceptable career for women; she proclaimed style in her surroundings, style in her dress, and she had long kept fit by performing daily exercises based on the Yogi method.

She's 91 [Colette reported to Marguerite], she's as slim as a young girl, and she keeps herself going almost entirely on alcohol. She was wearing white muslin, her throat was caught in a pillory of sapphires, and she wore a silk foulard tied like a turban to hide the absence of a wig. She was light and tottery in her green park, without a flower, [and with] hedges cut as they are in England, in the shapes of fantastic animals ... I should have liked you to be there.[32]

On 4 September she and Maurice left for Limas, near Villefranche. They were to stay with Jean Guillermet and his wife, 'very simple and very nice friends. From a chaise-longue, under a tree,' she wrote, 'I shall listen for a week to the distant sounds of the grape-gathering.'[33]

She stayed there for eleven days, and then returned to Paris, and to a world of literary activity. On 1 October the Académie-Goncourt held its first meeting of the season. Colette delighted in these *déjeuners*: in the company of the novelist Roland Dorgelès, and of her old friend Francis Carco, the poet and novelist who seemed to symbolise the *genius loci* of Montmartre in its wilder years. There was Léo Larguier, novelist, poet and literary journalist; there was André Billy, that other literary journalist, with his academic sympathies.

If Drouant hadn't had its lift, I should [confessed Colette] have been very deprived. But then I should count on six or eight men's hands, ready to haul me up to the salon adorned with the woolly portrait of Edmond de Goncourt ... We are diverse, we are fiercely unlike each other, we are rebels against cohesion. Dorgelès misses no occasion to burst like a chestnut on the embers. Carco sometimes sulks, and then he is silent and he deprives us of his enchanting, singing voice (the most beautiful voice on the radio!). Larguier has the humour and the manner of the playful lion, he roars in alexandrines. Billy? He knows everything of which I am ignorant – and how is that for handsome erudition? ...

It's no good pretending otherwise: I take a very feminine pleasure in being the only woman at the *déjeuners Goncourt* ... Do people think we are on a bed of roses when we come to the last hours of the competition? ... Oh no, it isn't as easy as that, the moment for the white wine and the vote. I agree about Salacrou, but I should have liked Anouilh, too ...[34]

The *déjeuners Goncourt* were Colette's last link with modern literature.

Since her return from Limas, in mid September, she had been caught up in a vortex of activity. The film rights of *Le Blé en herbe* had finally been sold.[35] It was a time of stringency, and for the moment the novel could not be filmed; but the project was to be resumed, and the film was to have its première in 1954.

Meanwhile, in 1947, in *Portraits de famille*, Léon-Paul Fargue published his impression of Colette. Fargue has been described as a latter-day François Villon; he reconciled in himself, it is said, his association with the Académie-Goncourt and the Faubourg Saint-Germain, and his role as a Bohemian, a poet of Montmartre.[36] A rebel in the literary establishment, he had much in common with Colette. He saw her, still, as a provincial in the heart of Paris; he remained aware, above all, of her sturdy and unerring common-sense.

Sometimes she talks about the letters she receives from her countless women readers. 'They confide about themselves, they question and listen. One of them asks me for a cat; another has fallen on hard times, and she complains that she has to move and to leave her dog. Look: an extraordinary large handwriting. It's knocking against the edges of the paper like a terrified bird ... It's the writing of an unknown and desperate mistress, crying out to me: "Madame, do you think he will come back?"' [37]

The genius of Colette, wrote Fargue, 'which Frenchwomen feel so close to their own, is that of answering every question about emotional life in the most precise way, like a generous Pythia. She is infallible ...' [38]

Colette was proud and delighted to be admitted to Fargue's 'family'. She went to dine with him in celebration. It was a meeting of invalids, for Fargue had suffered a severe stroke. However, one day, wrote Colette,

as I was in much less pain than usual, a journey was organised ... : a journey at the end of which I felt Fargue awaiting me.
In the rue du Montparnasse, they put me in the service-lift, all spangled with coal. The lift took me up to Fargue. Out of coquetry he was already seated, and so I believed that at any moment he could have risen to his feet – who knows? – and given me his arm to lead me to his table ...
Six guests, in all. But how many does Léon-Paul Fargue count for? Seated like Buddha, eloquent and gay? He was generous that evening, to the point of reassuring us, Goudeket and me ... He ate, grumbled, laughed like an intolerant prince ... He talked to the cat with tenderness ... [39]

It was an unrepeatable occasion; but Colette and Fargue continued to telephone one another, and to discuss their personal suffering. He died soon after her visit to the rue du Montparnasse.

Colette herself, disabled, ageing, often sleepless, still remained a symbol of ardent life. This year, 1947, in *Quarante contre un*, Paul Guth described a visit to the rue de Beaujolais. He made some curious factual errors, but he caught the magic of the place, the still astonishing vigour and charisma of its *châtelaine*.

At the end of a dark room, near the window, I catch sight of the illustrious shock of hair, and the raised chin and two interminable eyes which draw me from the darkness to the light.

Colette is lying on a divan, her body cut in half by a small movable table on which she is writing as if she were in a compartment in a railway train. From the waist down, she is immobile. But, above, the wonderful head shines out with a sparkling, passionate life.

The head of a Medusa, but not a terrifying Medusa vowed to the infernal regions. A radiant Medusa, belching fire...

She has been put by the window. She waits, all day, in her stone frame, flush with the Palais-Royal. Her feet do not move, but, like the bust of the swimmer emerging from the water, hers seems to rise from the trees, the stones, the urns...

'I haven't moved from here since the end of 1940 [sic]. It's easy to live in a window. I'm facing directly south. I can't be very unhappy, even if I am in pain.'

She talks to me about the pain, which follows a rhythm, like a dance. She amuses herself by training it, like a dog...

She dreams, and turns her heavy pepper-and-salt head of hair. It crackles with intelligence like the hair of the medicine-woman of negro tribes.

She looks at a dozen crystal balls on the mantelpiece. The Chinese read the future in them, but the future does not interest her. The present fills her to the brim. Beside her is a planisphere, blue, with the stars marked by yellow dots and the Milky Way aslant it...

She has in fact travelled little except once, by aeroplane, to follow a trial at the Court of Assizes in Fez [sic]...

She is not made *for depths or heights*. She didn't want to go down a mine.

'Between the grave and paradise, there is a place for me: the earth...'...

Suddenly, *tsss, tsss*. A fly is buzzing round. Colette seizes her fly-swatter: a little lattice framed in velvet, at the end of a stick. *Tsss, tsss*. The fly leaps on to the planisphere, among the planets. It settles on Mercury, brushes against Venus, skims the surface of Mars...

Colette always reaches all fruits and all living creatures. She finally reaches the fly in front of her, on a ranunculus in a bunch of flowers. One blow with the fly-swatter, as infallible as her sentences, and she knocks the fly and the flower into the vase. The water spatters us. And she looks at me with an air of triumph.[40]

On 4 November a letter arrived from Marguerite. Colette replied at once:

> ... We were talking about you, a few days ago. By 'we', I mean the invasion – very pleasant, however – of Yvonne de Bray, Jean Marais and Josette Day, who (especially Yvonne) had had a good lunch. I let them come in as I was feeling better. For of course I've had influenza and re-influenza. It's gone, now, let's forget about it. I think that Yvonne and Jean Marais are going to act *Chéri* on the radio.
>
> I spend the best part of my time reading the novels which aspire to the Prix Goncourt. I think that last year's total, terrifying as it was, has been exceeded. The fashion for *romans-fleuves* means that we have books of 700 and *800* pages, in close print. Tomorrow, at the last but one déjeuner Drouant, I shall say what I think of the *romans-fleuves*. I read day and night ...[41]

The penultimate *déjeuner* was held, and the reading continued.

> My Marguerite [this on 22 November], this is the beginning of a very short letter. I've come to the last days of the reading for the Goncourt, and they are still arriving, these novels which you can at least call numerous.
>
> So you're going to come. I shall believe you when I see you sitting beside my divan-bed ... My damned leg is terrible, I can hardly go down the stairs. B——r! Don't let's talk about it.[42]

Marguerite was now seventy-six. She had imposed herself on the public at an age when most actors have retired. She was in demand in the theatre and in the cinema. She even performed in cabaret; every night, about midnight, since the end of December, she had appeared at Liberty's Bar, in the place Blanche. There she delighted Tonton and his habitués with her recitations of Victor Hugo, Baudelaire and Verlaine. She was staying at a hotel in the avenue de l'Opéra; and she used to overcome her own tiredness and call, often late at night, at the rue de Beaujolais. 'I intensely regret that I can't go "up there" while she is still at Tonton's,' Colette told Pierre Moreno, 'but I'm in pain and Marguerite comes on late. People who've seen her say she is given an extraordinary reception – so it's worthy of her, then.'[43]

The letter was written on 15 January 1948. A fortnight later, on 28 January, Colette herself was seventy-five. Her birthday was the occasion for widespread celebration. She was acclaimed in the papers, deluged with letters and telegrams, postcards and photographs. One admirer sent her a dusty bottle of bordeaux of 1873, the year of her birth. Maurice gave her a gold bracelet; Bel-Gazou brought her a spray of orchids. There were countless flowers from the *quartier*, and a plump pork sausage, ready for cooking. There were a jeroboam of champagne, and 'a rampart of red azaleas' from the Académie-Goncourt, 'and newspapers spangled with the tenderly possessive "our Colette". How sweet it is to me,' she wrote, 'to be an unmixed blessing!'[44]

There was rarely a day when presents failed to come for Colette. They generally came from people who knew her well, and wanted to encourage her curiosity, inspire her memory and imagination. Like Proust, she needed only the taste of a madeleine to lose herself in her own private world. As she had written, long ago: 'My voracious wishes create what they need.' One day someone handed in the first chestnuts, small, hard and sombre brown, all packed in one green bur. 'The bur is half open, the three mahogany fruits are gleaming in the crack ... I don't need anyone to guide me on my walk. I only needed these chestnuts ... Goodbye, goodbye! I may be a little late for dinner.'[45] Colette was a wide-awake dreamer. She loved any present which brought nature to her solitude, swept her in spirit from the rue de Beaujolais. She loved the landscape painting which Jean Marais gave her. In the foreground, on a tree, he had written her name. She loved the stolen fruit which arrived for her. 'It was "someone in the *quartier*" ... who brought it. On a bare branch there hung, solidly, a rather wrinkled apple. "It is a Japanese apple," gossip murmured. "It comes from the gardens at the foot of the Eiffel Tower. It was stolen for Madame Colette, while the gardener was lighting his pipe." ... The apple had hardly been left with me,' reported Colette, 'before it gave out a fragrance half-quince, half-apple, which was enchanting ...'[46] One day Maurice brought her a small radio, 'which sang by itself as it came up the stairs. We set it on my divan, and what did it begin to spout but *L'Enfant et les sortilèges* ...'[47] Claude Chauvière brought Colette violets. 'Look,' said Colette, 'I'm depriving it of water so that it exhales all its fragrance. It's cruel, but necessary.'[48] She appreciated flowers, wrote Violet Trefusis, 'but her attitude was slightly that of the cannibal in relation to the missionary. Would he taste good in a stew?'[49]

⁕

On 16 March 1948, after a long interval, Marguerite arrived again at the rue de Beaujolais, where Colette had lingering influenza. The visit emphasised their profound affection for each other: an affection which had lasted, now, for over fifty years. Marguerite's friendship with Colette was not the unequal friendship which lesser, younger women formed with that formidable figure. Emotionally, at least, it was a relationship between equals. It had unique depth and authority. 'Well, here I am, my Marguerite,' wrote Colette soon afterwards. 'How could I, near as I am, deprive myself of you for so long, how could you do without me for all that time?'[50]

On 20 March Marguerite was belatedly appointed Chevalier de la Légion-d'honneur. The news appeared in the papers a few days later. 'My Marguerite, I don't read the evening papers enough,' went a brief confession from Colette. 'I'm not the first to tell you that I'm glad. But I am the most affectionate. No-one loves you better than I do.'[51]

She herself was to enjoy a rarer distinction: the publication, in her lifetime, of her *Œuvres complètes*. Maurice was, unlike his wife, an ardent bibliophile. He had spent nearly three years assembling and collating her works, seeking out and collecting unpublished texts, writing bibliographical notes. On 22 May Colette lamented: 'I am addle-headed with idiotic work. Thanks to the publication of the *Œuvres complètes*, I am obliged to correct typographically *everything* I've written from the very beginning until to-day! It's loathsome ... I'll write you a better letter next time. Maurice is working in silence; I am working, too, but I'm screaming.'[52]

It was not the only drama. Mermod, a publisher in Lausanne, had had an inspiration which had understandably charmed Colette. Once or twice a week, for a year and more, he had sent her flowers; and he had asked her, when she felt inclined, to draw their portraits. Colette had been enchanted by the continual bouquets, and her enchantment was to be reflected in *Pour un herbier*. Mermod was later to publish an edition illustrated by Raoul Dufy. However, in the summer of 1948 some of the manuscript was mislaid. 'I've just had a drama,' Colette reported on 7 June. 'I'd lost half the text of my little *Herbier*. Luckily Maurice is used to this kind of earthquake, from which he has rescued me until now. But while they last I lose all self-control.'[53]

On 1 July she and Maurice went, once again, to stay with Simone Berriau at Hyères. They planned to stay there for about a fortnight. 'Don't leave me without news,' Colette instructed Marguerite.[54]

On 8 July a letter duly arrived. It was dictated, and it announced that Marguerite was now out of danger. She was spending the summer at Touzac. She had caught cold at a charity performance at Cahors. The cold had been followed by congestion of the lungs and by pleurisy. On 14 July she died.[55]

V

Late in July Colette and Maurice returned to Les Aspres, to stay once again with Charles and Patat de Polignac. They were people of sensibility, and Colette could talk to them freely about Marguerite. At their country house, late in July and early in August, she wrote her tribute to her oldest and dearest woman friend.

The Polignacs did their best to distract and to comfort her. One evening, remembered Jacques Porel, son of the actress Réjane, he and Prince Pierre of Monaco went to dine and meet her.

We went up into the jasmine-scented hills where Colette was waiting...

When she embraced me, which she has consented to do for some years, I rediscovered the virile warmth of her welcome...

Just imagine that you arrive, one evening, at a friend's, and he leads you up to someone you haven't recognised in the darkness, and says: 'I don't know if you have met M. Jean-Jacques Rousseau?'

Well, that is about what I feel when I find myself beside Colette. Surprised, proud, reassured.

She is sitting in an armchair, with a tartan rug across her knees. Another tartan rug on the back of the chair.

'Well, Jacques, how's the book going?' ...

A brief glance of encouragement.

'Come on, tell me. How do you work? What do you write on?'

'I write in little school exercise-books. They don't make me so frightened, dear Colette.'

'Good. Personally, I write on loose sheets.'

She picks up a pile of big sheets of blue paper, and shows them to me, brandishes them at me.

'There you are, you see, I'm writing something on Moreno.'

I see, from a distance, the familiar writing. And the crossing out, crossing out, crossing out.

And immediately there's a magnificent outburst from the great writer: an outburst against the torture known as writing, and, in a chaos of interjections, I hear:

'No, it's frightful, it's idiotic, it shouldn't be allowed. It's a horror, it's disgusting, it's impossible!'[1]

Late that evening, when dinner was over and the guests had departed, Porel took a last look at Colette,

from a distance, a tartan rug round her shoulders, another over her legs, the twin sticks by her side. Colette, asking questions of the night and the fragrance of the jasmine.

Colette, alone, sitting on a height. As befits her. Wherever she may be.[2]

'I spend my time hitting against her absence, and it hurts me.' So Colette told Pierre Moreno as the new year began. 'But I so prefer my hurt to an indifference which had come too soon!'[3] 'I have really been rather ill, dear Pierre [this on 13 April]. And I have never thought so much about Marguerite ... Nothing, in the losses I have suffered, is like this shock which always comes when I think of Marguerite.'[4] On 20 October she added:

Dear Pierrou, ... I am in great pain, but that's no matter. I have had three injections: no effect at all. But you would laugh if you saw the cast of the revival of *Chéri* rehearsing round my bed – I mean *on* my bed! Yet I'm not sure that you would laugh ... Every day this revival, these characters bring forth memories which are dominated by the stature, the figure, of Marguerite, and by the sound of her voice ... I shall never understand anything about death, Pierre.[5]

The presence of Jean Marais at these rehearsals was itself a triumph for Colette. He considered, Cocteau said, 'that he was not the character in Colette's *Chéri*. He fought against every attempt to convince him. He created a thousand pretexts. His heart decided. He loved Colette. It was only out of affection and respect that he surrendered. From that moment, we saw him struggle not only to espouse the character, but to model it in his own image. The result was that Mme Peloux appeared to have sinned with a prince, that the gigolo became heroic, the alley-cat became a tiger-cat ...'[6] Colette had foreseen this. 'The most difficult thing for Jean Marais, if he plays Chéri, will be to abdicate, for a while, his basic purity.'[7]

In November *Chéri* was brilliantly revived at the Théâtre de la Madeleine, with Jean Marais as Chéri and Valentine Tessier as Léa. Colette, who attended the first night, now bore a prestigious new title. It was the honour, said Maurice, of which she was proudest. On the death of Lucien Descaves, she had been elected president of the Académie-Goncourt. As Janet Flanner, the American journalist, reported, Colette was the first woman ever to receive this literary honour.

The ovation given her on the opening night of *Chéri*, her own dramatization of her famous novel, at the Théâtre de la Madeleine was also unique. Elderly, arthritic, ensconced in a stage box, from which only her head was visible – her still mordantly witty face surrounded by its nimbus of radiant hair – she received the acclaim of what is left of the three generations of *tout Paris* she has known: of French government representatives, members of her own and other academies, the leading poets, writers, and artists, and less prosperous admirers, high in the gallery, who have loved her sad love stories of the froufrou days of gay Paris before the First World War.[8]

Since she and Maurice had moved to the rue de Beaujolais, Cocteau had become not only their neighbour but one of their most intimate friends. After the first performance of *Chéri*, he went on stage to say, briefly, what art owed to Colette. 'She has spoken, with truth and poetry, of men and animals and plants ... She has joined no literary school and she has charmed them all.'[9] Next day she wrote to him: 'Dear Jean, ... I was much too moved to say thank you. But we have never needed many words.'[10]

The critics paid their homage in the reviews of the play, though Janet Flanner thought that the novel's sombre shades of meaning and its emotional flow had been lost in adaptation. Valentine Tessier seemed to her a fine actress, not a convincing *demi-mondaine*. Jean Marais appeared not to know the more romantic tricks of the gigolo's trade. Perhaps, as Colette had surmised, he was too chivalrous for the part. When *Chéri* was filmed, he refused the leading rôle because they would not have Valentine Tessier.[11]

* * *

The year which had made Colette the president of the Académie-Goncourt and brought the revival of *Chéri* also brought the publication of the first of the fifteen volumes of her *Œuvres complètes*. There was even a film of her life, which used old photographs and newsreels, with scenes of herself and Maurice, Pauline and Cocteau, in the rue de Beaujolais.

In 1949 a booklet was published to mark the bicentenary of Le Grand Véfour: the restaurant in the Galerie Beaujolais, almost under Colette's apartment, which had long been part of French history. Victor Hugo had dined there on the night of the *bataille d'Hernani*. Now the chef created *Coulibiac de saumon Colette*. Raymond Oliver, the owner of the restaurant, explained that this hot salmon pie 'which the great Colette was so fond of, was only created so that during the last years of her life she could eat a lighter form of the *coulibiac* which she loved so much.'[12]

Cocteau – commemorated by *pintadeau farci Jean Cocteau* – was later to recall the Palais-Royal and its restaurant of historic splendour.

This Palais-Royal – whose inhabitants climb the few steps to the rue de Richelieu and say 'I am going up to Paris' – had elected Madame Colette as its president ...

In the centre of this village, the angle of the rue Montpensier where I live, and the rue de Beaujolais where Colette used to live, shelters the Restaurant Véfour, directed by Monsieur Oliver. There, at the bar, when the little cannon in the garden was fired, and aroused a silky squall of pigeons like the ones in the Piazza San Marco, a few aborigines would assemble, happy to clink glasses together.

Hardly had Madame Colette decided to leave her chaise-longue when, at a sign from Raymond Oliver, two sturdy scullions would go up with a kind of sedan-chair, and come down again ... with the president, in order that she could instal herself at a table which bore her name, and add to the lustre of a place where some of the glories of France, from Fragonard to Balzac, had been guests.[13]

Colette was fond of Le Grand Véfour; she felt a deep affection for the Palais-Royal: for 'the serene geometry of its arcades, which stretch out in the evening to infinity',[14] for its associations with her friends. She knew the window behind which Cocteau woke or slept, the window at which Christian Bérard, the stage designer, needed a good light on his sketches; she knew behind which half-lowered blind Mireille was working at her songs on a sky-blue grand piano. She loved the almost provincial intimacy of the Palais-Royal. To her it was an enclosed and magic world.

A spell keeps us all here, preserves in the heart of Paris what is going to ruin and what is lasting, what succumbs and what does not yield.

Some of my friends have seen me constantly, happily at my window, and sticking to my Palais-Royal like a periwinkle to its shell; they have suspected that some enlightened love attached me to it ... They showed little understanding, or a poor understanding, of me. I feel no reverence as I tread the soil which nurtured the Revolution, ... and the additional ghosts of the Regent and Camille Desmoulins are pale, when I recall that Marguerite Moreno lived in the rue de Valois with Marcel Schwob, and that, under the clipped elm-trees, Edmond Jaloux and Jean-Louis Vaudoyer savoured a delight like my own. I remember that Giraudoux, that casual stroller, used to raise his arm and point out my window, and tell his dog: 'Say good-morning to Madame Colette!' ...

'Have you found another province?' people ask me. God be thanked, provincial Paris will never be wanting for its Parisian lovers. They know how to discover it and, if need be, how to create it.[15]

The year 1949 saw the publication of *Le Fanal bleu*. The book of reminiscences and reflections took its title from the lamp that hung over Colette's divan; and this blue lamp, which kept her company during the long hours of sleeplessness, the lamp which shone on endless manuscripts, had long since become a symbol. To those who saw it from outside, it symbolised the continuation of French literature and, indeed, of the French genius; it was a symbol, too, of endurance.

While I await the day when I no longer move, I hardly move ...
 I rock at anchor, under the blue ship's lantern ... I make less and less distinction between the hours of night and the hours of day, the hour of reading, writing, looking, all of them are good ... The hour of surmising, of remembering ... Soon I shall finally confuse the hour of work and the hour of conjecture ...[16]

Sometimes she would ring for Pauline. 'Pauline, I must work. Give me some paper.'
 'Madame would do better to rest. Why must Madame write?'
 'Because it's my profession, Pauline.'[17]
 Colette had long ceased to keep animals in the rue de Beaujolais, for she could no longer look after them; she kept only one living creature, which was fire.[18] At night, the fire died down, and she was left to sleep – or to lie awake.

It's not more than three o'clock. Nothing is growing pale yet over the roofs. Since there is one lantern for every pillar, I could count the arcades of the Palais-Royal. The house is so peaceful that I can't hear anyone sleeping here, but the fall of the tongs in my fireplace would ruin the uneasy sleep of the man who sleeps two doors away ...
 Writing leads only to writing. I shall write on, with humility. There is no other destiny for me.[19]

'As for Maurice,' wrote Colette to Natalie Barney, on 18 January 1950, ' ... he is a man I should have adopted twenty years earlier ...; but then we should have been scandalous, perhaps.'[20] ('People have believed that she liked scandal,' wrote Maurice, mildly. 'She simply had her own ideas about what is scandalous, what is honourable or not.'[21]) Twenty-five years after she had met him,

Maurice remained the best friend, the perfect companion. He edited her works, he kept unwanted visitors at bay, and he treated her, she said, as if she were spun glass. They were, he wrote, united as few couples had been. 'Every moment that we lived together was a moment of plenitude and silent joy.'[22] When Cocteau paid tribute to Colette, he did not forget 'to salute the admirable and adorable man'.[23]

Cocteau was later to recall a visit to Colette, in her last years:

Let us go back to the Palais-Royal where Madame Colette, in bed, received us.

A little wooden bridge served her as a desk. Under this bridge she seemed to flow motionless, like certain rivers. The current was made of bedclothes, shawls, and the billows of the legs which she didn't know where to put to ease the pain. Day after day, ... I saw Madame Colette flow gently towards her death, under this little bridge on which, as on the Rialto or the bridge in Florence, there was a pile of graceful disorder. Fruit, flowers, a bunch of fountain-pens and a mountain of old scribbled-on paper in which she was lost, seeking in vain for what she wanted to show us ...

Her spirit was constantly alive, and her curiosity about everything, great and small, knew no rest at all. 'Oh, Maurice, look!' we heard her exclaim about a plant or insect.

The truth is that this plant or insect often managed to take first place ... And I don't know whether, if Goethe or Shakespeare had suddenly reappeared, they would have distracted Madame Colette from a spider in process of spinning its web ...[24]

On 7 April 1950 the Académie-Goncourt made a pilgrimage to the Goncourts' tomb at the Cimetière Montmartre; Colette regretted bitterly that she was too disabled to attend.[25] In mid May she and Maurice arrived at the Hôtel de Paris, Monte-Carlo, where they were to stay for two months. Colette had no illusions, now, about the permanence of her arthritis, but to please Maurice she had agreed to undergo yet another course of treatment. Every year, now, they were to pay a visit to Monte-Carlo. She could no longer travel, except by air, and her journeys demanded careful organisation. Her arrival was always announced at the airport at Nice, where journalists and flowers were waiting for her. On one occasion the Mayor of Nice, Monsieur Médecin, was there to welcome her. 'I am Médecin,' he explained. 'Thank you, doctor,' replied Colette, 'but I am not ill at the moment.'[26]

For five years she and Maurice had the same ground-floor apartment at the Hôtel de Paris; it looked over a garden where she could spend the days in the sunshine. She came in time to feel the tinsel charm of Monte-Carlo, the theatrical attraction of the Hôtel de Paris, its florid gilt decorations, its hall which was always full of bored millionaires and exotic Highnesses. It was to her the stuff of fiction.

It was in this hall, in the summer of 1950, that she made a discovery. Anita Loos was best known as the author of *Gentlemen Prefer Blondes*. During the 1930s and 1940s she had also written a number of screen-plays for Metro-Goldwyn-Mayer. She had now adapted *Gigi* for the stage, and she and her producer were desperately seeking a young actress for the title-rôle.

In Monte-Carlo itself, they were making a film, *Rendez-vous à Monte-Carlo*. Some of the scenes were being shot in the hotel as Colette arrived. A vivacious young English actress was speaking half in English, half in French. Colette turned to Maurice. 'That's our Gigi for America.' Audrey Hepburn had been discovered.[27]

On 18 July Colette returned, with Maurice, to the rue de Beaujolais; and here in September the English critic and francophile, Raymond Mortimer, came to see her. He was to be the general editor of an English edition of her works. Secker & Warburg, in London, hoped to bring out the first translated volume in June 1951. Raymond Mortimer found Colette 'invariably spirited. I wish, indeed,' he wrote, 'that more among the writers who enjoy excellent health could display anything approaching her gaiety and gusto.'[28] He explained that 'in France Madame Colette is accepted as a national glory, something to enjoy as well as to be proud of, like Chambertin or the Luxembourg Gardens or the Provençal spring. In the English-speaking countries she is very little known, except to those who like reading French ...'[29] This, indeed, was hardly surprising.

Her style [he continued] is an instrument most elaborately fashioned to reveal her temperament. Her immense prestige comes indeed largely from the quality of her prose, which is rich, flawless, intricate, audacious and utterly individual.

Her vocabulary is enormous ... From her imagination images rush profusely forth like bees from a hive, pollen from poplars, smoke from a cigarette, nudes from the staircase of the Moulin Rouge, platitudes from statesmen or paintings from Picasso. She can foreshorten the French language as boldly as Mallarmé; she has it trained to obey her caprices like a pony in a circus. All of which is a perpetual feast to the reader, a chronic headache to the translator ...[30]

However, she was now to reach a wider Anglo-Saxon audience. She was not only to be read in official translation. The American stage version of *Gigi*, that intensely Parisian short story, was first produced by Gilbert Miller at the Fulton Theatre, New York, on 24 November 1950. Audrey Hepburn took the leading part.

It was about now that a future biographer saw Colette herself as she left a Paris theatre,

after one of the last performances she had been able to attend (thanks to an invalid's chair) ... Conscious of the curiosity she aroused, she held her head very erect, so as not to meet people's gaze. From the side, I could see only a pointed chin and the extraordinary wild mop of hair like a magpie's nest that concealed a third of her face. For an instant I caught the gleam of her grey eye [*sic*] beneath the heavily made-up eyelid, and saw the dark patches of age, like mittens, that covered the still plump hands gripping the arm-rests of the chair. She looked like some strange ship's effigy, watching the waters close over her wake, as she neared the end of her life's voyage.[31]

It was in 1950 that Colette published another book of portraits and landscapes, *En Pays connu*. Chief among the familiar landscapes was Saint-Sauveur. 'Forty-five years of Paris,' so she confessed, 'haven't made me anything but a provincial, searching twenty *arrondissements* and two river banks for her lost province.'[32] She had found it at last; and she wrote touchingly, once again, of the Palais-Royal and its familiars. In the second part of the book, she collected her reminiscences of Debussy and Proust, of Anna de

Noailles and Sarah Bernhardt, and, from the distant days of her marriage to Willy, her recollections of Polaire. She added fifty pages or so of her *Journal intermittent*, brief impressions which covered nearly twenty years. *En Pays connu* is a 'made' book by an author who was old, now, and devoid of creative power.

━━━

On 13 March 1951 Paul Léautaud noted sharply: 'Colette, her books and her theatre, are commercial literature. There is only one great writer today, and that is François Mauriac.'[33] Presumably Léautaud was thinking only of French literature. Even so, his comment was debatable. That year a special issue of the magazine *Le Point* was devoted to Colette: to photographs of her, from childhood to prestigious old age, and to a number of tributes to her work. Among them was a tribute from Gide: 'I know few works which, in our day, have brought me such perfect and such amused delight.'[34]

Yet perhaps the most eloquent contribution to *Le Point* was the article 'Colette classique'.

What [enquired Claude Roy] is a classic? It's Colette ... Indeed perhaps Colette is the only classic writer of our time. The vague instinct of the public has made Madame Colette into a kind of national institution ... And the public is not mistaken. It has recognised in the author of *La Naissance du jour* all the features which make the true classic.

First and foremost among them: indifference as to whether one is a classic or not ...

Colette has the natural feeling of her perfection, and never does she cross the frontiers of the land where she is sovereign. She is almost the only writer who has never appreciated general ideas, or touched on politics, or toyed with philosophy.

When we have shut Colette's books, what remains to us? More than characters, more than places, actions, ideas, a morality or an anecdote, there remains Colette. Her readers are not mistaken. Colette is the writer who receives the most letters, the most *personal messages* ... She sees herself transformed into a sort of agony columnist, to whom *midinettes* and old ladies, young men and married women address their confidences, their requests and their cases of conscience ... One always wants to write to Virgil, Cervantes, Benjamin Constant, Stendhal or

Proust, to know *what they would do in our place*. The classics ... are those from whom one expects practical answers, particular directions and responses. Every classical work is read like a letter, a letter addressed to humanity.[35]

・──・

Colette herself was now clearly failing. On 19 March she had confessed to Claude Farrère: 'I've been out – an hour in a car – once in eighty days. Evidently I'd prefer not to suffer, or to suffer less. But my window faces south, over the Garden, towards the sun, have I the right to complain? And then I've married a saint.'[36]

That spring, again, Maurice took his wife to Monte-Carlo.

Huddled up in her wheelchair [wrote the novelist Henri Troyat], her triangular face under a froth of chestnut hair, her mouth mobile, her hands free, playful, Colette makes her entrance into the flower-decked salon of a big hotel in Monaco. There is a murmur of deferential curiosity. She recognises friends among the people and the things around her. It is with the same nod of the head that she greets a hoary-headed admirer, bent under the weight of memories, and a spray of lilies blooming in a vase ... By the virtue of her presence, as once by the virtue of her style, this old lady, imprisoned in her chair, reveals to the youngest among us the tastes, the smells, the colours and the music of a world in which, however, she no longer moves, except with difficulty. On the threshold of rest, she teaches us the devouring love of life.[37]

She and Maurice stayed in Monte-Carlo until early in July; and then, in order to avoid August in Paris, they went to the Hôtel Trianon at Versailles. Finally, without regret, they returned to the rue de Beaujolais. On 3 November, Colette invited Henri Mondor, the surgeon and expert on Mallarmé, to lunch. 'If you are not ashamed of my stretcher, oh! let's go down to my neighbour Véfour's, any day you like ...'[38] She kept her irrepressible love of life; she fought against her rapid and undeniable decline.

・──・

The new year, 1952, brought a documentary film about her. She attended the first performance in a wheelchair, and she clearly looked her seventy-nine years. But she had lost none of her spirit. 'What a wonderful life I've had!' she sighed, when the film was over. 'A pity I didn't realise it sooner!'[39] March found her, once again, with Maurice, at the Hôtel de Paris. On 6 March she 'talked a long time to Prince Pierre of Monaco about Marguerite.'[40]

The Prince came of a family which Colette knew well: the Polignacs, who could trace their ancestry back to the ninth century. Comte Pierre de Polignac had become Prince of Monaco on his marriage to the hereditary Princess Charlotte. He was the father of Prince Rainier; and in 1950, when Prince Rainier had become sovereign Prince of Monaco, Colette had recalled affectionately how his father had brought him to her bedside: 'a young lieutenant in the Armée des Vosges, adorned with a very ancient name and with a glory which he had just acquired.'[41] The shy young man and the shy and ageing woman had understood each other at once. Prince Rainier had happily returned to the rue de Beaujolais; and photographs show him in his principality, leaning attentively over her wheelchair, engrossed in conversation.

His parents had been important patrons of the Ballets Russes. In 1950 his father had become the president of the new Conseil littéraire de la principauté de Monaco; this had been established to award the annual Prix Rainier III. The prize was given every spring to a French writer, or to a foreigner writing in French, for the whole corpus of his work. As president of the Académie-Goncourt, Colette was honorary president of the council; and with her sat four of her fellow Academicians: André Billy, Roland Dorgelès, Gérard Bauer and Philippe Hériat. The five of them represented at the palace in Monaco the successors of Edmond de Goncourt, who had been the friend of Princess Mathilde.[42]

On 12 May, back in Paris, Colette had a visit from an English novelist. Kathleen Farrell was amazed by her still vigorous love of life, her pride in her appearance, her femininity. Colette was clearly satisfied with the photographs of herself in *Le Point*; she inscribed a copy for her visitor: 'To show her that there was a time – though distant! – when I was a pretty girl.' She asked to be kissed goodbye, and she seems to have been disappointed by the conventional kiss on both cheeks. 'Ah!' she muttered. 'Ces anglaises!'[43]

Another visitor that year was Glenway Wescott. He had met

Colette on her honeymoon in New York in 1935. Now he called on Cocteau, her neighbour in the Palais-Royal.

> He told me [recorded Wescott] that it had been one of her most dolorous weeks; her arthritis clamping down tight and chiselling away at her. In spite of which, he thought, surely she would receive me, especially if he telephoned and asked her ...
> Later in the week I found Anita Loos, the dramatiser of *Gigi* ... 'Don't write,' was her advice. 'M. Goudeket, the guardian husband, will think it his duty to ward you off. Just take a chance, ring the doorbell. At least you will see him, or you will see Pauline, the perfect servant. They're both worth seeing.'
> But I could not imagine myself standing all unannounced on their doorstep, nor think of any suitable initial utterance to the doorkeeper. Then I recalled the fact that when my young friend Patrick O'Higgins wanted to get in and take photographs of her, he armed himself with roses ... I sought out the major florist near the Palais-Royal, and asked if they knew which size and shape and shade and redolence of rose Mme Colette favoured. They knew exactly; I forget its name; it had a stout but inflexible stem, and petals wine-red on the inside, brownish on the outside ...[44]

Bravely, he went to the rue de Beaujolais, and handed the roses to Pauline. Standing by the door, he heard:

> 'What is it, Pauline? Who is it, Pauline? But no, but no, not that vase, not for roses. Oh, they're magnificent, aren't they? So long-legged and in such quantity! Leave them here on my bed, for the moment.'

Though the farthest thing in the world from a young voice, it had a sound of unabated femininity.[45]

Eventually he saw Colette; and,

> I have never seen a woman of any age so impeccable and immaculate and [so to speak] gleaming ... There was evidence of pain in her face but not the least suggestion of illness. What came uppermost in my mind at the sight of her was just rejoicing. Oh, oh, I said to myself, she is not going to die for a long while! ...
> 'Have you read *Le Pur et l'impur*?' she asked. 'I happened to read it myself the other day, and I took pride in it. I believe it to be my best book ... I am no thinker, I have no *pensées* ... Perhaps the most praiseworthy thing about me is that I have known how to write like a woman ...'[46]

The effect of the roses had been magical.

Colette, who always felt the cold, was now unable to bear the heat; and she was not inclined to spend the summer in the South of France. In this summer of 1952 Maurice took her to Deauville, wheeled her round in her invalid chair, took her to the cinema and even to the beach. She was usually lighthearted, but at times she was overcome by lassitude; and, when it was time to return to the Palais-Royal, she had no regrets. That was her real home, it was there that she surrounded herself with her permanent symbols and enchantments.

It was there, this autumn, that she received an apprehensive visit from a biographer, Margaret Crosland.

We discussed, not literature, not novels or plays, but knitting and crochet [wrote Miss Crosland, with evident surprise] ... We talked about food, and Colette told me how, when she was young, a bowl of *lait caillé* was kept in farmhouse kitchens and every visitor was expected to drink from it ...

Colette herself is a revelation. Her deeply emotional voice and her eyes are an indescribable mixture of vitality and sadness. The face is still recognisable as that piquant triangle of the Sem poster drawn when Colette Willy went on tour for Baret ...

There is talk in Paris that Colette had been so frightened of growing old that she has had injections of so-called rejuvenation serums and that she wears too much make-up and looks artificial. The only make-up she was wearing on this occasion was the blue eye-shadow skilfully giving value to her extraordinary eyes. After we had talked for some time she suddenly picked up a hand mirror from the table and was horrified that she had forgotten to put any rouge on. She seemed to think it might be impolite ...

After seeing and talking to Colette it is possible to understand something of the perpetual ecstasy of all French writing about her.[47]

'Colette,' said Maurice, 'c'est un phénomène.'[48] She herself returned the compliment. Writing to Lucie Saglio, she said: 'I have been bedridden for years, that is the truest thing about my life, with a *prodigious* person, Maurice, and Pauline.'[49]

Early in October, to her old and much respected friend, André Billy, she confessed that she was very ill; but she was learning to suffer honourably. She was also learning not to forget her friends, and she begged him to come and see her.[50] She had a particular affection for the Académie-Goncourt, '*mes petits* Goncourt', and André Billy was not the only member to return it. Sometimes the whole Academy assembled round her bed, and literature took second place while she delighted in their company.[51]

Gérard Bauer, who had known her in the days of Willy, was now one of her *petits* Goncourt. In *Rendez-vous avec Paris* he described his visit to her.

The door opens into the room which is hung with a thick red paper, red with the warmth of old bordeaux. At first you see these rich surroundings, then, sparkling on the marble mantelpiece, crystals and multicoloured glass balls; and in front of the window, stretched out on a divan bed fitted up with a small table, Colette, whose glance still burns with the old brilliance ...

The welcome contains affection, modesty, that coquetry which age converts into dignity and elegance. Without it, what should we become with the years? Immobile on this bed where she now spends most of her days, Colette keeps the same curiosity, the same lucid surveillance of people and of herself. The same as in her beginnings in literature, the woman whom I already saw, more than forty years ago, at our first meeting. It was at *L'Écho de Paris* ... She already had that triangular face whose obstinate bone structure has not moved under the pressure of the years, those silent eyes which have not ceased to fix on life their 'undeceivable' gaze. The years have passed, and they have made a woman of our time into a writer of all time.

When you are a friend, Colette talks to you about yourself, not about herself at all. She makes her confidences in her work; not in the exchanges of friendship. This modesty in which perhaps there enters a little peasant prudence has assumed with physical trial the force of a secret courage. It is hard to suffer as soon as one moves when one has so loved movement and everything which stirred under the sun, when one has restored an animal suppleness to the most weary words, and has aroused so many invisible spirits.

'You see,' she said, 'this is my world now; but it is enough for me!'

Through her window she pointed out the garden of the Palais-Royal. It might be a square without traffic, just as the *Piazza* in Venice is a square animated by passers-by, if a strange abandonment had not weighed on this space for the past century. Winter deadens it still further, gives it the languor of a park, with its anonymous statues and echoing galleries. But the spring reanimates these gardens with the cries of children and birds during the day, and of dogs and cats at night ... Swallows announce the summer, cross a sky without vibrations, and Colette may then think of everything that she has caught, that she has held under her glance and in her hand ...

I have known Claudine. I find her again in this face which speaks to me, in this shock of hair which is hardly grey, in the rather singing tone of the voice, sometimes mocking to feign surprise. But the pantheism of youth has turned into a grave acceptance of life, a profound dignity which always knows how to lavish the delicacies of friendship.[52]

Fauchier-Magnan, who had also known her for many years, still used to visit her in the rue de Beaujolais.

I have spent long hours at the foot of that divan where she was bound for so long by arthritis in the hip, an unrelenting pain which she bore with unheard-of courage, without complaint. Only a contraction of the face suggested that, at times, the pain became more acute. At about six o'clock, free from her daily task, Colette allowed you to visit her. I used to find her then in front of a writing-table which was laid across her knees, a table cluttered with sheets of blue paper covered with her fine clear handwriting and thick with crossings-out; for her incomparable style, which seemed to involve no effort, no hesitation, was the product of a painful birth. She loved and respected the French language, and she wrote it with a conscientiousness which allowed no concession. I remember that, one day, she pushed away the pages which she had just written, and sighed: 'And to think that, tomorrow, I may tear it all up!'[53]

She was acutely conscious of her style, and she was determined not to write to a formula, *faire du Colette*.[54]

Her conversation [wrote Fauchier-Magnan] was completely natural, and it showed that earthy commonsense which, like her accent, she owed to her Burgundian origins. Above all, she had ingenious opinions of her own, she was inquisitive about everything, she knew no conventions and no prejudices. I used to linger with her as long as possible, in the spring, as evening fell, in winter in the light of the blue lantern.[55]

There, among the glass paperweights with coloured snow whirling inside them, the knick-knacks which she lovingly collected,

Colette – 'an elderly and uncamouflaged Ceres'[56] – would herself prepare a big bowl of mulled wine, scented with cinnamon, on cold winter days. She had a new exotic enchantment. Mme Gaston Fournier, who had recently died, had given her some of her cases of butterflies. Colette delighted in their gouache wings.

Claude Gregory, who interviewed her in 1952, was amazed by her charisma. 'She is seventy-nine, and what struck me is the wonderful beauty of her face framed in a grey vapour. Not the beauty of an old woman who has remained very much alive, but simply that of a woman who revels in contact with everything, feels it within her, expresses its abundance and plentitude in her own features.'[57]

She was still vigorous in mind.

On my last visit to her [remembered Renaud de Jouvenel], I brought some Algerian flowers, called *strelitzia*, which brought back to her the smell and light of an African garden: she remembered what she had once told me, that the Ouled-Naïl dancers imitate with their fingers the shape of this flower and she tried to do so but could not as her hands were cramped with arthritis ...

During those long years of ceaseless physical pain, you might have seen her on her couch, sometimes with an apple or a shell in her hands, restoring to her the fullness of the orchard or of the sea which she would never gaze upon any more. Her gentle and attentive last husband would comfort her with these humble messengers from her true land: they meant far more to her than any praise of her work.[58]

VI

'In a few days,' wrote Colette to Pierre Moreno, on 9 January 1953, 'my fellow-writers want to celebrate (?) my eightieth birthday. I should indeed have embraced you all! Don't forget to send me another photo of Marguerite, the one I have never leaves me.'[1]

She had her moments of melancholy. Yet, even now, she had zest, and she fought her unremitting pain with unremitting courage. 'I can't walk. But I fly,' she told Henri Mondor a few days later. 'First into your arms. Then every day over my garden. Have no fears for me. I suffer and I discover, little by little, how to lessen physical suffering.'[2] She was increasingly hard of hearing. The world of sensations was closing about her. She hardly ever left her room; but it had become her private paradise, where everything remained for her a symbol and a perpetual wonder.

On 28 January she was eighty years old. Pierre Brisson hailed her in *Le Figaro*:

> Made contemplative by nature, she has installed herself by her window on what she calls her raft, a sort of corolla of a throne, padded with cushions, from which she emerges, like some Buddhist deity endowed, by miracle, with a Burgundian accent.
>
> Collecting, hour by hour, the sounds of the *quartier*, the differences in the days and seasons, watching her old friends the trees in the Palais-Royal, breathing in people and their adventures, the confidante of the shopkeeper on the corner, the charwoman on the third floor, the unhappy love-affairs of the bookseller's daughter, she remains closely bound to this provincial world which, immediately, becomes the world of Colette...
>
> In feminine literature, Colette, we owe you a ferment and a sap which had previously been unknown. The activities of the mind have scarcely concerned you. The activities of life have impassioned you, and they will impassion you till you draw your final breath.[3]

The literary weeklies fêted Colette with photographs of herself and with facsimiles of letters which had once been addressed to her by Gide and by Proust. Claudel and Valéry, Francis Carco and Pierre Fresnay published tributes to her; so did Mauriac and Anouilh, Rebecca West and Rosamond Lehmann. Intimate letters from Sido, written fifty years ago, were published for the first time, and also, reported Janet Flanner, 'like a third link in the female line of family sensibility, a paragraph from Colette's daughter, which terminates by quoting Saint Louis the King: "Merci, Mon Dieu, de m'avoir prêté Madame Ma Mère."'[4] One of the most disarming tributes was paid by the Académie-Goncourt. They arranged with the restaurant Drouant to hold their monthly luncheon at the rue de Beaujolais. There was even a presidential birthday cake with the requisite number of candles.[5] 'You are just a so-and-so,' Colette announced happily to her old friend Georges Wague, 'and I am a gracious young girl of 80.'[6] 'Eighty years old?' she added, on reflection. 'Of course I'm not eighty. I am twenty years old, four times over.'[7]

Among the letters of congratulation was one from Lucie Saglio. Early in February Colette replied to it.

How happy I am to have your letter! Dear Lucie, ... the strange thing is that, though I have been immobilised for so long, this letter only tells you of my departure, which I hope for and fear. Maurice has organised it for next Saturday. By air, that's all that's possible. Destination: Monte-Carlo; purpose: rest, and as much isolation as possible. But isolation with Maurice is never solitude. What a companion chance gave me there! ...

I shall write to you from Monte-Carlo, if I arrive there.[8]

When they reached the Hôtel de Paris, everyone in the foyer rose to greet her. 'Oh, look, Maurice!' exclaimed Colette. 'They remember me from last year!' Maurice was touched and amazed by her innocence.[9] Cocteau, recounting the same story, observed that 'Madame Colette was quite aware of the act which the politeness of kings inflicts upon them ... But it was her politeness to pretend, her way of avoiding the haughtiness of the parvenus of glory, never to display her wealth or the privileges of her rank.'[10]

On 19 February, during this visit to Monte-Carlo, Daisy Fellowes gave a luncheon for her. The only guests – other than Maurice – were James Lees-Milne, the English historian and man of letters, and his wife Alvilde, who had been a friend of Winnie de Polignac. Lees-Milne recorded:

We met Daisy in the hall of the Hôtel de Paris, went to the bar and were joined by Colette's husband, a nice, kind, attentive man of about 58 [Maurice was in fact 64]. Then Colette was wheeled up in a chair. There were no other guests. There was a procession to the dining-room, and as we followed the chair there was a wash of heads turned in our direction and a ripple of comments. I sat on her right. Under a fuzz of thin, greyish hair she has an oval, piquante little face: very pretty. Large eyes, expressive and beautiful and mascara'd. The skin round the right eye bruised black like a 'black eye' caused by a blow. Neatly shaped little nose; plump, expressive, pretty hands, ... and two large amethyst rings on the little and next finger of the left hand. She wore a blue blouse on which was pinned the new order she was awarded today, and over it a pretty deep blue coatee with a gold braid and blue-embroidered border.

Daisy was absolutely wonderful with her, for she told fanciful little stories to her and laughed in the most affectionate way about the things she chose to eat; and she pandered to her every whim. The luncheon ordered was exquisite, but Colette ordered china tea, then cheese. She is very frail and touchingly childlike, yet sharp still, and came out with pertinent little phrases and rather poetic expressions in a deep Burgundian voice. Her speech, like her style of writing, is clipped, economical and exact. She took a long time to warm up to conversation, and even so conversation did not exactly flow. She kept interrupting us with little bird-like cries of complaint about the spoon, or the salt, while looking bewildered and muddled ... She talked of fish and the superior intelligence of the pike. Her mother, she said, had a tortoise called Charlotte, which slept throughout the winter. There came a day every year when she heard her mother call out: 'Charlotte s'éveille. C'est le printemps!'

Colette reminded me of Gertie Millar when I met her staying with Patsy Ward. The same piquancy, candour, lack of society nonsense, gaiety, generosity – in fact the old music-hall qualities. Like someone left behind in an empty ball-room, someone to whom the silenced echoes of outdated music and song are still clinging. The ghost in fact from a departed époque more idyllic, more earthy even than our own.

It was rather touching to watch Willy Maugham, who was lunching nearby, come up to her and embrace her while she stroked his arm. Quite a flirtation took place between the two octogenarian novelists.[11]

It was now some thirty years since the end of her love-affair with Bertrand de Jouvenel; but the novel which it had inspired had at last reached the screen. The première of the film *Le Blé en herbe* took place in January 1954, in aid of the Caisse de Solidarité des Étudiants. Colette herself addressed a message to the assembled students. It was recorded at the rue de Beaujolais, and it was presented as an introduction to the film.

Throughout my existence [she said], I have studied flowering more than any other manifestation of life. It is there, for me, that the essential drama resides, and not in death which is just a banal defeat ...

Everything that surprised me when I was young surprises me much more today. There is never a time when discoveries end. The world is new to me when I wake each morning, and I shall only cease to flower when I cease to live.[12]

Her zest for life was unquenchable. On 22 February, adapted by Colette and Anita Loos, *Gigi* was first performed at the Théâtre des

Arts in Paris. The performance was televised, and in the interval there was a conversation between four members of the Académie-Goncourt, in the audience, and Colette, in the rue de Beaujolais.

My first three colleagues [remembered Philippe Hériat], talked with animation about this technical miracle. Colette herself did not seem captivated by a conversation in which the actual presence was lacking. Then the fourth Academician spoke, with less enthusiasm. He simply said that, if the evening had been a success, it was because one of Colette's great secrets had passed from her book into the play, and on to the stage, it was because one felt there the love of love. At that moment the image of Colette returned to the screen. The fine, wild, greying head was now erect, the eyes were sparkling with intelligence.

'Let me take up the word which you have just used,' said Colette. 'Love ... Love has never been a question of age. I shall never be old enough to forget love, and to stop thinking about it, and talking about it.'[13]

Every year, just after Easter, Colette and her colleagues used to go to Monte-Carlo to award the Prix du Prince. The principality used to put up the judges at the Hôtel de Paris. As soon as the choice had been made, remembered André Maurois, now a judge, it was the custom to telephone the winner, tell him that he had won his million francs, and ask him to fly to Monaco at once. On Palm Sunday, 11 April 1954, Maurois noted with regret that the annual meeting was ending. He added: 'At the Prince's I lunched beside Colette, whose beautiful eyes were tired but charming. "At my age," she said, "pleasure consists in not working." '[14] It was not simply a *boutade*. She was very tired. Maurois wrote later: 'Of those last days when I saw Colette so often at Monte-Carlo, I have kept a tender and touching memory. Her eyes, already strangely veiled, seemed to look, beyond us, at another world. But, as a traveller whose ship is moving out of harbour makes scarcely visible signs to the friends still standing on the quayside, she struggled to show us, smiling, more affectionate than ever, that she loved us and understood our emotion. It was delicate and it was devastating.'[15]

Just after her eightieth birthday, in spite of criticism from clerical quarters, and from the more orthodox establishment, Colette had been promoted to the highest rank which a woman had reached in the Légion-d'honneur. The Minister of National Education had presented her with the star of Grand Officier. The City of Paris had awarded her its Médaille d'Or; the American Ambassador had brought her the diploma of the National Institute of Art and Letters. Had she lived longer, thought Maurice, she would have had the Nobel Prize for Literature.[16]

She bore her burden of honours bravely. She was now incapable of moving, except to hoist herself by her arms from her divan to her wheel-chair.[17] Her writing, which had been so clear and so emphatic, betrayed her lassitude. She became vague about recent events, increasingly aware of the past. Early in June she found an old photograph taken of her school at Saint-Sauveur. It showed her among some thirty little girls, and she named them all without hesitation.

Gradually she became more silent. On two occasions Maurice took her out for a drive, but she came home exhausted. After May she kept to her apartment. Towards the end of June her weariness became more pronounced. She ceased to read the papers, she hardly opened her letters, and she very often slept. On about 20 July Maurice, Bel-Gazou and Pauline began a vigil whose issue was no longer in doubt.

On 2 August it was warm and overcast; the swallows flew chattering past the open windows. Colette gestured vaguely towards them and towards her cases of iridescent butterflies. She spoke for the last time: 'Regarde, Maurice! Regarde!'[18]

On the afternoon of Tuesday, 3 August, the temperature in Paris soared to 93°. Colette, her eyes half-closed, was lost in silent conversation: a clearly articulate conversation which was no longer addressed to those around her. She was radiant; and Maurice, who understood her every shade of feeling, divined that she had returned to the garden at Saint-Sauveur.[19] She had returned to her childhood, and regained her paradise: the paradise she had never really lost. Colette was talking to Sido, whom she had found again at last.

She died without pain, from cardiac arrest, at about half-past eight that evening. Her eyelids closed, wrote Gérard Bauer, 'over that undeceivable gaze'.[20]

Cocteau – who had had a heart attack – was convalescing at Cap Ferrat. He heard of her death the following afternoon. 'It is for me a family bereavement,' so he said. 'One cannot speak of the passing of someone so dear, someone who touches you so closely. I am too sad and too unhappy to say anything else. I used to see her every day. I feel as if I had lost my sister or my mother.'[21] Émile Henriot, the novelist and critic, declared that, alone among women writers, Colette could be set beside Proust and Claudel, Gide and Valéry.[22] André Billy said simply: 'She was the greatest writer of French prose of her day.'[23]

On 4 August a procession of friends came to pay their visits of condolence: Jean Berthoin, the Minister of National Education, André Dubois, the Prefect of Police, Julien Cain, Administrator-General of the Bibliothèque Nationale, the members of the Académie-Goncourt. Many unknown Parisians arrived with a bunch of flowers, to be received by Pauline. Colette had instructed her, firmly, in a moment of coquetry: 'People mustn't see me when I've died, you'll make sure of that, won't you? I don't want it.'[24] Yet, whatever her instructions, some were apparently allowed to see her after death. Pierre Mazars recorded in *Le Figaro littéraire*:

Pauline, the housekeeper, the confidante, is very red-eyed. She opens the door of the room. The shutters are closed, the window is half open and lets in the rustle of wings of the sparrows in the Palais-Royal. On the red bed, the bed where Colette used to read, and where she wrote, the head is leaning a little to one side. The black anthracite brilliance of the eyes is extinguished. There is a glitter on the black dress: the star of Grand-Officier de la Légion-d'honneur.[25]

There were more than five hundred telegrams of condolence. The death of Colette was the most significant literary loss in France since the death of Gide. Pierre Brisson, the editor of *Le Figaro*, wrote on the front page of that ultra-Catholic daily: 'There was something androgynous about her; she was masculine in her initiative and authority, and she was a woman by her intuition and assent; she was both vigorous and a dreamer.'[26] Germaine Beaumont recalled in *Les Nouvelles littéraires*: 'How alive she was! So alive that she made other people seem moribund.'²⁷ Louis Aragon wrote Colette a poem of farewell.²⁸

Colette was the first Frenchwoman to be given a State funeral. On Saturday, 11 August, a catafalque was set up in the *cour-d'honneur* of the Palais-Royal, and from 8.30 to 10 o'clock the public were allowed to file past. The oppressive heat of the previous days ended suddenly that morning. A wind, in the courtyard, gave a fluttering life to the great tricolour folds which draped the catafalque. Marlene Dietrich, who was present, assured Jean Cocteau (who was too unwell to attend) that the flag seemed to live and breathe as it enveloped the coffin.²⁹ Graham Greene, who had never known Colette, was in the crowd.³⁰

At half-past seven [wrote Philippe Hériat] a queue began to form in the rue Montpensier. It had been announced that the public would file past from half-past eight, they had to open the passage at quarter past ... Even the intimates of Colette, familiar with her glory, could only be astonished by this affluence, imposing, silent and extraordinary in its dignity. Valéry's funeral had been fine, but academic and hardly democratic in its pomp; Jouvet's funeral had been accompanied by jostling, by autograph books held out to the stars. This time it was Paris. Paris was in mourning for Colette.³¹

Janet Flanner reported:

Her glittering cross of a Grand Officer of the Legion of Honor and its scarlet ribbon were attached to a black velvet pillow that leaned against the coffin. Facing the catafalque sat her daughter, Mme Colette de Jouvenel; Pauline, her faithful maid for a quarter of a century [*sic*]; and her last husband, Maurice Goudeket. Facing them were members of the Goncourt Academy and other French notables. Across the court stretched a hedge of floral offerings with pale-blue and dark-blue gladioli predominant. (Blue was her favorite color, and she always wrote on blue paper.) There was a wreath from the French Parliament; one from the city of Lyons and its mayor, Édouard Herriot, an old friend of hers; a garland of roses with ribbons of the Belgian colors, marked 'Élisabeth', from the King's grandmother; a huge sheaf of lilies from the Association des Music-Halls et Cirques, since in her difficult young days she was a music-hall dancer and mime; and a big country bouquet of dahlias from her 'Compatriotes de Saint-Sauveur-en-Puisaye.'³²

The Minister of National Education, who spoke on behalf of the French Government, called her 'pagan, sensuous, Dionysiac'; Roland Dorgelès paid the affectionate homage of the Académie-Goncourt. Luc Hommel, permanent secretary of the Académie royale de Belgique, delivered a tribute on behalf of his colleagues. The President of the French Republic was represented by M. Friel, directeur du cabinet; Prince Pierre of Monaco had returned from Switzerland to attend the funeral. Military honours were accorded to Colette, as a Grand-Officier de la Légion-d'honneur.[33]

Colette's State funeral was the highest posthumous tribute that could be paid to a French citizen; it also emphasised the division between Church and State. Maurice Goudeket and Colette de Jouvenel had asked for a funeral service to be held at the Église Saint-Roch. This was refused by Cardinal Feltin, Archbishop of Paris, on the grounds that Colette had been twice divorced. Renaud de Jouvenel considered that the request itself had been 'a monumental gaffe. It is in bad taste to ask for a religious funeral for someone who has always lived outside the Church.'[34] Yet such was the intensity of public feeling at this refusal that Graham Greene admonished the Archbishop in an open letter on the front page of *Le Figaro littéraire*. 'To non-Catholics it could seem that the Church itself lacked charity ... Of course, upon reflection, Catholics can decide that the voice of an archbishop is not necessarily the voice of the Church ...'[35]

There was no religious ceremony. Colette was buried in the most absolute privacy in the cemetery of Père-Lachaise. The social and moral order for which she had shown a sceptical indulgence had had to wait until she was dead to take its revenge.

It was the absent Cocteau who sensed the atmosphere of the burial. 'It was not a question of funeral rites, but rather of gardeners digging, of the passing from one reign to another, of earth and flesh in collaboration.'[36] As Colette herself had written: 'Winter no more has an end than spring has a beginning, and the earth does not know either death or rest.'[37]

EPILOGUE

Claudine was one of those characters who exceed the bounds of their particular books and become a recognised type. Unmistakable in her appearance, unorthodox in her emotions and in her sexual behaviour, she had represented the emancipated woman of the turn of the century. In the first book she wrote, Colette had created a character who belonged to a definite moment in history; the sequels to *Claudine à l'école* established the heroine as a woman who voiced the troubled attitudes and the aspirations of many young contemporaries. Claudine was not the most touching person in the novels of Colette; she was far from being the deepest or the most deserving. But she had – and she still keeps – her significance. As Robert Sigl wrote, with a certain justice: 'The books of Colette will help us to study a period in the social life of women.'[1]

To say that Colette created Claudine is perhaps inaccurate, for Claudine is a distinct reflection of Colette herself; and most important women in the novels bear a certain likeness to their author. Renée Néré is the vagabond Colette of the music-hall years. Léa and Chéri may reflect Colette and Auguste Hériot; some say that they anticipate Colette and Bertrand de Jouvenel. Chéri is the only successful male character in the novels: the only man whom one can conceive existing beyond the confines of the book; and it has been observed, and rightly, that Chéri has something feminine about him. Larnac wrote that Colette could only attribute her own feelings to him. 'Chéri is not really a man. On the contrary, he has the coquetry, the bitterness, the emotional intuition of women.'[2] Léa is the mature Colette; she remains, without much question, the most deeply felt and the most convincing of Colette's creations. When Montherlant read *Chéri*, he said simply: 'C'est ça!'[3] Gérard Bauer declared that Colette's fine gaze

> never lost its penetrating calm; and even with the people she loved, of whom – like all women – she must sometimes have been the slave, she kept the sad and wonderful power of judgment. That is what assures such poignant perfection in a novel like *Chéri* and in its ineluctable end. The man who is loved is judged there, with his charm and with his weakness – judged with a precision, an art of detail and of feature which will always give the reader the sense of complicity.[4]

The work of Colette is largely a study of feminine psychology.

Chéri and *La Fin de Chéri* represent the height of Colette's achievement as a novelist. Raymond Mortimer observed that 'the Chéri novels form the classic analysis of a love-affair between a very young man and a middle-aged woman.'[5] Gonzague Truc took a wider view:

> We owe it to Madame Colette to lose all our illusions about love, about ourselves, about other people, and this is no small matter... Madame Colette strips the woman and, to use a term of which she does not in the least deprive herself, she allows the female to appear... Here, then [in the two *Chéri* books], posterity will find, with the lesson that we are given, the most perfect and the most sensitive pictures of our habits, our characters, our daily life and a faithful echo, across the ages, of our language. Madame Colette did not belong to any school, and, indeed, she was self-sufficient.'[6]

In its obituary of Colette, *The Times* observed:

> It is almost necessary to have lived in Paris, and to have known something of that side of it which is sometimes called Bohemian, but is really luxuriously immoral, if one is to appreciate the most vivid figure among Colette's literary creations – the portrait several times repeated, with slight variations, of the superannuated *demi-mondaine*... But even without that experience it is easy to feel that the portrait must be accurate because it is so human. Everything that Colette touched became human; human, that is to say, within the animal limits of humanity, but truly human within those limits.
>
> She felt deeply everything concerned with the senses – all the senses – and she had the literary instinct to be able to convey those feelings in her books. Everything that she did came from instinct rather than accomplishment, although she was a most conscientious artist... She

was all instinct, like the cats with which she loved to be surrounded, like the flowers that she loved to see and touch and smell. She was a complete sensualist; but she gave herself up to her senses with such delicacy of perception, with such exquisiteness of physical pain as well as physical ecstasy, that she ennobled sensualism almost into grandeur. The love-affairs of her novels were her own love-affairs. Everyone in Paris knew who 'Chérie' was [sic]. Everyone knew that she had suffered as she made her heroine suffer. And yet the thing never offended, as that sort of autobiography usually offends. She had transmuted it into art.[7]

Throughout her work, over more than half a century, Colette does more than simply reflect herself; she records her past with a nostalgia as deep as that of Proust. The whole work of Colette, as a critic once observed, was 'a fugue in a minor key on the theme of memory'.[8] The aroma of hot chocolate, the sight of a burnished chestnut in its shell, is enough to send her back, in imagination, to Saint-Sauveur. 'I belong,' she wrote, in her early days, 'to a country I have left ...'[9] Her roots remained there; she could not be uprooted without pain. Her childhood had been close to the earth, a childhood in the heart of nature. Saint-Sauveur was the place of her lost innocence; it was also the habitation of Sido, who was the dominant figure in her life. As Picon wrote, in *Humanisme actif*:

The world of Colette comes from childhood – although she goes beyond it and refrains from barren regrets. In childhood we are as close as possible to our true condition – which is the sensual condition. The house in the provinces, Sido, are not pictures of affection and nostalgia: instead they are keys, they are mythical figures which come from the very nature of things, which recall throughout the work this truth: that the human plant belongs to its soil.[10]

Violet Trefusis wrote that Colette's 'almost mythical love for her mother substituted itself early in life for other dogmas.'[11] Whether or not this was true, no-one, in more than eighty years, was to earn a comparable place in her heart and mind. Sido had given her love and security, an enchanted childhood; she had also given her the deep, poetic, questioning love of nature which was to inform her work, and to add a new dimension to French literature. No French writer before her had shown the same respectful affection for animals, felt them to be the equals of human beings, attempted to communicate with them, to effect 'an exchange of powers'.[12] Colette observed them closely, considered their habits and their ways of thought; she tamed them and she made friends of them. She described them with an affection which she did not always feel for her own kind. She watched not only animals but flowers and plants and trees; she surprised them in their most secret moments, heard the rose shed its petals: 'During a fit of silence, as thick as a mist, I have just heard them fall on the nearby table: the petals of a rose which was only waiting to be alone in order to shed its bloom.'[13]

Colette heard flowers as they died, and watched them as they came back to life: 'I do more than see the tulip come back to its senses: I hear the iris bloom. Its last protective silk grates and splits along a blue finger which itself unfurled a moment ago; and, retired in a small and silent room, one can shudder if one has forgotten that an iris, on a nearby console table, has decided suddenly to flower.'[14] Colette had an extraordinary and carefully developed sense of smell; she touched, she looked, she tasted. In her accounts of nature, as in some of her stories of human love, she was the most sensual of writers. 'Others, before her, have described with colours,' explained Roland Dorgelès. 'She was a woman, more delicate, and she added fragrances. That of the pinks in the flowerbed, the log blazing in the hearth, the damp linen spread out on the hedge, the apples in the attic, the lavender in the cupboard: you would think she gave us her books to inhale.'[15] Paul Chaponnière wrote that her work was radiant with health; her phrases seemed to have ripened in the sun and to sway with the blowing of the wind. Sido had once refused to visit Paris because she was waiting to see a rare lily burst into bloom. Colette was Sido's daughter, and her passion for nature, her enquiring mind, her poetic sense, made her the most original and powerful writer of natural history. She was sensitive, in this, to the point of genius. 'Poetry,' wrote Germaine Beaumont, 'is not a belated embellishment in the art of Colette, it is what at every moment she has perceived, seized, and keeps alive.'[16] Rousseaux went further:

The work of Colette does not recognise the presence of death. The inexhaustible life of nature has passed into it through the rhythms of art

... No-one has more really the feeling that art takes possession of all the perishable forces which linger here on earth, to endow them with wonderful survival. The world of Colette is a world of sensations which are living in an artist's memory.

That is her way of confronting immortality.[17]

In his introduction to Colette, Thierry Maulnier wrote that 'it seems we had to wait for her before French literature finally had its *Bucolics* or its Theocritus.'[18] Janet Flanner remarked that 'she even transferred to French readers her love for nature and for animals, domestic, or roaming country hills. Tastes such as these had been absent – in an almost too civilised omission – from French literature until she brought her Burgundian girlhood to Paris and put her rural sensibilities on paper.'[19] 'Madame Colette,' affirmed Cocteau, 'bristling with powerful instincts, registered nature with apparatuses a thousand times more sensitive than the mind.'[20] They were sensitive, and they were unerring. As Jacques Chenevière observed: 'Animals – and human beings – could not fail to be themselves in the presence of Colette. Of the manifold, transient, sometimes cruel truths of life, not one escaped her, she fixed them in a few words, in speech or on paper. And so she wrote like nobody else.'[21]

Colette had a passion for life itself.

Few of us – 'they have ears and hear not' – hearken to this song of all things created. Colette [wrote Bertrand de Jouvenel] has done nothing else in her eighty years of earthly pilgrimage ...

All that can be called 'doing', with the human interrelations and moral problems arising therefrom, has been completely foreign to Colette. Intentions, designs, which are the hallmark of men, have separated her from them to a far greater degree than has been understood; she had no intentions and could not easily grasp those of others. She has written most happily about the beings of Nature which have no plan of their own but merely follow their Creator's plan ... When she deals with people, she notes how they wither or bloom according to circumstances, like plants; they are not represented as doers ...

Things are, and they are good, such was her way of thinking. I knew her for some thirty-five years and never heard her speak of aught else than the beauty of things. She might sit in a sinister *café* and would not see there what a Simenon brings out: the goldenness of a piece of bread, a smile on the waiter's face, would please her. The charm of things never palled for her . . .

No-one was ever less unsatisfied, less revolted. There was no moment at which some little thing did not sing for her. It never came naturally to her to ask why, and any attempted statement of why was met by her as foreign language; and she had not the slightest curiosity about any foreign language. But, thanks to her, we may hearken to the song of Creation: Benedicite omnia . . .[22]

She was concerned with all nature, good and evil alike. As Cocteau insisted:

Madame Colette's greatness came from the fact that an inaptitude to distinguish good from evil set her in a state of innocence . . .

Let us salute in Madame Colette a wise woman who stopped her ears so as not to hear the sirens and refused none of the fruitful putrefactions of life. Like a true countrywoman, she guessed that everything that appears senseless in nature has in fact a secret meaning, and that correcting the slightest figure in it brings woeful errors in the total sum.[23]

Colette's appreciations of people, her appreciations of places – not only the countryside, but the Palais-Royal, in Paris – showed a sharp and delicate sense of character. She was a critic of the theatre and the cinema, a journalist who recorded contemporary events and *causes célèbres*; she was also, at a deeper level, a recorder of her times. She always made it clear, however, that she was not 'engaged' as a writer. She wisely recognised her limitations. She had, reported an English journalist on her death, 'an absolute trust in the intimations of her own senses; and when a reporter ventured not long ago to ask her opinion of some current political problem, she was quick to reply: "Young man, this is the first time that anyone has accused me of having any general ideas." '[24]

■▬■

Jean Vignaud said that the only reproach one could make to Colette was that she never rose above life; but her style clung to its subject like the peel to fruit.[25] Larnac observed that if the art of Colette revealed a great effort to find the right word and the right picture, it was none the less very clearly feminine.[26] Colette had a woman's perspective, said Maulnier, and man was only seen in that perspective.[27] Colette, wrote André Billy, enriched the sensibility of her contemporaries. She had, above all, a feminine genius. She held the first place among women writers; she was above George Sand, who aped men too much. This was a weakness which Colette always avoided. She had, to an incomparable degree, the intelligence of her sex.[28] André Maurois, writing on her death, repeated that for him her work was 'an essentially feminine work. She said what no man could have said, and she spoke of sensations and feelings as nobody had spoken of them before, for none of the great women of letters who had preceded her had lived in an age of such great freedom of expression. It was the first time that someone could say everything, and she said it to admiration.'[29]

She did not do so easily. When in 1924 André Billy sang her praises, she thanked him, rationally, for his article. 'The greatest living writer of French prose, myself? Even if that were true, I don't *feel* it deep down inside myself, you know what I mean. But the most miserable, the most desperate to write well, often the most disappointed – I have just finished *La Fin de Chéri*, and how I have toiled at it! It's true that it was too difficult a novel ...'[30] Writing did not come to her easily. She had had a minimal formal education, she had had her literary training, if such it can be called, from the facile, brutal and mediocre Willy. Yet, as Duhamel observed:

She was, from the very beginning, and she afterwards remained, an exemplary writer, a perfect servant of the language. She is among those who have not been marked by the humanist and classical culture, but prove that the French language is a classical language, and a living one, since the practice of it is, eventually, enough for the formation and the accomplishment of an artist in words ...

She was not one of those writers who give more attention and more time to personal influence than to the work itself. She did not found a school. She was not concerned with attaching pupils to her renown, with creating herself a following or a court. In any case, she is inimitable ...

I trust that the work of Colette may remain not only under the noble dust of libraries, which would not be enough, but intimately mingled with the thoughts of men who love nature, the beauty of the world: who, let me say, love life, sweet, agonising, incomprehensible life.[31]

Colette herself explained: 'As for me, it's my body which thinks. It's more intelligent than my mind. When my body thinks, all my flesh has a soul.'[32] She incorporated herself, body and soul, with everything that could be expressed. As Madeleine Jacob wrote: 'She violated the most secret thoughts. She took the husks off people to whom her genius had given life ... She leaves this highly personal imprint, this sensuality of mind, this power of evocation, for in fact she did not only describe the form and colour of things, she gave us the original emotion, re-created her memories of hearing, sight and touch. Her style, like Rimbaud's, synthesised the emotions, and touched at once on every mode of feeling.'[33] 'One doesn't read Colette,' confirmed Larnac. 'One sees what she sees. One breathes in what she breathes; one touches what she touches. And as she has much more perfect senses than her reader, he finds himself, for a few hours, living an intensified life: just like an ordinary violin which suddenly finds itself turned into a Stradivarius.'[34]

Maulnier recalled the decisive years of the 1930s when, as an adolescent, he had first read Colette. To him, and to his generation, she had given the world, a certain way of tasting it, of breathing, eating and drinking it. None of his contemporaries could read a book of hers for the first time 'without feeling the certainty that, until that actual moment, he had lacked sight and hearing and taste and touch, and that his senses had only just awakened.'[35] Colette described nothing that she had not seen, she considered human beings, nature itself, without the intermediary of any accepted idea. As Montherlant observed, there was nothing between her sensations and those of the reader. No work had ever reflected its author more clearly. She was the queen of a realm of feeling which no-one else had entered, in which no-one seemed able to contest her authority. To create a realm like this was, as Proust recognised, the test of a true writer. 'Style is not in the least an embellishment, as some people believe, it is not even a question of technique. It is, like colours with painters, a quality of vision, the revelation of a private world.'[36]

Colette, explained Boisdeffre, in his study of modern literature, saw her glory grow until her death. In her lifetime, she had given herself every licence except one: that of disowning the world in which she lived. And so people finally forgot the scandals of her private life, to accord her ... rewards which women rarely achieve. She used to speak of death with the affectionate irony with which she looked at men, happy to return to the good earth which she had not ceased to love. Instinctively, from childhood, she had wanted to relieve herself of the torments and risks inherent in human life, ... to keep just its animal gusto and its transient pleasures. Even when she speaks the language of passion, indeed the language of suffering, it is still with the feeling that the worst ills are relative and that the imperturbable cycle of Cybele will in due time bring good days ...

But the novelist to whom the cinema was to give a new public in her last years, is limited, and remains too indifferent to what makes the nobility of man. Who can love *Chéri* unless he is rather mean in spirit? And then, the style of Colette, with its chasing and its jewels, the style which is inordinately praised, risks succumbing to the pitiless erosion of time.

Unless the limits of the work are its best chance of survival.[37]

⁍━━⋅

It was easy to indicate the limits of her work. Yet the limitations were perhaps not so narrow or so rigid as they seemed.

People [wrote Du Gard] have said everything about Colette. They have even affirmed that she was not a novelist, and claimed that *La Vagabonde*, *L'Entrave* were only narratives and décors, sensitive sketches without significance, skilful impressions. Before *Chéri*, before *Le Blé en herbe*, this judgment may have been valid, at least in part; since the publication of these two books, perfectly composed dramas, one can read Colette with boundless admiration ...

Colette is indeed the representative type of our Third Republic. Among other things, she has discovered a sensuality which is not strictly speaking Latin, very different from the purely intellectual sensuality of a Stendhal. And the great art of this born writer is that, while she admits a rather plebeian taste for the flesh, she has imposed on it a rank among the most delicate masterpieces.[38]

Colette, added Picon,

never wrote anything but her own story, she only puts on stage the characters and the experiences of her own life. Under the anecdotal surface, how can one not become aware, very quickly, of the deep waters? ... If Colette has seduced and fascinated so many readers, it goes without saying that it is first and foremost for this reason: for the first time, this experience of love, which men never cease to describe, is written as they cannot ever write it. It is written for the first time with this precision, this determination, by the other partner, the mysterious partner who is so often silent.[39]

Jean Cocteau enlarged on the statement:

No doubt one must hail Madame Colette as the liberator of a feminine psychology emasculated by the scruples of Mesdames de Clèves and de Chasteler, and no doubt by renouncing the pride which makes these ladies set their virtue very high, Madame Colette has changed the place of virtue and opened vaster and more complex horizons than the rectangular canopy of the bed.

Madame Colette doesn't need to be whitened, because she is white. She detested black as much as the Impressionists – to whom she is related, although she was never concerned with the group and she was indifferent to their researches. She is alone. Alone she was. Alone she remains.[40]

NOTES

ABBREVIATIONS

BN = Bibliothèque Nationale, Paris
C = Colette
LDV = Colette: *Lettres de la Vagabonde*
LHP = Colette: *Lettres à Hélène Picard*
LMM = Colette: *Lettres à Marguerite Moreno*
LPC = Colette: *Lettres au Petit Corsaire*
LSP = Colette: *Lettres à ses Pairs*

Quotations from the works of Colette are taken from her *Œuvres complètes*, published in fifteen volumes by Flammarion, 1948-51.

SIDO'S DAUGHTER

1 Mitchell: *Colette*, pp. 11-12
2 Ibid., p. 12
3 C in *Bulletin de l'Académie Royale de Langue et de Littérature Françaises de Belgique*, avril 1936, pp. 67 sqq.
4 C: *La Maison de Claudine*, pp. 15 sqq.
5 Lefèvre: *Une Heure avec*..., 4e série, p. 135
6 C: *Le Fanal bleu*, pp. 102 sqq.
7 [16 October 1904.] C: LSP, p. 109
8 C: *Le Voyage égoïste*, pp. 9-10
9 Ibid., pp. 10-11
10 Ibid., p. 11
11 *Mercure de France*, 1 août 1930, pp. 678-9
12 21 August 1907 (*Le Figaro littéraire*, 24 janvier 1953)
13 C: *Le Voyage égoïste*, pp. 15 sqq.
14 Ibid.
15 C: *Mélanges*, p. 361
16 C: *Les Vrilles de la vigne*, p. 228

17 To Pierre Blanchar [December 1947]. LSP, p. 283
18 To Lucie Delarue-Mardrus [12 December 1940]. Ibid., p. 177
19 Colette claimed this in later life; yet she also claimed that she had not thought of a literary career.
20 Faure-Favier: 'La Muse aux violettes' (*Mercure de France*, 1 décembre 1953, p. 653)
21 *Bulletin de l'Académie Royale...*, loc. cit.
22 Albert: *Willy*, pp. 5-8
23 C: *Mes Apprentissages*, p. 19
24 Rosny: *Portraits et Souvenirs*, pp. 81 sqq.
25 Ibid.
26 Ibid.
27 Escholier: 'La véritable histoire de Sido et du Capitaine.' (*Le Figaro littéraire*, 24 novembre 1956)
28 *La Revue illustrée*, 15 janvier 1905
29 C: *Noces*, p. 251
30 C: *Mes Apprentissages*, p. 19
31 C: *Noces*, p. 252

COLETTE WILLY

1 Charpentier: 'Colette' (*Mercure de France*, 1 février 1931, p. 590)
2 C: *Mes Apprentissages*, pp. 24-5
3 Ibid., p. 26
4 Ibid.
5 Ibid., p. 64
6 Ibid., p. 36
7 Ibid., p. 37
8 [September 1894?] LSP, p. 26
9 26 June 1936. C: *La Jumelle noire*, p. 341
10 Rosny: op. cit., p. 83
11 Gregh: *L'Âge d'or*, pp. 208-9
12 To Marcel Schwob [27 June 1894]. LSP, p. 15
13 LMM, p. 9, note
14 Ibid., pp. 10, 11
15 6 November 1894. Renard: *Journal*, pp. 246-7
16 C: *Mes Apprentissages*, p. 18
17 Ibid., p. 21
18 Ibid.
19 Ibid., p. 52
20 [Summer 1895?] LSP, p. 27
21 Angue: 'La Jeunesse de Colette' (*Les Nouvelles littéraires*, 4 juillet 1925)
22 Ibid.
23 Quoted by Albert: op. cit., p. 32
24 Barney: *Souvenirs indiscrets*, p. 190
25 Gauthier-Villars: 'Willy et Colette' (*Les Œuvres libres*, octobre 1959, p. 175)

26 Ibid.
27 Quennell: 'Colette at Home' (*Spectator*, 23 November 1956, p. 733)
28 Lees-Milne: unpublished diary, 19 February 1953
29 Boulestin: *Myself, my two countries*..., p. 62
30 Gauthier-Villars: op cit., pp. 186, 188–9
31 Cocteau: *Portraits-souvenir*, pp. 7–8
32 C: *Mes Apprentissages*, p. 50
33 Ibid., p. 59; for the origins of Claudine's father, see Fabureau: 'Robineau-Desvoidy, le père de Claudine à l'école' (*Mercure de France*, 1 janvier 1950, pp. 188–90)
34 Quoted by D'Hollander: *Colette, ses apprentissages*, p. 183
35 Renaud de Jouvenel: supplementary note to the author, 1982
36 Lees-Milne: loc. cit.
37 *Mercure de France*, n.d.; quoted by Chauvière: op. cit., p. 131
38 Albert: op. cit., pp. 14–15
39 Walzer: *Paul-Jean Toulet*, pp. 70–1
40 [Early June 1902?] LSP, p. 52
41 [Mid July 1902.] Ibid., p. 54
42 [1902.] LMM, pp. 31–2
43 Quoted by Chauvière, op. cit., pp. 56–9; where it is attributed, I think mistakenly, to the later days of the rue de Courcelles.
44 C: *Mes Apprentissages*, p. 25
45 Ibid., p. 28
46 Chauvière: loc. cit.
47 C: *Mes Apprentissages*, p. 60
48 Miomandre: *Figures d'aujourd'hui et d'hier*, p. 211
49 Ernest-Charles: *Les Samedis littéraires*, 5e série, pp. 125–7
50 Ibid.; Albert: op. cit., 47; and Colette Willy to Nadar [14 June 1897]. N.A. Fr. 24266 f. 40
51 Colette, quoted by Chauvière: op. cit., p. 56
52 Delarue-Mardrus: *Mes Mémoires*, p. 141
53 C: *Mes Apprentissages*, p. 66
54 C: *Le Fanal bleu*, p. 233
55 *Mercure de France*, April 1904, pp. 181–2
56 The journal of Paul Léautaud records many disparaging comments by Rachilde.
57 Albert: op. cit., p. 19
58 Rosny: op. cit., p. 84
59 Brisson: 'Colette et l'amour' (*Le Figaro littéraire*, 10 août 1957)
60 [Mid-May 1904.] LSP, p. 106
61 *La Revue illustrée*, 15 janvier 1905.
62 *Bulletin de l'Académie Royale*..., avril 1936, pp. 70–1
63 23 March 1903. Léautaud: *Journal littéraire*, I, pp. 66–7
64 *Bulletin de l'Académie Royale*..., loc. cit.
65 Barney: *Souvenirs indiscrets*, pp. 188–90
66 Ibid., p. 192
67 Colette gave this account in her *Renée Vivien*: an essay published in Abbeville

by Les Amis d'Edouard in 1928. The reference occurs on pp. 3-5; the essay was later reissued in her *Œuvres complètes*. See also Billy: 'Paris littéraire en 1910' (*Les Œuvres libres*, 1945. No. 229, pp. 5 sqq.).
68 C: *Renée Vivien*, loc. cit.
69 C: *Les Heures longues*, p. 350
70 Rosny: op. cit., p. 84
71 C: *Mes Apprentissages*, p. 125
72 Ibid., p. 127
73 *Mercure de France*, 1 décembre 1913, p. 588

LA VAGABONDE

1 Parturier: *Morny*, p. 238; see also Lanoux: *Amours 1900*, p. 334
2 Weiss: *Souvenirs littéraires*, Vol. II, février 1950. Complément du portrait de Mathilde de Morny. Papiers Louise Weiss. B.N., N.A. Fr. 17794 fos. 54-7
3 Ibid.
4 4 October 1924. Liane de Pougy: *My Blue Notebooks*, p. 179
5 Bonmariage: op. cit., p. 82
6 Weiss: loc. cit., and ibid., fo. 005
7 Fouquières: *Cinquante ans de panache*, pp. 92, 93
8 Liane de Pougy: op. cit., p. 110
9 Weiss: loc. cit.
10 C: *Les Vrilles de la vigne*, p. 215
11 Ibid., pp. 219-20
12 Ibid., p. 222
13 Weiss: N.A. Fr. 17794, fo. 026; *Paris-Match*, 17 septembre 1982, p. 83
14 Brisson: 'Colette et l'amour' (*Le Figaro littéraire*, 10 août 1957.)
15 C: *Le Voyage égoïste*, pp. 7-8
16 B.N. N.A. Fr. 15260 fo. 131. Copy of undated letter, sent from 44 rue de Villejust. See also N.A.Fr. 15155 fos. 181-2, 183-4; N.A.Fr. 15301 fos. 110, 113-4; N.A.Fr. 15293 fo. 100; N.A.Fr. 15161 fo. 151
17 Rémy: *Wague*, p. 67
18 Boulestin: op. cit., pp. 95-6
19 Unidentified press-cutting. B.N., N.A.Fr. 15301 fo. 122
20 *Gil-Blas*. Undated cutting. Ibid.
21 Boulestin: op. cit., pp. 97-8
22 Léautaud: *Journal littéraire*, I, p. 8
23 Rémy: op. cit., p. 73
24 Chevalier: *Ma Route et mes chansons*, p. 180
25 Maurice Martin du Gard: *Les Mémorables*, I, p. 141
26 Boulestin: op. cit., pp. 90, 93
27 [23 June 1910.] LSP, p. 151
28 24, 30 June 1924. Liane de Pougy: op cit., pp. 173, 174
29 5 April [1909]. LMM, p. 34
30 [28 February 1909.] LDV, p. 30
31 [28 July 1910.] LSP, p. 152
32 Larnac: *Colette*, pp. 76-7

33 Gauthier-Villars: op. cit., p. 196
34 Polaire: op. cit., p. 258
35 Bonmariage: op. cit., pp. 218-19
36 Ibid., pp. 220-1
37 [12 November 1910.] LDV, p. 42
38 [19 November 1910.] Ibid., p. 45
39 Cocteau: *Bulletin de l'Académie Royale...*, p. 194
40 Chevalier: op. cit., pp. 179-80
41 Rémy de Gourmont: *Promenades littéraires*, 4e série, pp. 96-7
42 Claretie: *La Vie à Paris, 1911*, pp. 8-11
43 [14 February 1911.] LDV, pp. 45-6
44 [22 February 1911.] LSP, pp. 160, 161
45 [21 March 1911.] LDV, p. 46
46 [31 March 1911.] Ibid., p. 48
47 [25 June 1911.] LSP, p. 155
48 Binion: *Defeated Leaders*, pp. 117 sqq.
49 Bertry: *Vie de Léon de Jouvenel*, p. 23
50 Binion: loc. cit.
51 Beneš: *Souvenirs*, I, p. 222
52 Renaud de Jouvenel to the author; complementary note on Claire Boas de Jouvenel
53 Renaud de Jouvenel: notes on Henry de Jouvenel
54 Ibid.; and notes on Isabelle de Comminges. Letter to the author, 27 June 1982
55 Renaud de Jouvenel: notes on Isabelle de Comminges
56 Renaud de Jouvenel: 'Mon Enfance à l'ombre de Colette' (*La Revue de Paris*, décembre 1966, p. 6)
57 Ibid., p. 7
58 [22 July 1911.] LSP, p. 156
59 LDV, p. 55, note
60 [31 July 1911.] Ibid., pp. 55 sqq.
61 Renaud de Jouvenel: letter to Yvonne Mitchell, 26 October 1975
62 Renaud de Jouvenel to the author, 15 July 1982
63 Ibid.
64 27 July 1920. Liane de Pougy: op. cit., p. 110
65 LDV, pp. 55-7
66 Renaud de Jouvenel: op. cit., p. 17
67 [19 August 1911.] LDV, p. 58
68 [29 August 1911.] Ibid., pp. 59-60
69 N.d. *Le Figaro littéraire*, 24 janvier 1953
70 Rémy: op. cit., p. 75
71 Ibid.
72 [17 August 1912.] LLV, pp. 74-5
73 [26 August 1912.] Ibid., p. 76
74 [29 August 1912.] Ibid., p. 77
75 Larnac: *Colette - Sa vie, son œuvre*, p. 28
76 [27 September 1912.] LDV, p. 80
77 Renaud de Jouvenel: Letter to the author, 24 July 1982

78 [Undated.] LDV, p. 217
79 C: *De ma fenêtre*, p. 302
80 C: *Belles saisons*, pp. 460-1
81 C: *Journal à rebours*, p. 80
82 [14 October 1912.] LDV, p. 81
83 Renaud de Jouvenel: notes on Mamita
84 [14 October 1912.] LDV, p. 81. Édith de Jouvenel, half-sister of Henry de Jouvenel, was to die at the age of twenty-two
85 Rémy: op. cit., pp. 76-7
86 Renaud de Jouvenel: notes to the author

MADAME LA BARONNE DE JOUVENEL

I

1 [27 December 1912.] LDV, p. 86
2 [Late January 1913.] Ibid., pp. 87-8
3 [11 July 1913.] LSP, p. 158
4 [16 September 1913.] LDV, p. 96
5 Ibid.
6 C: *L'Entrave*, p. 254
7 Ibid., p. 290
8 Ibid., p. 349
9 B.N., N.A.Fr. 17794 fo. 021
10 C: *L'Étoile vesper*, p. 277
11 Renaud de Jouvenel: letter to the author, 27 June 1982
12 Chauvière: op. cit., pp. 123-4
13 [11 February 1914.] LMM, pp. 36-8
14 [April 1914.] Ibid., p. 44
15 Renaud de Jouvenel: notes to the author
16 Quoted by Mitchell: op. cit., p. 128
17 Renaud de Jouvenel: letter to Yvonne Mitchell, 26 October 1975; letter to Michèle Sarde, 4 June 1978
18 [30 August 1914.] LDV, p. 107
19 [16 October 1914.] Ibid., p. 111
20 C: *Les Heures longues*, pp. 328 sqq.
21 [20 December 1914.] LDV, pp. 112, 114
22 Ibid., p. 118
23 [28 June 1915.] Ibid., p. 119
24 C: *Journal intermittent*, p. 246
25 C: *La Paix chez les bêtes*, p. 215
26 25 January 1916. Léautaud: op. cit., III, p. 220
27 [22 September 1916.] LDV, p. 121
28 Binion: loc. cit.
29 Renaud de Jouvenel: letter to Yvonne Mitchell, 26 October 1975
30 [July 1918.] LSP, p. 205
31 [9 August 1918.] Ibid., p. 206

32 Du Gard: *Impertinences*, pp. 61–3
33 Hermant: *La Vie littéraire*, 2e série, p. 231
34 Renaud de Jouvenel: letter to the author, 27 June 1982
35 Chauvière: op. cit., pp. 65–6
36 Beaumont: *Colette par elle-même*, p. 6
37 Ibid., pp. 6–8
38 Ibid., pp. 18–19
39 Ibid., p. 25
40 Ibid., pp. 25–6, 27, and undated letter: B.N., N.A.Fr. 16870 fo. 209
41 C: *L' Étoile vesper*, p. 212
42 Renaud de Jouvenel: letter to the author, 27 June 1982
43 LSP, p. 216, note
44 Liane de Pougy: *My Blue Notebooks*, p. 252
45 [Late August 1919.] LSP, p. 216

II

1 C: Preface to *Chéri*, pp. 7 sqq.
2 Ibid.
3 [28 August 1921.] Maurice Martin du Gard: *Les Mémorables*, I, pp. 136–7
4 Polaire: op. cit., pp. 259–60
5 Maurice Martin du Gard: loc. cit.
6 Renaud de Jouvenel: letter to Yvonne Mitchell, 26 October 1975
7 Renaud de Jouvenel: letter to the author, 27 June 1982
8 C: Preface to *Chéri*, pp. 9, 10–11
9 C: *Mes Cahiers*, pp. 358 sqq.
11 Renaud de Jouvenel: letter to the author, 26 July 1982
12 Bertrand de Jouvenel: *Un Voyageur dans le siècle*, pp. 54 sqq., and in conversation with the author, 20 September 1982
13 Bertrand de Jouvenel: op. cit., p. 55
14 [Early June 1920.] LHP, p. 33
15 [June 1920.] Ibid.
16 [June 1920.] LSP, p. 38
17 Goudeket: *Près de Colette*, p. 18
18 Ibid., p. 21
19 Ibid.
20 Cocteau: 'Colette' (*Bulletin de l'Académie Royale...*, p. 197)
21 C: *Chéri*, p. 134
22 Ibid., p. 141
23 Ibid., p. 127
24 C: *Mes Cahiers*, pp. 387–90
25 Cocteau: op. cit., p. 198
26 Vandérem: *Le Miroir des lettres*, 3e série, pp. 157, 160
27 *Le Journal des Débats*, 13 octobre 1920
28 [Mid October 1920.] LSP, p. 280
29 [Summer 1920?] LHP, p. 36
30 Bertrand de Jouvenel: op. cit., pp. 54 sqq.
31 Ibid., p. 56

32 Ibid.
33 Bertrand de Jouvenel, in conversation with the author, 20 September 1982
34 Ibid.; and Mme Jeannie Malige, in conversation with the author, 20 September 1982
35 Bertrand de Jouvenel: op. cit., p. 56
36 [Early September 1920.] LSP, p. 219
37 [1 October 1920.] LMM, p. 48
38 [c. 10 November 1920.] LSP, p. 40
39 11 December 1920. Quoted by Chauvière: op. cit., pp. 148-9
40 Chauvière: op. cit., p. 156
41 C: *L'Étoile vesper*, p. 281
42 Ibid., p. 280

III

1 B.N., N.A.Fr. 16533 fo. 305, n.d.
2 Ibid., fos. 303-4., n.d.
3 Mitchell: op. cit., p. 146
4 Renaud de Jouvenel: supplementary notes to the author
5 Renaud de Jouvenel: notes
6 Renaud de Jouvenel: op. cit., p. 7
7 Ibid., pp. 3-4
8 Binion: loc. cit.
9 Faure-Favier: 'La Muse aux violettes' (*Mercure de France*, 1 décembre 1953, p. 654)
10 Barney: *Souvenirs indiscrets*, p. 198
11 Renaud de Jouvenel: letter to the author, 24 July 1982
12 Renaud de Jouvenel: letter to the author, 15 July 1982
13 [c. 10 March 1921.] LMM, pp. 48-9
14 [28 April 1921.] Ibid., p. 50
15 [2 June 1921.] LSP, p. 125
16 [June 1920.] Ibid., p. 38
17 [Early June 1920.] Ibid., pp. 42-3
18 Renaud de Jouvenel: notes
19 [Early August 1921.] LMM, p. 53
20 Sachs: *La Décade de l'illusion*, p. 99
21 [17 August 1921.] LMM, pp. 54, 55
22 Bertrand de Jouvenel: 'Colette' (*Time and Tide*, 14 August 1954)
23 Renaud de Jouvenel: op. cit., p. 5
24 [Autumn 1937.] Ibid., p. 17
25 Mitchell: op. cit., p. 139
26 Renaud de Jouvenel: letter to the author, 27 June 1982
27 Ibid.
28 Vandérem: *Le Miroir des lettres*, 3e série, pp. 27-8
29 [1922.] LSP, pp. 169-70
30 [Early July 1922?] Ibid., p. 60
31 [10 July 1922.] LHP, p. 41
32 [1 August 1922?] LMM, p. 62

33 Mme Jeannie Malige, in conversation with the author, 20 September 1982
34 Lefèvre: *Une heure avec...*, pp. 129 sqq.
35 [23 [?] September 1922.] LDV, p. 156
36 Maurice Martin du Gard: *Les Mémorables*, I, p. 137
37 Bertrand de Jouvenel: loc. cit.
38 Lefèvre: loc. cit.
39 MacOrlan: 'La Femme la plus libre du monde' (*Paris-Presse*, 5 août 1954)
40 *La Revue de Paris*, 1 mars 1923, pp. 204-5
41 22 February 1920. Liane de Pougy: op. cit., p. 91
42 [Spring 1923.] LHP, p. 48
43 Renaud de Jouvenel: letter to the author, 1 July 1982
44 Renaud de Jouvenel: notes
45 Bertrand de Jouvenel: conversation with the author, 20 September 1982
46 [May or June 1923.] LMM, pp. 64, 65
47 Bertrand de Jouvenel: *Un Voyageur dans le siècle*, p. 36
48 Vandérem: *Le Miroir des lettres*, 6e série, pp. 299-301
49 [July 1923.] LMM, p. 67
50 [31 July 1923.] Ibid., pp. 69, 70
51 [18 August 1923.] Ibid., p. 71
52 [30 August 1923.] Ibid., p. 72
53 Renaud de Jouvenel: op. cit., p. 9
54 [October 1923?] LMM, pp. 73-4
55 [20 October 1923.] Ibid., p. 75
56 [23 November 1923.] Ibid., pp. 76-7
57 [16 December 1923.] Ibid., p. 77
58 Renaud de Jouvenel: notes
59 [6 January 1924.] LDV, p. 171
60 Bertrand de Jouvenel: op. cit., p. 57

IV

1 Renaud de Jouvenel: letter to the author, 27 June 1982
2 Bertrand de Jouvenel: *Time and Tide*, loc. cit.
3 Barney: op. cit., pp. 194, 199-200
4 Renaud de Jouvenel: letter to the author, 27 June 1982
5 Renaud de Jouvenel: letter to the author, 27 July 1982
6 Cocteau: 'Colette', (*Bulletin de l'Académie Royale...*, XXXIII, p. 186)
7 Renaud de Jouvenel: letter to the author, 26 July 1982
8 [12 January 1924.] LHP, pp. 62-3
9 Renaud de Jouvenel: notes
10 [22 January 1924.] LMM, p. 78
11 [8 February 1924.] LHP, p. 65
12 [23 February 1924.] LMM, p. 80
13 Bertrand de Jouvenel: *Un Voyager dans le siècle*, p. 57
14 Hitchcock: *Beneš*, p. 229
15 [2 July 1924.] LMM, p. 81
16 Renaud de Jouvenel: op. cit., p. 13
17 [10 July 1924.] LMM, p. 83

18 [12 August 1924.] Ibid., pp. 85-6, 86
19 [30 August 1924.] Ibid., p. 87
20 [28 December 1924.] Ibid. p. 99
21 Renaud de Jouvenel: letter to Yvonne Mitchell, 26 October 1975
22 Bertrand de Jouvenel: *Un Voyageur dans le siècle*, p. 57
23 Ibid., p. 58
24 Bertrand de Jouvenel in conversation with the author, 20 September 1982
25 Renaud de Jouvenel: letter to the author, 27 June 1982
26 Bertrand de Jouvenel in conversation with the author, 20 September 1982
27 Quoted by Larnac: op. cit., p. 131
28 Chalupt: op. cit., p. 120 and passim
29 [Summer 1924.] LSP, p. 267
30 *La Revue de Paris*, 15 avril 1925, pp. 897 sqq.

THE DARK YOUNG MAN

I

1 Goudeket: *Près de Colette*, passim; *La Douceur de vivre*, passim
2 Goudeket: *Près de Colette*, p. 8
3 Ibid., pp. 9-10
4 Ibid., p. 12
5 [14 April 1925.] LHP, pp. 72, 73
6 Goudeket: *Près de Colette*, p. 15
7 [7 May 1925.] LMM, p. 101
8 [11 May 1925.] Ibid., p. 102
9 [13 May 1925.] Ibid., pp. 102-3
10 [18 May 1925.] Ibid., p. 104
11 [Early June 1925.] Ibid., p. 107
12 [11 June 1925.] Ibid., pp. 107-8
13 Chauvière: op. cit., p. 125
14 Léautaud: op. cit., V, pp. 55-7
15 [21 June 1925.] LMM, p. 108
16 [23 June 1925.] Ibid., pp. 109-10
17 [15 August 1925.] LSP, p. 80
18 [14 September 1925.] LMM, p. 116
19 [28 September 1925.] Ibid., pp. 116-17
20 [1 October 1925.] Ibid., p. 118
21 [3 October 1925.] Ibid., pp. 119-20
22 [22 October 1925.] Ibid., p. 124
23 [24 April 1929.] LSP, p. 171
24 [18 November 1925.] LHP, p. 76
25 Quoted by Chauvière: op. cit., p. 259
26 [c. 15 December 1925.] LHP, pp. 76-7
27 Ibid., p. 79
28 Goudeket: *La Douceur de vivre*, pp. 97, 98, 99
29 [c. 20 January 1926.] LHP, pp. 79, 80

30 [20 January 1926.] LMM, p. 126
31 [c. 20 January 1926.] LHP, p. 80
32 *Libération*, 4 août 1954
33 *La Revue de Paris*, avril 1926, pp. 690 sqq.
34 Ibid., 1 mars 1926, pp. 180-1
35 *Mercure de France*, 15 mars 1926, p. 704
36 Vandérem: *Le Miroir des lettres*, 8e série, p. 196

II

1 C: *Mes Cahiers*, p. 375
2 Charpentier: 'La Fin de Chéri' (*Mercure de France*, 15 mai 1926, pp. 151-2)
3 Lefèvre: *Une Heure avec...*, 4e série, pp. 129 sqq.
4 Ibid.
5 Ibid.
6 Goudeket: *Près de Colette*, pp. 145-6
7 Beaumont: op. cit., p. 31
8 Trefusis: *Prelude to Misadventure*, p. 146
9 [12 April 1926.] LMM, p. 127
10 [April 1926.] LHP, pp. 81-2
11 *Mercure de France*, 1 juin 1926, pp. 427-30
12 [14 June 1926.] LMM, p. 128; see also, Riverain: 'Chez les poètes d'Auteuil' (*Les Nouvelles littéraires*, 15 avril 1948)
13 Renaud de Jouvenel: notes on his family
14 [14 June 1926.] LMM, p. 130
15 [c. 12 July 1926.] LHP, pp. 83-4
16 [13 July 1926.] LMM, pp. 130-1
17 [c. 10 August 1926.] LHP, pp. 84-5
18 C: *La Fin de Chéri*, p. 240
19 [Late August 1926.] LHP, p. 86
20 [14 September 1926.] LMM, pp. 136-7
21 Goudeket: *Près de Colette*, p. 17
22 Trefusis: op. cit., p. 150
23 This and the following letter, both undated, are quoted by Chauvière: op. cit., pp. 249-50 and pp. 252-4
24 Cocteau: loc. cit.
25 Renaud de Jouvenel: letters to the author, 24 and 26 July 1982
26 [5 November 1926.] LHP, p. 86
27 [30 November 1926.] Ibid., p. 87
28 Goudeket: *Près de Colette*, pp. 63-4
29 Brasillach: *Œuvres complètes*, X, p. 455
30 11 April 1927. Léautaud: op. cit., V, pp. 375-6
31 Billy: *Intimités littéraires*, pp. 149-54
32 *L'Action Française*, n.d. Quoted by Chauvière: op. cit., p. 62

III

1 Mauriac: *Le Roman d'aujourd'hui*, pp. 265-6
2 Undated. LHP, p. 91

3 [21 July 1927.] LMM, pp. 146-7
4 Renaud de Jouvenel: letter to Yvonne Mitchell, 26 October 1975
5 *Libération*, 5 août 1954
6 Leroy: op. cit., p. 83
7 [3 August 1927.] LMM, p. 148
8 [28 August 1927.] Ibid., pp. 149-50, 151
9 [14 September 1927.] Ibid., p. 152
10 [23 December 1927.] Ibid., p. 153
11 [27 December 1927.] Ibid., pp. 154-5
12 5 January [1928.] Ibid., p. 156
13 [11 January 1928.] Ibid., p. 158
14 [28 January 1928.] Ibid., pp. 158-9
15 [Between 18 and 24 April 1928.] LSP, pp. 194-5
16 *Mercure de France*, 1 avril 1928, p. 173
17 Marsan: 'Du sentiment de la personne' (*Les Cahiers d'occident*, 2e série, No. 9, 1930, pp. 129-30)
18 [25 March 1928.] LMM, p. 162
19 [c. 14 April 1928.] LHP, pp. 95-6
20 [17 April 1928.] LMM, pp. 166, 167
21 [21 April 1928.] Ibid., p. 168
22 Gramont: op. cit., pp. 243-5
23 [22 July 1928.] LMM, p. 178
24 Quoted by Chauvière: op. cit., pp. 70 sqq.
25 [Late August 1928.] LHP, pp. 104, 105
26 *Le Figaro littéraire*, 26 janvier 1953
27 [10 September 1928.] LMM, p. 187
28 [24 December 1928.] Ibid., p. 188
29 [Late December 1928.] LSP, p. 91
30 [10 January 1929.] Ibid., p. 93
31 [Late December 1928.] LHP, p. 105
32 [31 December 1928.] LMM, p. 189
33 [2 January 1929.] Ibid.
34 [First half of January 1929.] LSP, pp. 187-8

IV

1 [Early January 1929.] LSP, p. 196
2 Renaud de Jouvenel: letter to the author, 1 July 1982
3 Brasillach: *Une Génération dans l'orage*, pp. 73-4
4 13 August 1929. Brasillach: *Œuvres complètes*, X
5 Brasillach: op. cit., p. 74
6 Flanner: loc. cit.
7 Wescott: *Images of Truth*, p. 88
8 [1 April 1929.] LHP, p. 108
9 [3 April 1929.] LMM, p. 191
10 *Gringoire*, 29 mars 1929; quoted in Prévost: *Marcel Prévost et ses contemporains*, I, p. 272
11 Prévost: op. cit., I, p. 274 [undated]

12 [Early May 1929.] LHP, pp. 109-10
13 Tuesday [9 or 16 July 1929.] LMM, p. 197
14 Tuesday [23 July 1929.] Ibid., p. 198
15 [11 August 1929.] Ibid., p. 201
16 [12 September 1929.] Ibid., p. 203
17 [21 September 1929.] LHP, p. 112
18 [23 October 1929.] LMM, p. 204
19 Goudeket: *Près de Colette*, p. 53
20 Lang: *Tiers de siècle*, pp. 166-7
21 [10 February 1930.] LMM, p. 206
22 [Spring 1930.] LHP, p. 114
23 [Spring 1930.] Ibid., p. 115; [April 1930.] LMM, p. 206
24 [Late June or early July 1930.] LHP, p. 119
25 [Early July 1930.] Ibid., p. 120
26 [18 July 1930.] Ibid., p. 121
27 Binion: loc. cit.
28 Renaud de Jouvenel: notes on his family
29 Binion: loc. cit.
30 Ibid.
31 Goudeket: *La Douceur de vivre*, pp. 46-7
32 [15 August 1930.] LMM, p. 208
33 Ibid.
34 [August 1930.] LHP, p. 122
35 [31 August 1930.] LMM, pp. 210-11
36 Billy: *Intimités littéraires*, pp. 149-54
37 [22 September 1930.] LMM, p. 212
38 [Late 1930 or early 1931.] LDV, p. 218

v

1 [Late January or early February 1931.] LHP, p. 127
2 Pringué: *Trente ans de dîners en ville*, p. 240
3 Fauchier-Magnan: op. cit., p. 108
4 Ernest-Charles: op. cit., p. 132
5 Rosny: *Portraits et Souvenirs*, pp. 84-5
6 [3 November 1927.] Léautaud: op. cit., VI, pp. 101-2
7 Leroy: op. cit., p. 60
8 [12 February 1931.] LMM, pp. 212-13
9 Beaumont: 'La Leçon de Colette' (*La Table ronde*, octobre 1954, p. 126)
10 Reprinted in *Hommage à Colette* (Monaco 1955). No page given.
11 [27 February 1931.] LHP, pp. 129-30
12 [1 March 1931.] LMM, p. 213
13 [18 March 1931.] LHP, pp. 130-1
14 [Spring 1931.] Ibid., p. 135
15 [Spring 1931.] Ibid., p. 137
16 Fauchier-Magnan: op. cit., p. 108
17 Renaud de Jouvenel: supplementary note to the author
18 [10 August 1931.] LMM, p. 219

19 [July/August 1931.] Poulenc: *Correspondance*, pp. 83-4
20 [1 September 1931.] LMM, p. 220
21 Ibid.
22 [5 September 1931.] Ibid., p. 221
23 [6 September 1931.] Ibid., p. 222
24 Maurice Martin du Gard: *Les Mémorables*, III, p. 203
25 [October 1931.] LHP, p. 140
26 [October or November 1931.] Ibid., p. 141
27 [5 November 1931.] LMM, p. 224
28 [Late November or early December 1931.] LHP, p. 145
29 [December 1931.] B.N. Rothschild AXX fo. 46; see also AXX fos. 47, 48
30 [12 December 1931.] LMM, p. 225

VI

1 Renaud de Jouvenel: letter to the author, 27 June 1982
2 Fillon: *Colette*, pp. 39-40
3 Liane de Pougy: *My Blue Notebooks*, pp. 244-5
4 [27 July 1932.] LMM, p. 229
5 Barney: op. cit., pp. 199-200
6 Sorel: *Les Belles Heures de ma Vie*, p. 280
7 Barney: loc cit.
8 [22 November 1932.] LHP, p. 156
9 [Mid December 1932.] Ibid., p. 157
10 [c. 1 January 1933.] Ibid., p. 158
11 [c. 20 January 1933.] Ibid., p. 159
12 Ibid.
13 Renaud de Jouvenel: letter to the author, 27 June 1982
14 [c. 20 January 1933.] LHP, p. 159
15 Renaud de Jouvenel: letter to the author, 26 July 1982
16 [c. 20 January 1933.] LHP, p. 159
17 [25 January 1933.] Ibid., p. 160
18 [1 May 1933.] Ibid., p. 161
19 Goudeket: *Près de Colette*, pp. 35, 41
20 Trahard: *L'Art de Colette*, pp. 87, 88
21 LSP, p. 364, note
22 [Early July 1933.] Ibid., p. 364-5
23 Aumont: *Souvenirs provisoires*, pp. 83-4
24 [5 August 1933.] LMM, p. 234
25 B.N., N.A.Fr. 15950. n.d.
26 B.N., N.A.Fr. 16870. fo. 210 [July 1933.]
27 Bourdet: *Édouard Bourdet*, pp. 79-82
28 Goudeket: *Près de Colette*, pp. 111, 112
29 C: *La Jumelle noire*, p. 44
30 Ibid., pp. 344-5
31 Ibid., p. 264; see also ibid., pp. 406-7
32 Leroy: 'Colette au Claridge en juin 1934' (*Femmes d'aujourd'hui*, pp. 17 sqq.)
33 Marcel: '*Duo*, par Colette' (*L'Europe nouvelle*, 12 janvier 1935)

34 Brasillach: *Les Quatre Jeudis*, p. 349
35 [July/August 1934.] Montherlant: *Carnets, 1930-1944*, p. 165
36 Ibid., p. 166
37 Leroy: op. cit., p. 81
38 Blanche: *La Pêche aux souvenirs*, p. 289
39 Gramont: *La treizième heure*, p. 186
40 Bauer: *Les Billets de Guermantes*, p. 129
41 Ibid.
42 14 November 1935. Léautaud: op. cit., XI, p. 103
43 [Mid March 1935.] LHP, p. 173
44 Goudeket: *La Douceur de vieillir*, p. 120
45 Ibid., p. 21
46 Goudeket: *Près de Colette*, p. 240
47 Ibid., pp. 97-8
48 Ibid., p. 98

MADAME MAURICE GOUDEKET

I

1 Goudeket: *Près de Colette*, pp. 99 sqq.
2 C: *Mes Cahiers*, p. 426
3 Ibid.
4 Wescott: introduction to *Short Novels of Colette*
5 Goudeket: loc. cit.
6 Renaud de Jouvenel: letter to Yvonne Mitchell, 26 October 1975
7 Ibid.
8 Mitchell: op. cit., p. 194
9 Renaud de Jouvenel: letter to Yvonne Mitchell, 26 October 1975
10 Mme de Comminges to Renaud de Jouvenel: letter of 7 July 1935
11 Mitchell: op. cit., p. 194
12 Ibid.
13 Renaud de Jouvenel: letter to Yvonne Mitchell, 26 October 1975
14 Renaud de Jouvenel: letter to the author, 27 June 1982
15 Renaud de Jouvenel: letter to the author, 13 July 1982
16 Binion: loc. cit.
17 *Le Temps*, 6 octobre 1935.
18 Binion: op. cit., p. 375, note
19 Bibesco: *La Vie d'une amitié...*, III, p. 259
20 [c. 8 October 1935.] LHP, p. 175
21 Renaud de Jouvenel: letter to Michèle Sarde, n.d.
22 [3 [?] January 1936.] LHP, p. 181
23 Marks: op. cit., p. 246
24 Papiers Louise Weiss. B.N., N.A.Fr. 17794, fo. 012
25 Goudeket: *Près de Colette*, p. 133
26 C: *Mes Apprentissages*, p. 19
27 Léautaud: op. cit., XI, pp. 140-1
28 Brasillach: *Les Quatre Jeudis*, p. 359

29 Gide: *Journal 1932-1939*, p. 183
30 [c. 1 April 1936.] LHP, pp. 181-2
31 Académie Royale: *Bulletin*, avril 1936, pp. 60, 63
32 Ibid., pp. 65-6
33 Rosamond Lehmann: letter to the author, 11 January 1981
34 Brasillach: *Œuvres complètes*, XII, pp. 122, 123
35 Goudeket: *Près de Colette*, pp. 143-4
36 Ibid., p. 144

11

1 [January 1938.] LSP, pp. 130-1
2 Trefusis: *Don't Look Round*, pp. 89-90
3 Beaumont: op. cit., pp. 32-3, 39-40
4 Cain: 'Ma Voisine' (*Les Lettres françaises*, 12-18 août 1954)
5 [12 November 1938.] LHP, pp. 195-6
6 [4 December 1938.] Ibid., pp. 196-7
7 Goudeket: *Près de Colette*, p. 28
8 [26 March 1939.] LSP, p. 310
9 C: *Le Fanal bleu*, pp. 77-8; *L'Étoile vesper*, pp. 266-8
10 Goudeket: *Près de Colette*, p. 238; Bénisti: *La Main de l'écrivain*, pp. 63 sqq.
11 Brasillach: *Œuvres complètes*, XII, pp. 279
12 [21 August 1939.] LHP, p. 197
13 [3 September 1939.] Unpublished letter (Mrs James Lees-Milne)
14 Undated (Mrs James Lees-Milne)
15 [September 1939.] LHP, p. 199
16 [Winter 1939-40.] Ibid., pp. 199-200
17 Undated (Mrs James Lees-Milne)
18 Undated (Mrs James Lees-Milne)
19 2 March 1940. (Mrs James Lees-Milne)
20 Ibid.
21 [Mid March 1940.] LHP, pp. 200-1
22 Renaud de Jouvenel: supplementary note to the author
23 [July 1940.] LSP, p. 134
24 Ibid.
25 Renaud de Jouvenel: supplementary note to the author
26 C: *Journal à rebours* pp. 96-7. However, in 'Ma Mère et les livres', in *La Maison de Claudine*, Colette makes clear how her mother fostered her love of literature.
27 C: *L'Étoile vesper*, p. 190
28 [24 March 1941.] LPC, p. 103
29 [29 May 1941.] LHP, p. 202
30 Mitchell: op. cit., p. 194
31 Renaud de Jouvenel: letter to the author, 26 July 1982
32 Renaud de Jouvenel: letter to Yvonne Mitchell, 26 October 1975
33 Undated extract from letter to Renaud de Jouvenel
34 Renaud de Jouvenel: supplementary note to the author
35 Renaud de Jouvenel: letter to the author, 24 July 1982

36 [25 June 1941.] LMM, p. 239
37 [29 July 1941.] Ibid.
38 [July/August 1941.] LHP, pp. 202-3
39 [Between 12-19 December 1941.] Ibid., p. 204
40 [23 December 1941.] Ibid., pp. 205-6
41 Goudeket: *La Douceur de vieillir*, p. 79

III

1 Bonmariage: op. cit., pp. 25-6; Gold and Fizdale: *Misia*, pp. 281-2
2 [12 January 1942.] LSP, pp. 179-80
3 Barney: op. cit., p. 204
4 Beaumont: op. cit., pp. 40-1
5 Goudeket: *Près de Colette*, p. 34
6 31 January 1942. Léautaud: op. cit., XIV, pp. 159-60
7 [13 February 1942.] LMM, p. 241; [19 February 1942.] LHP, pp. 206-7
8 [27 May 1942.] LMM, p. 242
9 Goudeket: *Près de Colette*, p. 47
10 [Early December 1942.] LSP, pp. 180-1
11 Guitry: *Quatre ans d'occupations*, pp. 306-7; see also Lorcey: *Sacha Guitry*, p. 235
12 [4 February 1943.] LMM, pp. 244-5
13 Bertrand de Jouvenel in conversation with the author, 20 September 1982
14 [23 February 1943.] LMM, p. 245
15 [29 January 1938.] LPC, p. 41
16 [9 April 1943.] LSP, p. 417
17 [23 June 1943.] LMM, pp. 248-9, 250
18 [28 July 1943.] Ibid., p. 252
19 [21 September 1943.] Ibid., pp. 254-5
20 [6 October 1943.] Ibid., p. 256
21 [25 January 1944.] Ibid., p. 265
22 [3 February 1944.] Ibid., p. 269
23 [3 March 1944.] Ibid., p. 271
24 [12 March 1944.] Ibid., p. 273
25 [Undated.] Renaud de Jouvenel: op. cit., p. 18
26 [4 April 1944.] Ibid., p. 279
27 [23 April 1944.] Ibid., pp. 280-1
28 [28 April 1944.] Ibid., p. 282
29 [1 May 1944.] Ibid., p. 283
30 [9 May 1944.] Ibid., pp. 284-5
31 [25 May 1944.] Ibid., p. 285
32 C: *Paris de ma fenêtre*, p. 335
33 Ibid., p. 358
34 Ibid., p. 353
35 Ibid., p. 375
36 Cocteau: loc. cit.
37 [7 June 1944.] LMM, pp. 287-8
38 Ibid.

39 Fouquières: op. cit., pp. 93-4
40 Ibid., p. 94
41 Goudeket: *Près de Colette*, pp. 217-18

IV

1 Brasillach: *Œuvres complètes*, X, p. 606
2 [Mid March 1945?] LMM, p. 303
3 LSP, p. 413, where it is improbably dated 'late May 1945'
4 [23 April 1945.] LMM, p. 304
5 Dorgelès: oration at Colette's funeral. Printed in *Hommage à Colette:* the collection of tributes published in Monaco, 1955. No pages given.
6 [6 May 1945.] LMM, p. 305
7 [6 May 1945.] LSP, p. 139
8 [1945.] LMM, p. 306
9 C: *L'Étoile vesper*, p. 278
10 Or what she had called 'the spherical world, packed full with savour' (Davies: *Colette*, p. 102).
11 Beaumont: op. cit., p. 40; Dorgelès: loc. cit.
12 Cocteau: loc. cit.
13 [6 August 1945.] LMM, p. 307
14 [18 August 1945.] Ibid., p. 308
15 [28 August 1945.] Ibid., p. 309
16 [January or February 1946.] Ibid., pp. 311-12
17 [February or March 1946.] Ibid., p. 312
18 C: *Le Fanal bleu*, p. 47
19 [2 July 1946.] LMM, p. 313
20 C: *L'Étoile vesper*, p. 309
21 Ibid., p. 176
22 Ibid., pp. 290, 332
23 [Late July 1946.] LMM, pp. 313-14
24 [16 August 1946.] Ibid., pp. 314, 315
25 Quennell: loc. cit.
26 Goudeket: *Près de Colette*, pp. 239-41
27 Gide: *Journal, 1942-1949*, p. 256
28 Goudeket: *Près de Colette*, p. 110
29 [21 April 1947.] LMM, pp. 317-18
30 [1 May 1947.] Ibid., p. 319
31 [17 July 1947.] Ibid., p. 322
32 [7 August 1947.] Ibid., pp. 324-5
33 [28 August 1947.] Ibid., p. 327
34 C: *Le Fanal bleu*, pp. 223 sqq.
35 [5 October 1947.] LMM, p. 331
36 Cossart: p. 193
37 Fargue: *Portraits de famille*, pp. 19-20
38 Ibid., pp. 22-3
39 C: *Le Fanal bleu*, pp. 65-8
40 Guth: *Quarante contre un*, pp. 71 sqq.

41 [4 November 1947.] LMM, p. 332
42 [22 November 1947.] Ibid., pp. 333-4
43 [15 January 1948.] Ibid., p. 335
44 C: *Le Fanal bleu*, pp. 102-7
45 Ibid., pp. 119-21
46 Ibid., pp. 123-4
47 Ibid., pp. 77-8
48 Chauvière: op. cit., p. 19
49 Trefusis: *Prelude to Misadventure*, pp. 147-8
50 [c. 18 March 1948.] LMM, pp. 336, 337
51 [c. 25 March 1948.] Ibid., p. 338
52 [22 May 1948.] Ibid., p. 339
53 [7 June 1948.] Ibid., p. 342
54 [24 June 1948.] Ibid., p. 343
55 [14 July 1948.] Ibid., p. 344

V

1 Porel: *Fils de Réjane*, I, pp. 99-100
2 Ibid., pp. 104-5
3 [8 January 1949.] LMM, p. 351
4 [13 April 1949.] Ibid., p. 352
5 [20 October 1949.] Ibid., pp. 352-3
6 Cocteau: *Jean Marais*, p. 79
7 C: *Le Fanal bleu*, p. 75
8 Flanner: *Paris Journal*, p. 110
9 LSP, p. 442, note
10 [29 November 1949.] Ibid. Presumably the date should be October
11 Cocteau: loc. cit.
12 Oliver: *The Art and Magic of Cooking*, translated by Ambrose Heath (Muller 1959), p. 75
13 Cocteau: 'Colette' (*Bulletin de l'Académie Royale*..., pp. 184-5)
14 C: *L'Étoile vesper*, p. 202
15 C: *Mélanges*, p. 350
16 C: *Le Fanal bleu*, pp. 86-7
17 Goudeket: *Près de Colette*, p. 135
18 C: *Le Fanal bleu*, p. 237
19 Ibid., pp. 241-2
20 Barney: op. cit., p. 205
21 Goudeket: *Près de Colette*, pp. 30-1
22 Goudeket: *La Douceur de vieillir*, p. 159
23 Cocteau: 'Colette' (*Bulletin de l'Académie Royale*..., p. 94)
24 Cocteau: Ibid., pp. 187 sqq.
25 *Le Figaro littéraire*, 8 avril 1950
26 Goudeket: *Près de Colette*, pp. 254 sqq.
27 Ibid., pp. 256 sqq.
28 Mortimer: *Introduction*, p. 4
29 Ibid., p. 3

30 Ibid., pp. 6-7
31 Le Hardouin: *Colette*, p. 17
32 C: *En Pays connu*, p. 392
33 Léautaud: op. cit., XVIII, p. 126
34 *Le Point* XXXIX, p. 4
35 Ibid., pp. 25 sqq.
36 [19 March 1951.] LSP, pp. 166
37 Troyat in *Hommage à Colette* (Monaco 1955). No page given.
38 [3 November 1951.] LSP, p. 394
39 MacOrlan in *Paris-Presse*, 5 août 1954
40 [8 March 1952.] LMM, p. 355
41 Colette: Message on the accession of Prince Rainier III, 11 April 1950. (*Hommage à Colette*. Monaco 1955. No page given.)
42 Hériat: *Retour sur mes pas*, p. 85
43 Kathleen Farrell, in conversation with the author
44 Wescott: *Images of Truth*, pp. 142 sqq.
45 Ibid.
46 Crosland: *Colette: a Provincial in Paris*, pp. 213, 214, 215
47 Ibid., p. 216
48 Ibid.
49 [1952.] LSP, pp. 141, 142
50 [Early October 1952.] Ibid., p. 203
51 Goudeket: *Près de Colette*, pp. 229-30
52 Bauer: *Rendez-vous avec Paris*, pp. 30-4
53 Fauchier-Magnan: op. cit., pp. 106-7
54 Goudeket: *Près de Colette*, p. 179
55 Fauchier-Magnan: loc. cit.
56 Trefusis: *Prelude to Misadventure*, p. 149
57 Gregory in *Arts*, 17-23 avril 1952
58 Renaud de Jouvenel: op. cit., p. 19

VI

1 [9 January 1953.] LMM, p. 355
2 [15 January 1953.] LSP, pp. 396-7
3 *Le Figaro littéraire*, 24 janvier 1953
4 Flanner: *Paris Journal 1944-1965*, pp. 193-4
5 Goudeket: *Près de Colette*, p. 230
6 [8 or 9 April 1953.] LLV, p. 284
7 MacOrlan in *Paris-Presse*, 5 août 1954
8 [Early February 1953.] LSP, pp. 142-3
9 Goudeket: op. cit., pp. 255-6
10 Cocteau: 'Colette' (*Bulletin de l'Académie Royale*, loc. cit., p. 195)
11 James Lees-Milne: unpublished diary
12 In *Hommage à Colette* (Monaco 1955). No page given.
13 Hériat: *Retour sur mes pas*, p. 180
14 Maurois: *Memoirs 1885-1967*, pp. 382, 383
15 In *Hommage à Colette* (Monaco 1955). No page given.

16 Goudeket: op. cit., p. 277
17 Ibid.
18 Ibid., p. 282
19 Ibid.
20 *Le Figaro littéraire*, 7 août 1954
21 Quoted by Beaumont: op. cit., p. 191
22 *Le Monde*, 5 août 1954
23 *Libération*, 5 août 1954
24 Ibid.
25 *Le Figaro littéraire*, 7 août 1954
26 Flanner: op. cit., pp. 236 sqq.
27 Ibid.
28 Ibid.
29 Hériat: op. cit., pp. 181 sqq.; Cocteau: op. cit., pp. 188
30 Greene: letter to the author, 11 February 1981
31 Hériat: loc. cit.
32 Flanner: op. cit., pp. 236 sqq.
33 *Libération*, 6, 8 août 1954; and see Académie Royale de Belgique: *Bulletin*, XXXII, No. 4, pp. 289-90
34 Renaud de Jouvenel: letter to the author
35 'À propos des obsèques de Colette. Lettre à Son Éminence le Cardinal-Archevêque de Paris' (*Le Figaro littéraire*, 14 août 1954). See also Maurice Druon: 'Un destin parfait' (*Les Lettres françaises*, 12-19 août 1954).
35 Cocteau: op. cit., p. 196
36 C: *Belles Saisons*, p. 429

EPILOGUE

1 Sigl: *Colette*, p. 52
2 Larnac: op. cit., p. 232
3 Montherlant: 'En relisant Colette' (*Arts*, 22 février 1952)
4 Bauer: 'Visages de Colette' (*Le Figaro littéraire*, 7 août 1954)
5 Mortimer: op. cit., p. 8
6 Truc: *Madame Colette*, pp. 129, 133, 144
7 *The Times*, 4 August 1954
8 Quoted by Leroy: op. cit., p. 92
9 C: *Les Vrilles de la vigne*, p. 222
10 Picon: *Humanisme actif*, I, pp. 215-16
11 *The Times*, 10 August 1954
12 For Colette's understanding of animals, see Goudeket: *Près de Colette*, pp. 36 sqq.
13 C: *L'Étoile vesper*, p. 198
14 C: *Aventures quotidiennes*, pp. 415, 416
15 *Hommage à Colette* (Monaco 1955). No page given.
16 'Colette n'est plus'. *Journal de Genève*, 7-8 août 1954; Beaumont: op. cit., p. 24
17 Rousseaux: *Le Paradis perdu*, pp. 56-7

18 Maulnier: *Introduction*, p. 16
19 Flanner: loc. cit.
20 Cocteau: op. cit., p. 191
21 *Hommage à Colette* (Monaco 1955). No page given.
22 Bertrand de Jouvenel: *Time and Tide*, loc.cit.
23 Cocteau: 'Colette' (*Bulletin de l'Académie Royale...*, loc. cit.)
24 *Sunday Times*, 8 August 1954
25 Vignaud: op. cit., pp. 94, 98
26 Larnac: op. cit., p. 272
27 Maulnier: op. cit., p. 58
28 *Libération*, 5 août 1954
29 *Hommage à Colette* (Monaco 1955). No page given.
30 [February 1924?] LSP, pp. 193-4
31 Duhamel: *Souvenir de Colette*, pp. 289 sqq.
32 Chauvière: op. cit., p. 101
33 *Libération*, 4 août 1954
34 Larnac: *Colette*, p. 213
35 Maulnier: op. cit., pp. 12-13
36 Montherlant: 'En relisant Colette' (*Arts*, 22 février 1952); Proust, quoted by Chauvière: op. cit., pp. 222-3
37 Boisdeffre: *Une histoire vivante...*, pp. 205-6
38 Du Gard: *Impertinences*, pp. 63-5
39 Picon: op. cit., I, p. 214
40 Cocteau: 'Discours de réception' (*Bulletin de l'Académie Royale...*, loc. cit.)

SELECT BIBLIOGRAPHY

English books are published in London, French books in Paris, unless otherwise stated.

BOOKS

Albalat, Antoine. *Trente Ans de Quartier Latin. Nouveaux Souvenirs de la Vie littéraire*. Société Française d'Éditions Littéraires et Techniques, 1930.
Arland, Marcel. *Essais critiques*. N.R.F., Gallimard, 1931.
—. *Lettres de France*. Albin Michel, 1951.
Aumont, Jean-Pierre. *Souvenirs provisoires*. Julliard, 1957.
Barney, Natalie Clifford. *Aventures de l'esprit*. Émile-Paul, 1929.
—. *Souvenirs indiscrets*. Flammarion, 1960.
Bauer, Gérard. *Rendez-vous avec Paris*. Albin Michel, 1959.
—. *Les Billets de Guermantes*. Plon, 1937.
Beaumont, Germaine, et Farinaud, André. *Colette par elle-même*. Éditions du Seuil, 1954.
Beneš, Édouard. *Souvenirs de Guerre et de Révolution (1914–1918)*, I. Leroux, 1928.
Bénisti, Edmond. *La Main de l'écrivain*. Préface de Gabriel Marcel. Avec des portraits inédits par Laure Albin. Stock, 1939.
Bertry, Abbé L. *Vie de Léon de Jouvenel, Député de la Corrèze (1811–1886)*. Imprimerie Chastrusse, Praudel, 1931.
Bibesco, Princesse Marthe. *La Vie d'une amitié. Ma correspondance avec l'abbé Mugnier, 1911–1944*. III, Plon, 1957.
Billy, André. *Intimités littéraires*. Flammarion, 1932.
Binion, Rudolph. *Defeated Leaders. The political fate of Caillaux, Jouvenel, and Tardieu*. N.Y., Columbia University Press, 1960.
Blanche, Jacques-Émile. *La Pêche aux souvenirs*. Flammarion, 1949.
Boisdeffre, Pierre de. *Une Histoire vivante de la littérature d'aujourd'hui*. Le Livre contemporain, 1959.
Bonmariage, Sylvain. *Willy, Colette et moi*. Éditions Charles Fremanger, 1954.
Boulenger, Jacques. ... *Mais l'Art est si difficile!* Ire série. Plon-Nourrit, 1921.
Boulestin, X. M. *Myself, my two countries* ... Cassell, 1936.
Bourdet, Denise. *Édouard Bourdet et ses amis*. Préface de Jean Cocteau. La Jeune Parque, n.d.

Brasillach, Robert. *Portraits*. Plon, 1935.
—. *Une Génération dans l'orage. Mémoires. Notre avant-guerre. Journal d'un homme occupé*. Plon, 1968.
—. *Les Quatre Jeudis. Images d'avant-guerre*. Les Sept couleurs, 1951.
—. *Œuvres complètes*. Tomes X, XII. Au Club de l'honnête homme, 1964, 1965.
Brisson, Pierre. *Autre Temps*. N.R.F., Gallimard, 1949.
—. *Vingt Ans de Figaro, 1938-1958*. N.R.F., Gallimard, 1959.
Carco, Francis. *Ombres vivantes*. Ferenczi & Fils, 1948.
Cecil of Chelwood, Viscount (Lord Robert Cecil). *A Great Experience*. Jonathan Cape, 1941.
Champion, Pierre. *Marcel Schwob et son temps*. Grasset, 1927.
Chastener, Jacques, *Une époque pathétique. La France de M. Fallières*. Fayard, 1949.
Chauvière, Claude. *Colette*. Firmin Didot, 1931.
Chevalier, Maurice. *Ma Route et mes chansons*. Julliard, 1946.
Claretie, Jules. *La Vie à Paris, 1911-1912-1913*. Charpentier, 1914.
Cocteau, Jean. *Portraits-souvenir, 1900-1914*. Illustrés par l'auteur. Grasset, 1935.
—. *La Difficulté d'être*. Paul Morihen, 1947.
—. *Jean Marais*. Calmann-Lévy, 1951.
Colette. *Œuvres complètes*. Flammarion, 1948-50.
—. *Lettres à Hélène Picard*. Texte établi et annoté par Claude Pichois. Flammarion, 1958.
—. *Lettres à Marguerite Moreno*. Texte établi et annoté par Claude Pichois. Flammarion, 1959.
—. *Lettres de la vagabonde*. Texte établi et annoté par Claude Pichois et Roberte Forbin. Flammarion, 1961.
—. *Lettres au petit corsaire*. Texte établi et annoté par Claude Pichois et Roberte Forbin. Préface de Maurice Goudeket. Flammarion, 1963.
—. *Lettres à ses pairs*. Texte établi et annoté par Claude Pichois et Roberte Forbin. Flammarion, 1973.
Cossart, Michael de. *The Fool of Love: Princess Edmonde de Polignac (1865-1943) and her Salon*. Hamish Hamilton, 1978.
Cottrell, Robert D. *Colette*. N.Y., Ungar, 1974.
Crosland, Margaret. *Madame Colette: A Provincial in Paris*. Peter Owen, 1953.
—. *Colette: The Difficulty of Loving. A Biography*. Peter Owen, 1973.
Daguesseau, André. *À l'ombre de Colette. Poèmes*. Éditions de la Revue Moderne, 1959.
Davies, Margaret. *Colette*. Oliver & Boyd, 1961.
Deharne, Lise. *Les Années perdues. Journal. (1939-1949)*. Plon, 1961.
Delarue-Mardrus, Lucie. *Mes Mémoires*. N.R.F., Gallimard, 1938.
Du Gard, Maurice Martin. *Impertinences. Portraits contemporains*. Camille Bloch, 1924.
—. *Harmonies critiques*. Editions du Sagittaire, 1936.
—. *Les Mémorables*. Tomes I, II. Flammarion, 1957, 1960; Tome III. Grasset, 1978.
Dumas, F. Ribadeau. *Carrefour de Visages*. Nouvelle Société d'Éditions, 1929.
Ernest-Charles, J. *Les Samedis littéraires*. 5e série. Sansot, 1907.
Fargue, Léon-Paul. *Portraits de Famille. Souvenirs*. J. B. Janin, 1947.

Fauchier-Magnan, Adrien. *C'était hier . . . (Souvenirs d'un demi-siècle)*. Éditions du Scorpion, 1960.
Fillon, Amélie. *Colette*. Éditions de la Caravelle, 1933.
Flanner, Janet. *Paris Journal. 1944-1965*. Victor Gollancz, 1966.
Fouquières, André de. *Cinquante ans de panache*. Horay, 1951.
Gide, André. *Journal. 1932-1939*. Rio de Janeiro, Americ-Edit, n.d.
—. *Journal. 1939-1942*. N.R.F., Gallimard, 1946.
—. *Journal. 1942-1949*. N.R.F., Gallimard, 1950.
Giry, Jacqueline. *Colette et l'Art du discours interieur*. La Pensée universelle, 1980.
Gold, Arthur, and Fizdale, Robert. *Misia: The Life of Misia Sert*. Macmillan, 1980.
Goudeket, Maurice. *Près de Colette*. Flammarion, 1956.
—. *La Douceur de vieillir*. Flammarion, 1965.
Gourmont, Rémy de. *Promenades littéraires*. 4e série. Mercure de France, 1912.
Gramont, Élisabeth de [Duchesse de Clermont-Tonnerre]. *Mémoires. Les marroniers en fleur*. Grasset, 1929.
—. *Mémoires. Tome IV. La treizième heure*. Grasset, 1935.
—. *Souvenirs du monde de 1890 à 1940*. Grasset, 1966.
Green, Julien. *Journal. 1928-1934*. Plon, 1938.
—. *Journal. 1950-1954*. Plon, 1955.
Gregh, Fernand. *L'Âge d'or*. Grasset, 1947.
Guitry, Sacha. *Quatre ans d'occupations*. L'Élan, 1947.
Guth, Paul. *Quarante contre un*. Éditions Corrêa, 1947.
Hériat, Philippe. *Retour sur mes pas*. Namur, Wesmael-Charlier, 1959.
Hermant, Abel. *La Vie littéraire*. 2e série. Flammarion, 1928.
Hitchcock, Edward B. *Beneš. The Man and the Statesman*. Hamish Hamilton, 1940.
Hollander, Paul d'. *Colette. Ses Apprentissages*. Montréal, Les Presses de l'Université de Montréal, 1978.
Houssa, Nicole. *Le souci de l'expression chez Colette*. Bruxelles. Académie Royale de Langue et de Littérature Françaises de Belgique, 1958.
Jouhandeau, Marcel. *Carnets de l'écrivain*. N.R.F., Gallimard, 1957.
Jouvenel, Bertrand de. *Un Voyageur dans le siècle*. Laffont, 1979.
Keller, Fernard, et Lautier, André. *Colette (Colette Willy). Son Œuvre*. Éditions de La Nouvelle Revue Critique, 1923.
Lang, André. *Tiers de siècle*. Plon, 1935.
Lanoux, Armand. *Amours 1900*. Hachette, 1961.
Larnac, Jean. *Colette. Sa vie, son œuvre*. Kra, 1927.
—. *Histoire de la littérature féminine en France*. Kra, 1929.
Léautaud, Paul. *Journal littéraire*. 19 tomes. Mercure de France, 1954-66.
—. *Lettres à Marie Dormoy*. Albin Michel, 1966.
Lefèvre, Frédéric. *Une heure avec . . .* 4e série. N.R.F., Gallimard, 1927.
Le Hardouin, Maria. *Colette. A biographical study*. Translated from the French by Erik de Mauny. Staples, 1958.
Leroy, Paul. *Femmes d'aujourd'hui. Colette. Lucie Delarue-Mardrus*. Rouen, Éditions Maugard, 1936.
Lorcey, Jacques. *Sacha Guitry*. La Table Ronde, 1971.
Marks, Elaine. *Colette*. Secker & Warburg, 1961.

Maulnier, Thierry. *Introduction à Colette*. La Palme, 1954.
Maurois, André. *Memoirs, 1885-1967*. Translated from the French by Denver Lindley. The Bodley Head, 1970.
Miomandre, Francis de. *Figures d'hier et d'aujourd'hui*. Dorbon-Aîné, n.d.
Mitchell, Yvonne. *Colette. A taste for life*. Weidenfeld & Nicolson, 1976.
Montfort, Eugène de. *Vingt-cinq ans de littérature française*. Tome II. Librairie de France, n.d.
Montherlant, Henry de. *Carnets. Années 1930 à 1944*. N.R.F., Gallimard, 1957.
Moreno, Marguerite. *Souvenirs de ma vie*. Préface de Colette. Introduction de Robert Kemp. Éditions de Flore, 1948.
Parturier, Maurice. *Morny et son temps*. Hachette, 1969.
Pascal, André (Henri de Rothschild). *Croisière autour de mes souvenirs*. Préface de Mme Colette. Émile-Paul Frères, 1932.
Phelps, Robert. *Colette. Earthly Paradise*. An Autobiography drawn from her lifetime writings by Robert Phelps. Secker & Warburg, 1966.
Polaire. *Polaire par elle-même*. Figuière, 1933.
Polignac, Hedwige de. *Les Polignac*. Fasquelle, 1960.
Porel, Jacques. *Fils de Réjane. Souvenirs*. 2 tomes. Plon, 1951, 1952.
Pougy, Liane de. *My Blue Notebooks*. Translated by Diana Athill. André Deutsch, 1979.
Poulenc, Francis. *Correspondance, 1915-1963*. Réunie par Hélène de Wendel. Préface de Darius Milhaud. Éditions du Seuil, 1967.
[Prévost, Marcel]. *Marcel Prévost et ses contemporains*. 2 tomes. Les Éditions de France, 1943.
Pringué, Gabriel-Louis. *Trente ans de dîners en ville*. Éditions Revue Adam, 1950.
Raaphorst-Rousseau, Madeleine. *Colette. Sa vie et son art*. Nizet, 1964.
Rachilde. *Portraits d'hommes*. Mercure de France, 1930.
Ravon, Georges. *L'Académie Goncourt en Dix Couverts*. Aubanel, 1946.
Rémy, Tristan. *Georges Wague. Le Mime de la Belle Époque*. Girard, 1964.
Renard, Jules. *Journal, 1887-1910*. Texte établi par Léon Guichard et Gilbert Segaux. Préface, Chronologie et Index par Gilbert Segaux. N.R.F., Bibliothèque de la Pléiade, 1960.
Renaud, Paul. *Mémoires*. 2 tomes. Flammarion, 1960.
Rosny, J.-H., aîné, *Portraits et souvenirs*. Compagnie Française des Arts Graphiques, 1945.
Rousseaux, André. *Le Paradis perdu*. Grasset, 1936.
Sachs, Maurice. *La Décade de l'illusion*. N.R.F., Gallimard, 1950.
Sarde, Michèle. *Colette, libre et entravée*. Stock, 1978.
Sigl, Robert. *Colette*. Les Éditions de Belles-Lettres, 1924.
Sorel, Cécile. *Les Belles Heures de ma Vie*. Monaco, Éditions du Rocher, 1946.
Souday, Paul. *Les Livres du temps*. 2e série. Émile-Paul Frères, 1914.
Strowski, Fortunat. *La Renaissance littéraire de la France contemporaine*. Plon, 1922.
Thiébaut, Marcel. *Entre les lignes*. Hachette, 1962.
Trahard, Pierre. *L'Art de Colette*. Éditions Jean-Renard, 1941.
Trefusis, Violet. *Prelude to Misadventure*. Hutchinson, n.d.
—. *Don't Look Round*. Hutchinson, 1952.
Treich, Leon. *L'Esprit de Willy*. N.R.F., Gallimard, 1926.

Truc, Gonzague. *Madame Colette*. Corrêa, 1941.
Vandérem, Fernand. *Le Miroir des lettres*. 3e série. Flammarion, 1921.
—. *Le Miroir des lettres*. 5e série. Flammarion, 1923.
—. *Le Miroir des lettres*. 6e série. Flammarion, 1924.
—. *Le Miroir des lettres*. 8e série. Flammarion, 1927.
Viel, Marie-Jeanne. *Colette au temps de Claudine. Récit*. Les Publications Essentielles, 1978.
Vignaud, Jean. *L'Esprit contemporain*. Éditions du Sagittaire, 1938.
Virmaux, Alain et Odette. *Colette au cinéma. Chroniques, dialogues, scénarios*. Flammarion, 1975.
Walzer, Pierre-Olivier. *Paul-Jean Toulet. L'Œuvre, l'Écrivain*. Éditions des Portes de France, 1949.
Wescott, Glenway. *Images of Truth. Remembrances and Criticism*. Hamish Hamilton, 1963.
West, Rebecca. *Ending in earnest. A Literary Log*. N.Y., Doubleday, 1931.
Willy. *Souvenirs littéraires ... et autres*. Éditions Montaigne, 1925.

ARTICLES AND PAMPHLETS

Aghion, Max. Mme Colette Willy. En mémoire de trois rencontres. *Journal de Genève*, 28-9 décembre 1963.
Albert, Henri. Willy. *Les Célébrités d'aujourd'hui*. Sansot, 1904.
Angue, Fernand. La Jeunesse de Colette. *Les Nouvelles Littéraires*, 4 juillet 1925.
Arland, Marcel. La Naissance du Jour. *La Nouvelle Revue Française*, 1 juillet 1928, pp. 127-9.
Autant-Lara, Claude. Colette de France. *Les Lettres Françaises*, 12-19 août 1954.
Bauer, Gérard. Visages de Colette. *Le Figaro Littéraire*, 7 août 1954.
Beaumont, Germaine. Esquisse pour un portrait de Colette. *Les Nouvelles Littéraires*, 12 août 1954.
—. La leçon de Colette. *La Table Ronde*, octobre 1954, pp. 126 sqq.
Bidou, Henry. La Semaine dramatique. Chéri. *Le Journal des Débats*, 19 décembre 1921.
Billy, André. Paris littéraire en 1910. *Les Œuvres Libres*, 1945. No. 229, pp. 5 sqq.
—. Vraiment pas de rue Willy? *Le Figaro Littéraire*, 22 août 1959.
Boulenger, Marcel. Claudine en ménage. *La Renaissance Latine*, 15 juin 1902, pp. 254-5.
Bourin, André. Colette. *Larousse Mensuel*, octobre 1954, pp. 533-5.
Brasillach, Robert. Colette et son univers. *La Revue Universelle*, 1 octobre 1935.
Brisson, Pierre. Colette et l'amour. *Le Figaro Littéraire*, 10 août 1957.
Cain, Julien. Ma voisine. *Les Lettres Françaises*, 12-19 août 1954.
Calderon, Ventura Garcia. Colette en sandales. *Le Figaro Littéraire*, 16 août 1958.
Carco, Francis. Mon 'Ami' Colette. *Le Figaro Littéraire*, 28 mai 1955.
Casella, Georges. Chronique littéraire. *La Revue Illustrée*, 1 octobre 1903.
Chaponnière, Paul. Colette n'est plus. *Journal de Genève*, 7-8 août 1954.

Charensol, G. La première rencontre de Colette et de Jean Larnac. *Les Nouvelles Littéraires*, 28 novembre 1927.

Charpentier, John. Colette: *La Fin de Chéri*. *Mercure de France*, 15 mai 1926, pp. 151-2.

—. Sido. *Mercure de France*, 1 août 1930, pp. 678-9.

—. Colette. *Mercure de France*, 1 février 1931, pp. 590 sqq.

Chonez, Claudine. Hier, aujourd'hui, demain. *La Table Ronde*, mars 1956, pp. 60-4.

Clouard, Henri. La Ronde autour de Colette. *La Revue Critique des Idées et des Livres*, 10 novembre 1913, pp. 268 sqq.

Cocteau, Jean. Colette. Bruxelles, *Bulletin de L'Académie Royale de Langue et de Littérature Françaises*, XXXIII, pp. 154 sqq.

Colette (Willy). L'Ouvreuse, jugée par Colette Willy. *Revue Illustrée*, 15 janvier 1905.

Colette. Claude Chauvière. *Les Nouvelles Littéraires*, 20 juillet 1929.

—. Discours de réception. *Bulletin de l'Académie Royale de Langue et de Littérature Françaises de Belgique*, XV, No. 2.

Crémieux, Benjamin. Colette: *Le Blé en herbe*. *Les Nouvelles Littéraires*, 25 août 1923.

Dalby, Henry. Au Pays de Colette. *Les Nouvelles Littéraires*, 5 novembre 1927.

Diard, Alfred. Au temps de Claudine. *Les Nouvelles Littéraires*, 1 juin 1950.

Dorgelès, Roland. Adieu à Colette. *Le Figaro Littéraire*, 14 août 1954.

Druon, Maurice. Un destin parfait. *Les Lettres Françaises*, 12-19 août 1954.

Duhamel, Georges. Le souvenir de Colette. *Mercure de France*, 1 octobre 1954, pp. 289 sqq.

Escholier, Raymond. Le Drame secret de Sido. *Le Figaro Littéraire*, 17 novembre 1956.

—. La véritable histoire de Sido et du Capitaine. *Le Figaro Littéraire*, 24 novembre 1956.

Fabureau, Herbert. Robineau-Desvoidy, le père de Claudine à l'école. *Mercure de France*, 1 janvier 1950, pp. 188-90.

—. Le terroir de Colette. *Mercure de France*, 1 février 1950, pp. 381-4.

Fargue, Léon-Paul. Colette et la sensibilité féminine française. *Adam*, November-December 1946.

Faure-Favier, Louise. La muse aux violettes. *Mercure de France*, 1 décembre 1953, pp. 633-54.

Fernandez, Raymon. Colette. *La Nouvelle Revue Française*, 1 mars 1942, pp. 348-53.

Flament, Albert. Tableaux de Paris. Colette ou l'écrivain-Protée. *La Revue de Paris*, 1 mars 1923.

—. Tableaux de Paris. *La Revue de Paris*, 1 mars 1926.

—. Tableaux de Paris. *La Revue de Paris*, 1 avril 1926, pp. 690 sqq.

Gandon, Yves. Critique romancée. Au Jardin de Colette. *Les Nouvelles Littéraires*, 31 août 1929.

Gauthier-Villars, Jacques. Willy et Colette. Un couple parisien de la Belle Époque, ou Willy vu par son fils. *Les Œuvres Libres*, octobre 1959, pp. 175 sqq.

Gautier, Félix. Henry Gauthier-Villars (Willy). *La Revue Illustrée*, 15 juillet 1902.

Georgin, René. En lisant Colette. *La Parisienne*, mai 1953, pp. 649 sqq.

Gilbert, Eugène. Dix années de roman français. *Revue des Deux Mondes*, 1 mars 1908, pp. 159 sqq.
Goudeket, Maurice. Colette son amie. *Le Figaro Littéraire*, 19 octobre 1963.
Gourmont, Jean de. Colette. *Mercure de France*, 1 avril 1926, pp. 145-7.
Greene, Graham. Lettre à Son Éminence le Cardinal-Archevêque de Paris. *Le Figaro Littéraire*, 14 août 1954.
Gregory, Claude. Le leçon d'interview chez Madame Colette. *Arts*, 17-23 avril 1952.
Hayes, Richard. The Wisdom of Colette. *The Commonweal*, 5 September 1952, pp. 536 sqq.
Henriot, Émile. Colette. *Le Monde*, 5 août 1954.
—. Colette. *Le Monde*, 11 août 1954.
Hériat, Philippe. Colette, la femme cachée. *La Revue de Paris*, septembre 1954, pp. 9 sqq.
—. Rien n'aura manqué à cette vie exemplaire. *Les Lettres Françaises*, 12-19 août 1954.
—. Colette et ses secrets. *Le Figaro Littéraire*, 11 mars 1965.
Hirsch, Charles-Henry. De Mademoiselle de Maupin à Claudine. *Mercure de France*, juin 1902, pp. 577 sqq.
Houville, Gérard d'. Théâtre Daunou et de la Renaissance. Colette dans *Chéri*. *La Revue de Paris*, 15 avril 1925, pp. 897 sqq.
Jaloux, Edmond. Colette. La Femme cachée. *Les Nouvelles Littéraires*, 21 juin 1924.
Jourdan-Morhange, Hélène. La regarder vivre etait plus beau que tout. *Les Lettres Françaises*, 12-19 août 1954.
Jouvenel, Renaud de. Mon Enfance à l'ombre de Colette. *La Revue de Paris*, décembre 1966.
Lanco, Yvonne. Colette à Belle-Isle-en-Mer. *Mercure de France*, 1 mars 1955, pp. 556-7.
Lefèvre, Frédéric. Une heure avec Colette. *Les Nouvelles Littéraires*, 27 mars 1926.
L'Herbier, Marcel. En souvenir... *Les Lettres Françaises*, 12-19 août 1954.
MacOrlan, Pierre. La Femme la plus libre du monde. *Paris-Presse L'Intransigeant*, 5 août 1954.
Marcel, Gabriel. Duo par Colette. *L'Europe Nouvelle*, 12 janvier 1935.
Marcenac, Jean. Le cristal de Colette. *Les Lettres Françaises*, 12-19 août 1954.
Marnold, Jean. Opéra-Comique: *L'Enfant et les sortilèges*, fantaisie lyrique en 2 parties, poème de Mme Colette, musique de M. Maurice Ravel. *Mercure de France*, 15 mars 1926, pp. 701 sqq.
Marsan, Eugène. Du sentiment de la personne. *Les Cahiers d'Occident*, 2e série, No. 9, 1930, pp. 129-30.
Martin Du Gard, Maurice. Colette. *Les Nouvelles Littéraires*, 26 janvier 1924.
—. Colette au *Matin*. *La Parisienne*, novembre 1954, pp. 1216 sqq.
Mauriac, François. Le Roman d'aujourd'hui. *La Revue Hebdomadaire*, 19 février 1927, pp. 259 sqq.
Mazars, Pierre. Les derniers moments de Colette. *Le Figaro Littéraire*, 7 août 1954.
Montherlant, Henry de. En relisant Colette. *Arts*, 24 février 1952.
Mortimer, Raymond. An Introduction to Colette. Secker & Warburg, 1951.
Musidora. Colette scénariste. *Les Lettres Françaises*, 12-19 août 1954.

Olken, I. T. Imagery in *Chéri* and *La Fin de Chéri*. Taste and Smell. Oxford, *French Studies*, Vol. XVI, No. 3, July 1962, pp. 245 sqq.
Phelps, Robert. The Genius of Colette – an Appreciation. N.Y., *New Republic*, 6 September 1954.
Picon, Gaëtan. Songeant à l'œuvre de Colette. In *Humanisme actif. Mélanges d'art de littérature offerts à Julien Cain*. 2 tomes. Hermann, 1968. Tome I, pp. 213 sqq.
Pierrefeu, Jean de. La Vie littéraire. *Chéri. Le Journal des Débats*, 13 octobre 1920.
Quennell, Peter. Colette at Home. *Spectator*, 23 November 1956, pp. 733-4.
Rachilde. Les Romans... *L'Entrave*, par Colette. *Mercure de France*, 1 décembre 1913, pp. 587 sqq.
Riverain, Jean. Chez les poètes d'Auteuil. *Les Nouvelles Littéraires*, 15 avril 1948.
Rousseaux, André. Colette aux derniers rivages. *Le Figaro Littéraire*, 13 décembre 1958.
Rouveyre, André. Colette actrice. À propos de la reprise de *Chéri*, au Théâtre des Maturins. *Mercure de France*, 1 juin 1926, pp. 427 sqq.
Roy, Claude. Classique Colette. *Le Point*, XXXIX, pp. 25 sqq.
Sadou, Georges. Colette collaboratrice de Delluc. *Les Lettres Françaises*, 12-19 août 1954.
Truc, Gonzague. L'unique héroïne de Madame Colette. *La Revue Critique des Idées et des Livres*, 25 février 1920, pp. 34-44.
Venaissin, Gabriel. Colette toute bleue. *Critique*, juin 1952, pp. 491-7.
Viel, Marie-Jeanne. La Naissance de Claudine à Paris. *Paris-Presse L'Intransigeant*, 6 mars 1957.
—. Un Mariage pas comme les autres. *Paris-Presse L'Intransigeant*, 7 mars 1957.
Wague, Georges. Elle savait ce qui ne s'apprend pas. *Les Lettres Françaises*, 12-19 août 1954.
Willy. Quelques détails sur la collaboration Colette-Willy. *Les Nouvelles Littéraires*, 3 avril 1926.
Wurmser, André. Le respect fanatique de la vie. *Les Lettres Françaises*, 12-19 août 1954.

PUBLICATIONS DEVOTED TO COLETTE

Le Figaro Littéraire, 24 janvier 1953.
Le Point. Revue Artistique et Littéraire, XXXIX. Mai 1951. Souillac (Lot). Mulhouse, 1951.
Hommage à Colette. Conseil littéraire de la Principauté de Monaco, Imprimerie Nationale de Monaco, 1955.
Cahiers Colette. Société des Amis de Colette, 1977-.

INDEX

C = Colette

Académie-Française, 45, 159-60
Académie-Goncourt, 45, 187, 193-4, 199-200, 204, 208, 223
Académie Royale de Langue et de Littérature Françaises de Belgique, 160, 168-9
Action Française, L', 122-3, 170-1
Albert, Henri, 21, 27
Alençon, Émilienne d', 35, 186
Annales, Les, 132
Anouilh, Jean, 156, 223
Apollinaire, Guillaume, 45
Arnyvelde, André, 171
Aumont, Jean-Pierre, 153-4

Balzac, Honoré de, 200
Barbusse, Henry, 82
Barney, Natalie, 29-30, 83, 149-50, 184, 211
Barthou, Léon, 127
Barthou, Louis, 127, 131
Bauer, Gérard, 159, 200-1, 232
Beardsley, Aubrey, 36
Beaumont, Germaine, 68-9, 70, 80, 143-4, 172, 184-5, 228-9, 234
Beaunier, André, 15-16
Belboeuf, Marquis de (Missy): 32 sqq., 33-5, 40, 145, 191-2
Bénisti, Edmond, 173-4, 188
Bernhardt, Sarah, 81
Berriau, Simone, 193, 195, 206
Berthelot, Philippe, 48
Bibesco, Princess Marthe, 91, 92, 166

Bibliothèque Doucet, 185
Bibliothèque Nationale, 172
Billy, André, 122, 139-40, 200, 220, 228, 237
Blanche, Jacques-Émile, 22-3, 159
Bloch-Levallois, Andrée, 103, 104
Bloch-Levallois, Bernard, 103, 104
Boas, Alfred, 48
Boas, Claire, *see* Jouvenel, Mme Henry de (1)
Boisdeffre, Pierre de, 239
Bonmariage, Sylvain, 43
Boulestin, Marcel, 17, 38
Bourdet, Édouard, 154-5
Bouteron, Marcel, 172-3
Brasillach, Robert, 121, 133, 158, 168, 170-1, 174, 192-3
Brisson, Pierre, 27, 35, 223, 228

Caillaux, Joseph, 65
Caillavet, Mme Arman de, 12-13, 114
Cain, Julien, 172-3, 228
Carco, Francis, 65, 70, 139, 200
Castel-Novel, 47, 53, 56 and *passim*, 61-2
Cecil, Lord Robert, 89
Chaponnière, Paul, 234
Charpentier, John, 4
Châtillon-Coligny, 6, 8, 12
Chauviere, Claude, 35, 60-1, 67-8, 69, 107, 204
Chennevière, Jacques, 235
Chevalier, Maurice, 40, 44, 156

Cocteau, Jean, 13, 18, 75, 97, 136, 195, 209-10, 212, 228, 230, 235, 236, 240
Colette, Captain Jules-Joseph (father) 2-3, 31
Colette, Mme Jules-Joseph (mother) 1, 2, 4, 5, 8-9, 11-12, 23, 55-6, 136-7, 227
Colette, Léopold (brother), 3, 6, 175, 179
Colette, birth, 3; childhood, 3 sqq.; education, 5; visits Brussels, 5-6; moves to Châtillon-Coligny, 6; meets Willy, 6; marries Willy, 8-9; early years in Paris, 10 sqq.; at 28 rue Jacob, 10-17; illness of, 11-12; social life of, 12, 13-14; meets Marguerite Moreno, 13; begins literary career, 14; at 93 rue de Courcelles, 17; at 177, *bis*, rue de Courcelles, 25; and stepson, 16, 17-18; and Marcel Boulestin, 17; and Mme Raoul-Duval, 19-20; visits Les Monts-Boucons, 21-2; failure of marriage, 22-3, 27-8; and Robert de Montesquiou, 28-9, 31-2; and Renée Vivien, 30-1; separation from husband, 31-2; divorce, 42; at 25 rue de Villejust, 32; at rue Saint-Senoch, 42; liaison with Missy, 32 sqq.; performs with Missy in *Rêve d'Égypte*, 37-9; theatrical career, 32 sqq.; liaison with Auguste Hériot, 42-6; contributes to *Le Matin*, 45; liaison with Henry de Jouvenel, 46-57; breaks with Missy, 52; settles at 57 rue Cortambert, 54; pays last visit to mother, 55; death of mother, 55-6; marries de Jouvenel, 57; gives birth, 58; career as lecturer, 60-1 and *passim*; wartime experiences, 63; correspondent in Italy, 63-4; literary editor of *Le Matin*, 65-6; moves to 69 boulevard Suchet, 67; friendships with women, 69-70, 127; relationship with Bertrand de Jouvenel, 73-4, 79-80, 85-7, 88-9, 96-7, 98-100; marital problems, 82-4; friendship with Proust, 84-5, 114-15; returns to the stage, 91; separation from de Jouvenel, 95-6; as mother, 97-8, 119-20; has rejuvenation treatment, 101; collaborates with Ravel, 101; as Léa in *Chéri*, 99, 101-2, 108 and *passim*; meets Goudeket, 102-4; liaison with Goudeket, 104 sqq.; buys house at Saint-Tropez, 110; moves to *entresol* at 9 rue de Beaujolais, 118; financial questions, 124, 167; visits Belgium, 131; visits École Normale, 132-3; visits Spain and Morocco, 133-4; visits Berlin, 135; on cruise to Norway, 137; life at Saint-Tropez, 138-40; moves to Hôtel Claridge, 141; visits Austria and Roumania, 144; lectures in North Africa, 144; fractures fibula, 147; becomes beautician, 148-51; becomes dramatic critic of *Le Journal*, 155; elected to Académie Royale de Langue et de Littérature Françaises de Belgique, 160; moves to 33 Champs-Élysées, 160; marries Goudeket, 160-1; visits New York, 162-3; and daughter's marriage, 163-5; and death of Henry de Jouvenel, 166; received at Belgian Academy, 168-9; meets Rosamond Lehmann, 169-70; offered apartment at 9 rue de Beaujolais, 171; moves to Palais-Royal, 171; celebrated visitors, 172-3; has hand read, 173-4; in wartime Paris, 175 sqq.; broadcasts to America, 176-7; fall of France, 179-80; in occupied Paris, 180 sqq.; arrest of Goudeket, 183-6; increasing ill-health and immobility, 184-5; return of husband, 186; Liberation of Paris, 192; aftermath of war, 192-3; elected to Académie-Goncourt, 193-4; has arthritis treatment in Geneva, 196; in Uriage, 196-7; again in Geneva, 198-9; friendship with Léon-Paul Fargue, 200-1; C aged 75, 204; publication of *Œuvres complètes*, 205, 209; and death of Marguerite Mor-

INDEX

eno, 206-8; elected president of Académie-Goncourt, 208; affection for Palais-Royal, 209, 210; visits Monte-Carlo, 212-13; discovers Audrey Hepburn, 213; described by Raymond Mortimer, 213-14; second visit to Monte-Carlo, 216; third visit to Monte-Carlo, 217; friendship with Prince Pierre and Prince Rainier, 217; described by Kathleen Farrell, 217; by Glenway Wescott, 217-19; by Margaret Crosland, 219; by Gerard Bauer, 220-1; by Fauchier-Magnan, 221; by Renaud de Jouvenel, 222; C aged 80, 222-3; fourth visit to Monte-Carlo, 224-5; described by James Lees-Milne, 224-5; fifth visit to Monte-Carlo, 226; described by André Maurois, 226; increasing honours, 227; gradual decline, 227; final illness, 227; death, 227-8; funeral, 228-30.

Works: *Bella-Vista*, 170-1, 180; *Belles Saisons*, 55, 193; *Ces Plaisirs ...* see *Le Pur et l'impur*; *Chambre d'hôtel*, 180; *Chéri* (novel), 70-3, 74-9, 80, 81-2, 84, 194-5, 231-3; *Chéri* (play), 88, 99, 100, 101, 155, 195, 207-8; *Chéri* (film), 209; *Claudine à l'école*, 14, 15-16; *Claudine amoureuse*, see *Claudine en ménage*; *Claudine à Paris* (novel), 19; *Claudine à Paris* (play), 21, 40; *Claudine en ménage*, 19-21; *Claudine s'en va*, 24; *De ma fenêtre*, see *Paris de ma fenêtre*; *Dialogues de bêtes*, 26, 27; *Duo*, 157-8, 174; *En Camarades* (play), 40; *En Pays connu*, 214-15; *Gigi* (novella), 121, 186-7, 193; *Gigi* (American stage version), 213, 214; *Gigi* (French stage version), 225-6; *Journal à rebours*, 180-1; *Journal intermittent*, 215; *Julie de Carneilhan*, 181-2; *La Chambre éclairée*, 82; *La Chatte*, 64, 150, 152-3, 154, 174; *Lac aux dames* (film scenario), 152, 153; *La Femme cachée*, 100-1; *La Fin de Chéri*, 100, 108, 109-10, 112-14, 237; *La Jumelle noire*, 155-6; *La Maison de Claudine*, 90; *La Naissance du jour*, 125-6, 135; *La Paix chez les bêtes*, 64; *La Retraite sentimentale*, 39, 98; *La Seconde*, 92, 127, 131, 132, 134; *La Treille Muscate*, 129, 135; *La Vagabonde* (novel), 42, 44-5; *La Vagabonde* (play), 96, 120, 121; *La Vagabonde* (film), 64, 143; *Le Blé en herbe* (novel), 80, 93-4; *Le Blé en herbe* (film), 225; *Le Fanal bleu*, 211; *Le Képi*, 187; *L'Enfant et les sortilèges*, 101, 111-12; *L'Enfant malade*, 189; *L'Entrave*, 58, 59-60; *L'Envers du Music Hall*, 59; *Les Vrilles de la vigne*, 35, 40; *L'Étoile vesper*, 195, 196-7; *Le Voyage égoïste*, 3, 90; *L'Ingénue libertine*, 26, 40; *Le Pur et l'impur*, 144-5, 147-8, 218; *Les Égarements de Minne*, 26; *Le Toutonier*, 174; *Mes Apprentissages*, 11, 167-8; *Mes Cahiers*, 180; *Minne*, 26; *Mitsou*, 66-7; *Notes de Voyage*, 137; *Nudité*, 187; *Paradis terrestres*, 145; *Paris de ma fenêtre*, 191; *Pour un herbier*, 205-6; *Sept Dialogues de bêtes*, 98; *Sido*, 136-7; *Trois ... Six ... Neuf*, 189

Comminges, Isabelle de, 50-1, 52, 53, 87, 145, 164, 181
Crosbie, Alba, 117, 118
Crosland, Margaret, 219

D'Annunzio, Gabriele, 64
Daragon, Jean, 40
Dausse, Dr (son-in-law), 163, 165
Dausse, Mme: see Jouvenel, Colette de
Debussy, Claude, 7, 13
Delarue-Mardrus, Lucie, 25-6, 70, 88, 184
Derval, Suzanne, 38, 73
Dietrich, Marlene, 229
Dorgelès, Roland, 193-4, 195, 200, 230, 234
Dormoy, Marie, 185-6
Draper, Miss (Nursie-dear), 62
Drieu La Rochelle, Pierre, 71-2, 89

Ducharne, M., 90
Duhamel, Georges, 237-8
Dunoyer de Segonzac, A. 129-30, 135-6

Fargue, Léon-Paul, 200-1
Farrell, Kathleen, xi, 217
Farrère, Claude, 46, 216
Fauchier-Magnan, Adrien, 141-2, 221
Fellowes, Mrs Daisy, 224-5
Feltin, Cardinal, 230
Fischer, Max, 110, 124
Flament, Albert, 91, 111
Flanner, Janet, 133, 229
Foucault, André, 81
Fouquières, André de, 34, 192
Fournier, Mme Gaston, 190
France, Anatole, 12
Franck, César, 13

Gauthier-Villars, Albert (father-in-law), 6, 7
Gauthier-Villars, Henry (*known as* Willy; 1st husband): birth, 6; education, 6-7; career, 7-8; marries C, 8; married life, 10 sqq.; and C's career, 14, 16; break-up of marriage, 31-2; divorce, 42; later life, 142-3; death, 143
Gauthier-Villars, Jacques (stepson), 16, 17-18, 42
Gautier, Judith, 13, 194
Gellhorn, Martha, 100
Geneva, 57, 196, 198-9
Géraldy, Paul, 128-9, 193
Gide, André, 13, 81, 198, 223
Gille, Valère, 169
Goudeket, Maurice, birth, childhood, education, career, 103; meets C, 102, 103-4; relationship with C, 104 sqq.; marries C, 160-1; arrested and interned by Gestapo, 183-4; freed from prison camp, 186
Gourmont, Rémy de, 29
Gramont, Élisabeth de (Duchesse de Clermont-Tonnerre), 70, 127-8
Grand Véfour, Le, 209-10
Greene, Graham, 229, 230

Gregh, Fernand, 12
Gregory, Claude, 222
Guillermet, Jean, 199
Guitry, Lucien, 73
Guitry, Sacha, 183, 187, 192
Guth, Paul, 201-2

Hall, Radclyffe, 70
Hamel, Léon, 37, 52
Hamon, Renée, 69
Henriot, Émile, 228
Hepburn, Audrey, 213, 214
Hériat, Philippe, 226, 229
Hériot, Auguste, 42-6, 53, 71
Hermant, Abel, 66-7
Hirsch, Charles-Henry, 126
Houville, Gérard d', 102

Jaloux, Edmond, 173
Jammes, Francis, 27
Jaworski, Dr, 101
Jourdain-Morhange, Hélène, 143
Jouvenel, Bertrand de (stepson), xi, 48, 73-4, 79-80, 85-7, 88-9, 96-7, 98-100, 235-6
Jouvenel, Colette de (daughter): birth, 58; childhood, 62, 97-8, 119-20, later life, 150-1; marriage and divorce, 163-5
Jouvenel, Henry de (2nd husband): family history, 46-7; birth, 47; childhood and education, 47-8; career, 49, 65, 82-3, 89, 94, 111, 117, 137-8, 151, 165-6; first marriage, 48; liaison with Mme de Comminges, 50; liaison with C, 46-57; marries C, 57; marital problems, 82-4; separates from C, 95-6; divorce, 108; third marriage, 137-8; death, 166
Jouvenel, Mme Henry de (1), 48-9, 73, 110-11
Jouvenel, Mme Henry de (2), *see* Colette
Jouvenel, Mme Henry de (3), 137-8, 166
Jouvenel, Léon de, 47
Jouvenel, Raoul de (father-in-law), 47

Jouvenel, Mme Raoul de (Mamita), (mother-in-law), 47, 56, 137
Jouvenel, Renaud de (stepson), xi, 50-1, 52, 60, 62, 72, 73, 83-4, 87-8, 92, 96, 97, 100, 116-7, 163, 164, 165, 179, 222
Jouvenel, Robert de (brother-in-law), 47, 64-5, 85, 99
Jullien, Dr, 11

Lamy, Dr Marthe, 196
Landoy, Adèle-Eugénie-Sidonie (mother): *see* Colette, Mme Jules-Joseph
Landoy, Adèle-Sophie (grandmother), 1
Landoy, Henri-Marie (grandfather), 1
Lang, André, 154
Larguier, Léo, 200
Larnac, Jean, 231, 236-7, 238
Léautaud, Paul, 29, 39, 64, 107, 143, 168
Lees-Milne, James, 17, 224
Lees-Milne, Mrs James, 224
Lefèvre, Frédéric, 90-1, 114
Légion-d'honneur, 2, 81, 131, 154, 168, 227, 230
Lehmann, Rosamond, 169-70, 223
Leroy, Paul, 156-7
Loos, Anita, 213, 225

Malige, Mme Jeannie, xi
Manson, Colonel, 17
Marais, Jean, 203, 204, 208
Marcel, Gabriel, 158
Marchand, Léopold, 55, 85-6, 89, 94
Marrakesh, Pasha of (the Glaoui), 200
Martin du Gard, Maurice, 65-6, 239
Mata-Hari, 30
Matin, Le, 45, 48, 49, 52, 58, 60, 63, 65, 69, 70, 73, 74, 82, 84, 89, 91, 93, 95, 98
Maugham, Somerset, 225
Maulnier, Thierry, 235, 237
Mauriac, François, 13, 123, 188, 223
Maurois, André, 226, 237
Mazars, Pierre, 228
Mendès, Catulle, 7, 12, 13

Mendl, Lady, 199
Menkes, Dr, 198
Mercure de France, Le, 13, 111-12, 113, 115-16
Metegnano, 2
Mézilles, 1
Miomandre, Francis de, 24
Mistinguett, 138, 155-6
Monceau, Marguerite, *see* Moreno, Marguerite
Mondor, Dr Henri, 216, 222
Monte-Carlo, 212-13, 216, 217, 224-5, 226
Montesquiou-Fezensac, Comte Robert de, 28-9, 36
Montherlant, Henry de, 158-9, 238
Monts-Boucons, Les, 21-2
Moreau, Dr, 147
Moreau, Luc-Albert, 135-6
Moreno, Marguerite, 13, 22, 37, 40, 103, 104, 105 sqq. and *passim*, 206
Moreno, Pierre, 190, 191, 207, 222
Mortimer, Raymond, 213-14, 232
Moulin-Rouge, Le, 37-9
Mugnier, Abbé, 56, 166
Muhlfeld, Jeanne, 13, 22
Muhlfeld, Lucien, 13

Naples, 43
New York, 162-3
Nice, 45, 84, 110, 178-9
Noailles, Comtesse de, 29, 160, 168-9
Normandie, 162

Oliver, Raymond, 209, 210

Paris-Midi, 171
Patat, Germaine, 89, 92, 150
Pène, Annie de, 68
Picard, Hélène, 69, 79 and *passim*
Picon, Gaëtan, 233, 239-40
Pierre, Prince of Monaco, 206, 217, 230
Pierrefeu, Jean de, 79
Pillet-Will: *see* Comminges, Isabelle de
Poiret, Paul, 121
Polaire, 21, 42-3, 71

Polignac, Charles de, 197, 206
Polignac, Princess Edmond de, 70, 170, 175-6, 177-9 and *passim*
Porel, Jacques, 206-7
Pougy, Liane de (Princess Georges Ghika), 33-4, 35, 38, 40, 91, 149, 186
Poulenc, Francis, 146
Prévost, Marcel, 134
Primoli, Joseph, 64
Pringué, Gabriel-Louis, 142
Proust, Marcel, 12, 70, 74-5, 84-5, 114-15, 223, 238

Quennell, Peter, 16-17, 198

Rachilde, 13, 20, 27
Rainier III, Prince of Monaco, 217
Raoul-Duval, Mme, 19-20, 35
Ravel, Maurice, 13, 101
Rême, Lily de, 45, 46
Renard, Jules, 13-14
Renoir, Pierre, 139
Robert, Thérèse, 35
Robineau-Duclos, Dr Achille (half-brother), 2, 6
Robineau-Duclos, Jules, 1-2
Robineau-Duclos, Mme Jules, *see* Colette, Mme Jules-Joseph
Robineau-Duclos, Juliette (half-sister), *see* Rocher, Mme
Rocher, Dr (brother-in-law), 6
Rocher, Mme (half-sister), 2, 6, 31
Roman, Dr, 196, 197
Rosny, J.-H., 7, 8, 12, 27
Rothschild, Henry de, 134, 137, 148
Rousseaux, André, 234-5
Rouveyre, André, 42, 46, 52, 116
Roy, Claude, 215-16
Rozven, 46, 52, 53, 61, 85

Sachs, Maurice, 85-6
Saglio, Charles, 84, 171-2, 194
Saglio, Lucie, 84, 171-2, 224
Saint-Marceaux, Mme de, 13, 101

Saint-Sauveur, 1-6, 15, 19, 31, 90, 106, 171, 174, 179-80, 214, 227, 229, 233
Saint-Tropez, 110, 116, 121, 125, 126, 127, 128, 130, 135-6, 138-40, 147, 149, 153-5, 164, 173, 175, 186
Sauerwein, Charles, 52, 53
Schwob, Marcel, 7, 12
Sert, Jose-Maria, 183-4
Sert, Misia, 184, 189
Sido, *see* Colette, Mme Jules-Joseph
Sigl, Robert, 231
Simenon, Georges, 82
Sorel, Cécile, 149-50
Soulié de Morant, 188

Tati, Jacques, 156
Tessier, Valentine, 208, 209
Tissandier, Mme, *see* Verine, Pauline
Trahard, Pierre, 152-3
Trefusis, Violet, 66, 70, 118-19, 172, 205, 233
Troubridge, Lady, 70
Troyat, Henri, 216
Truc, Gonzague, 232

Valdrôme, M. Chevandier de, 56
Valdrôme, Édith Chevandier de, 56
Valéry, Paul, 12, 223
Vallette, Alfred, 13
Vallette, Mme Alfred, *see* Rachilde
Vandérem, Fernand, 79, 88, 93-4, 112, 154
Verine, Pauline, 62, 161, 198, 211, 218, 228
Vignaud, Jean, 153, 236

Wague, Georges, 37, 223
Weiss, Louise, 33, 34-5, 167
Wescott, Glenway, 163, 217-19
West, Rebecca, 133, 223
Willy, *see* Gauthier-Villars, Henry

Zouze, Émilie, *see* Polaire